The

SUPREME COURT *of the* UNITED STATES

An Introduction

The

SUPREME COURT *of the*

UNITED STATES

An Introduction

Thomas G. Walker

EMORY UNIVERSITY

Lee Epstein

WASHINGTON UNIVERSITY

ST. MARTIN'S PRESS
NEW YORK

Senior editor: Don Reisman
Managing editor: Patricia Mansfield-Phelan
Project editor: Suzanne Holt
Production supervisor: Alan Fischer
Text design: Leon Bolognese & Associates
Cover design: Sheree L. Goodman
Cover photo: Jim Finlayson

For information, write:
St. Martin's Press, Inc.
175 Fifth Avenue
New York, NY 10010

ISBN: 0-312-06269-9

For Mark, Mike, and Pat
T. G. W.

For Jay
L. E.

Preface ✑

Scholars have many reasons for writing textbooks. For us, *The Supreme Court of the United States* grew out of a frustration with existing volumes. This is not to say that books already on the market are inferior—quite the contrary. There are several excellent texts on the Supreme Court, ably written by leading scholars of the judicial process.

Rather, our frustration emanated from the types of books available. We found them to be too lengthy and too comprehensive for our purposes. We wanted a book that would provide a basic introduction to the Supreme Court, that would review the essential information, but do so in a relatively concise fashion. Why? The answer is simple: Unless we were teaching courses specifically on the Supreme Court, where we wanted a core, comprehensive text, there was no need for a long and detailed treatment of the institution. For many of our classes—those providing general introductions to American government and its political institutions, those on public law (e.g., constitutional law, civil liberties), and those on judicial process and behavior—we could not find a book that provided a concise introduction to the Court. So we wrote one.

Accordingly, our goal in *The Supreme Court of the United States* is to impart, in a straightforward manner, essential knowledge about the Supreme Court, including its history, justices, agenda, procedures, impact, and role in the American polity. The book does not assume any previous coursework on the judiciary. Instructors with little experience teaching about American judicial institutions can readily use it. Still, we have incorporated the findings of the latest legal and political science scholarship, so that veteran instructors in the field will find it attractive.

Finally, we recognize that those who teach courses on American government, public law, and judicial process, as well as students who take such courses, are a diverse lot, representing a wide array of theoretical approaches, academic backgrounds, and scholarly interests. As a result, we avoid imposing any particularly structured approach or rigid theme. Rather, we introduce (and integrate throughout the volume) the important and sometimes overlooked view that the Supreme Court is both a political branch of the government and a legal institution. We hope that this approach will provide instructors with a "handle" of sorts, a theme around which they can build lectures and discussions; and that it will also give them sufficient flexibility to adapt the book to their own classroom needs.

Many people have had a hand in moving *The Supreme Court of the United States* from a concept to a bound volume. Although we would like to take sole credit for the idea of the book, it actually emerged from a "brainstorming" session with Joanne Daniels and Don Reisman of St. Martin's Press. They have been with us every step of the way since then. Frances Jones and Suzanne Holt, also of St. Martin's, were very helpful in keeping us abreast of the book's progress.

Several of our colleagues took the time to read and comment on the manuscript: Robert A. Carp, University of Houston; Phillip J. Cooper, The University of Kansas; Robert L. Dudley, George Mason University; Kent A. Kirwan, University of Nebraska at Omaha; Samuel Krislov, University of Minnesota; David Robinson, University of Houston–Downtown; Elliot E. Slotnick, The Ohio State University; Harold W. Stanley, University of Rochester. We also received a great deal of help from Amy Hendricks, Liane Kosaki, and Tracey E. George. We are grateful to all of these individuals for helping us to improve many portions of the book. But, of course, we fully exonerate them from any errors that it may still contain.

Thomas G. Walker
Lee Epstein

Contents ∽

The

SUPREME COURT *of the* UNITED STATES

An Introduction

One ❧

AN OVERVIEW OF THE SUPREME COURT: ITS DEVELOPMENT, POWERS, AND ROLES

I n a recent survey, pollsters asked Americans this question: In what branch of government do you have the most confidence? The overwhelming winner? The Supreme Court of the United States. Around the same time, the *Washington Post* asked people to name the current chief justice of the United States. Was William Rehnquist the overwhelming response? No. Only 9 percent could correctly identify him as chief justice. But fully 54 percent knew that Joseph Wapner was the presiding judge on television's "The People's Court"![1]

The gap here—Americans think highly of the Court even though they know little about it—is just one of the many puzzles surrounding the Supreme Court. It is, in short, a part of the most misunderstood branch in the governmental system. But why? We think the answer lies somewhere in the unique character of the institution. Like the legislature and the executive, the judiciary is a political creature, meaning that the ordinary ebb and flow of politics affects the Court and its members in everything from who gets nominated and confirmed to what cases get decided and how disputes are resolved. Nonetheless, the Court is different from the other political branches because it is ultimately a court, a legal institution. As a result of its combined political and legal nature, the Court in some respects is more constrained than the Congress and the president, but in other ways has more discretion. For example, as we shall consider in Chapter 3, the justices cannot simply rule on just any issue. The traditions and norms of the law require that the Court wait for cases to come to it. This *may* act to constrain the Court. Yet because the justices maintain their positions for life, they do not have to satisfy constituents and accede to their demands as members of Congress must. Hence, the justices may be somewhat freer than their legislative counterparts to resolve disputes and set policy.

---

[1] Gregory A. Caldeira, "Courts and Public Opinion," in *The American Courts: A Critical Assessment,* John B. Gates and Charles A. Johnson, eds. (Washington, D.C.: CQ Press, 1991), 303.

The dual roles played by the Court may be puzzling to many, but they also empower the institution, creating the potential for it to play key roles in both the legal and larger governmental process. The Supreme Court sits atop the American legal system, presumably setting policy for all state and federal courts to follow. At the same time, perhaps because the justices can reach decisions without the fear of electoral reprisal, they have become enmeshed in some of the great issues of our times. We might go so far as to say that lately the other branches of government, whose members' jobs depend on constituent approval, have tended to let the Court act before they do, particularly on controversial issues. This, in turn, has allowed the justices to set the political agenda for decades to come on policy matters like religious liberty, desegregation, abortion, affirmative action, and so forth.

Yet, for all its importance—as both a legal and political institution—the Court remains misunderstood. It is our objective to clear up some of the confusion surrounding it. We think, of course, that it is best to begin at the beginning, with an examination of the Framers' reasons for creating the Supreme Court and their blueprint for its function in the new government. After that, we move to the controversy surrounding judicial review, the Court's power to evaluate the acts of the other branches for their compatibility with the Constitution. This leads us to conclude with a discussion of the Court's history and its current role within the American legal system and in the governmental process.

THE CREATION AND DEVELOPMENT OF THE FEDERAL JUDICIARY: THE FRAMERS' BLUEPRINT

When the Framers met in Philadelphia in 1787, they had some vision of the kind of government they did and did not want. After all, it was their dissatisfaction with the existing one, formulated under the Articles of Confederation, that largely produced the need for the convention in the first place. For instance, most of the delegates recognized that the Articles not only failed to provide sufficient power to the national legislature but also excessively constrained those powers it did authorize. The exercise of most national authority required the approval of at least nine states, which was virtually impossible to obtain on any matters of importance. Amending the Articles required the unanimous approval of the states. Consequently, most who gathered in Philadelphia knew that a stronger Congress—one that could act authoritatively on matters of national concern—would be an important element in the new order.

When it came to creating a judiciary, the Framers lacked that sort of hindsight. The Articles of Confederation did not provide for national courts, so the delegates had no experience with a federal judiciary. However, each of the states had its own operating judicial system. These court structures varied from state to state but shared common elements flowing from the English legal tradition. Consequently, the delegates to the Philadelphia convention brought with them a knowledge of courts based on their experiences in their respective states. Debates over the judiciary were, as a result, among the least contentious. However, a core issue was how to structure the system. Delegates had several options: allow the states to retain their existing systems, eradicate state systems in favor of a national judiciary, or create a new federal system that would coexist with those of the states. In the end, they chose the latter option, but they left their work somewhat incomplete. In Article III of the Constitution they drew a blueprint for a federal court system but described only the Supreme Court. The creation of a lower court structure was left to Congress. In the words of the Constitution:

> The judicial Power of the United States, shall be vested in one supreme Court, and in such inferior Courts as the Congress may from time to time ordain and establish.

The decision to give Congress the power to create a lower court system was a matter of some debate and controversy. The final decision was made on June 5. On that day, South Carolina delegate John Rutledge, who was later to become a member of the Supreme Court, proposed that there be no lower federal courts, but that the state judiciaries decide all cases below the national Supreme Court. He argued that "the State Tribunals might and ought to be left in all cases to decide in the first instance the right of appeal to the supreme national tribunal being sufficient to secure the national rights & uniformity of Judgmts."[2] In part, Rutledge feared that the creation of lower federal courts, with their potential of encroaching on the powers of the state judiciaries, might be objectionable to the states and make ratification more difficult. Rutledge's proposal received only the support of five of the smaller states and was defeated. Immediately thereafter James Wilson of Pennsylvania and James Madison of Virginia moved that "the National Legislature be empowered to institute inferior tribunals."[3] This proposal served two purposes. First, it provided for the future creation of a lower court system, an action most of the delegates thought would be necessary. And second, it avoided the immediate imposition of such courts by the proposed Constitution, thereby disarming a potential threat to ratification in some states. Not all the delegates were convinced, however. Pierce Butler of South Carolina declared, "The people will not bear such innovations. The States will revolt at such encroachments."[4] But the motion carried with the support of eight states.

Clearly, the majority of the Founders fully anticipated that Congress would indeed establish a federal court structure. This expectation is demonstrated by the balance of Article III, which defines the jurisdiction—the authority to hear cases—of the federal courts. That is, the Founders did not create lower federal

---

[2] Quoted in Daniel A. Farber and Suzanna Sherry, *A History of the American Constitution* (St. Paul, Minn.: West Publishing Co., 1990), 55.

[3] Ibid.

[4] Ibid., 56.

courts, but they did provide operational rules for Congress to establish them. In essence, the Constitution provided the federal courts with the authority to hear cases involving certain subjects or certain parties:

Subjects Falling under Federal Authority

▶ Cases involving the U.S. Constitution, federal laws, and treaties

▶ Cases affecting ambassadors, public ministers, consuls

▶ Cases of admiralty and maritime jurisdiction

Parties Falling under Federal Authority

▶ United States

▶ Controversies between two or more states

▶ Controversies between a state and citizens of another state[5]

▶ Controversies between citizens of different states

▶ Controversies between citizens of the same state claiming lands under grants of different states

▶ Controversies between a state, or the citizens thereof, and foreign states, citizens, or subjects

The Framers also defined the jurisdiction of the U.S. Supreme Court, the one judicial body mandated by the Constitution. First, they provided the Supreme Court with original jurisdiction—the power to hear cases before any other judicial body. Article III states:

> In all Cases affecting Ambassadors, other public Ministers and Consuls, and those in which a State shall be a Party, the supreme Court shall have original Jurisdiction.

And second, they gave the Supreme Court appellate jurisdiction—the power to hear cases on review—over all those disputes falling within the subject/party jurisdiction of the lower federal courts. As a counterbalance, the delegates also provided Congress with a potential weapon over the Court's exercise of its appellate (but not original) jurisdiction:

> In all the other Cases before mentioned, the supreme Court shall have appellate Jurisdiction, both as to Law and Fact, with such Exceptions, and under such Regulations as the Congress shall make.

---

[5] In 1795, this was modified by the Eleventh Amendment, which removed from federal jurisdiction those cases in which a state is sued by the citizen of another state.

Scholars and justices have debated the precise meaning of this Exceptions Clause. Under certain interpretations it provides Congress with a serious check on the Court's authority. The legislature could take away the justices' ability to hear certain kinds of cases. This is a subject we consider later in this chapter. Suffice it to say for now that Congress has proposed to do so many times, but has taken such action only once, during the Civil War. Still, the Exceptions Clause remains a functioning part of the Constitution.

Beyond these explicit discussions of jurisdiction, Article III is rather vague, providing Congress with the wherewithal to create a federal court system, but not with specific instructions as to its ultimate design and structure. This, of course, is hardly surprising. The Framers disagreed over how states would react to the new court system; and as was the case with other key constitutional issues, balance and compromise guided the Convention's decisions.

In other sections of the Constitution, however, the Founders were somewhat more explicit about the federal judiciary. Most important is Article II's description of the judicial selection process, a Court issue hotly debated by the delegates. Though some wanted judges selected by the legislature, in the end it was decided that the president would nominate and, "by and with the Advice and Consent of the Senate, . . . appoint" federal judges. The division of the selection power between the legislative and executive branches means that federal judges need not feel indebted to any single party for attaining their positions. This helps keep the judiciary independent of the other two branches of government.

The value the Framers placed on judicial independence can be seen in two other constitutional provisions as well. First, Article III stipulates that judges may hold their offices for terms of good behavior. This means that federal judges may continue in office for as long as they desire, capable of being removed only by impeachment for gross misbehavior. Unlike the president or members of Congress, federal judges do not have fixed terms or limitations on their tenure. They are not required to undergo periodic reconfirmation by other government bodies or the electorate, and they cannot be challenged by any opponents who might want to replace them. Second, the Framers made sure that federal judges could not be made the target of economic attacks by Congress. Article III prohibits the legislature from reducing the salaries of federal judges during their tenure of active service. These job security and economic protections allow federal judges considerable independence from the other branches as well as from public opinion and the electorate. The Framers clearly thought it necessary to establish the independence of the judiciary so that the judges would be able to execute their duties without being unduly influenced by inappropriate external pressures.

Debates over the Ratification of the Constitution

When the Framers left Philadelphia in 1787 they did so with confidence that the U.S. Constitution would obtain quick approval by the states. At first, their optimism did not seem misplaced: four states ratified it almost immediately. But by January of 1788 the drive for ratification had slowed; a strong opposition movement was growing in size and generating an array of arguments to deter state convention delegates. Most of all, these opponents, the so-called Anti-Federalists, did not believe that the Constitution's new balance of powers was equitable. They argued that it favored a strong national government when it was the states that "provided the only sure defense of their liberties against a potentially tyrannical central authority."[6] Those favoring ratification—the self-labeled Federalists—were quick to respond. Although their arguments and writings took many forms, among the most important was a series of eighty-five articles published in New York newspapers under the name Publius. Written by Alexander Hamilton, James Madison, and John Jay, *The Federalist Papers* continue to provide great insight into the objectives and intent of our nation's founders.

To be sure, the emphasis of the *Papers* was not on the courts, in particular, but on the underlying theories embraced by the Constitution. For example, when the opponents of ratification clamored for a listing of specific individual rights, which at that time the proposed Constitution did not contain, Alexander Hamilton responded that "the Constitution is itself . . . a Bill of Rights." Under it the government could exercise only those functions specifically bestowed upon it; all remaining rights lay with the people. He and others felt that a laundry list of such rights might even be dangerous because it would inevitably omit some. Still, in *Federalist* no. 78, Alexander Hamilton did discuss the legal system and, in so doing, provided a classic explication of judicial power and justified why the Framers made the decisions they did.

From that discussion we learn that the Framers made decisions concerning the federal judiciary with the desire to make it a significant part of the new system; that is why they gave it potential jurisdiction over a wide range of disputes.[7] Yet in Hamilton's estimation that was still insufficient; a strong judiciary also required the power of *judicial review,* the "duty" to declare all acts contrary to the manifest tenor of the Constitution void, to be a coequal branch of the national government. To animate this, the Court would need to be far different in character from the other institutions; if it had the same constituencies as the other branches, it might be hesitant to strike down the improper acts of Congress and the president. And it was for that reason, Hamilton suggested, the Framers developed the unique selection and retention system of our federal judiciary: presidential nomination, Senate confirmation, and life tenure. By eradicating any electoral connection, the Framers felt they had accomplished the all-important end: the judiciary's constituency was now very different from that of the other institutions of the government. Congress and the president would

---

[6] Melvin I. Urofsky, *A March of Liberty* (New York: Knopf, 1988), 97–98.

[7] We adopt this discussion from Lee Epstein and Joseph F. Kobylka, *The Supreme Court and Legal Change* (Chapel Hill: University of North Carolina Press, 1992).

respond to the ebb and flow of ordinary politics and reflect public opinion. The Court, on the other hand, would confine its attention to the law. It would stand above the political fray and interpret the law free from overt political forces and influence.

To be sure, Hamilton's assertion that the Framers intended for the courts to exercise the power of judicial review has been, as we shall see later in this chapter, the subject of some scholarly debate. Suffice it to say for now that, at the time, it was not the potential power of the courts that deterred states from ratifying the Constitution. Rather, it was the fact that it did not contain a bill of rights. When the Federalists agreed to develop one, states began to approve the Constitution and it was eventually ratified in the summer of 1788.

Judiciary Act of 1789

Although those in favor of ratification had promised the states the immediate proposal of a bill of rights, this did not occur until the fall of 1789. Rather, the First Congress of the United States—full of Federalists of the Hamiltonian bent— quickly turned their attention to fulfilling the promise of Article III. This they did in the first major law passed in the United States (enacted several weeks before George Washington transmitted the Bill of Rights to the states), the Judiciary Act of 1789, which developed a federal court system and provided some additional rules and regulations to govern it.

The first five sections defined the structure of the new system in this way:

1 U.S. Supreme Court
(1 chief justice, 5 associate justices)

3 Circuit Courts (one for each of three geographical circuits)	**13 District Courts** (one per state)
• no separate judges; cases heard by 2 Supreme Court justices and 1 district court judge	• 1 judge per district
• heard major criminal and civil cases, and had appellate jurisdiction over the district courts	• heard minor criminal and civil cases

Other important sections expanded the power of the federal courts and of the Supreme Court in particular. For example, section 25 gave the Supreme Court the power to hear appeals from state supreme courts if they involved issues of federal concern. Section 13 added the power to issue writs of mandamus to the Court's original and appellate jurisdiction. That is, if a citizen wanted a court to issue an order to a public official commanding the performance of some task, that litigant could go either directly to the U.S. Supreme Court or to the lower federal courts. Seen in this way, the 1789 Judiciary Act was something of a victory for those in favor of a strong federal judicial system. Not only did

Congress create federal courts, but it also expanded the kinds of disputes such bodies could hear.

As important as this act was, though, perhaps its greater significance comes from the way in which the Supreme Court interpreted part of it. Indeed, section 13 gave rise to the landmark decision issued by Chief Justice John Marshall in *Marbury v. Madison* (1803), firmly establishing what Hamilton had assumed: the power of judicial review.

Marbury v. Madison

Judicial review, as Hamilton suggested, would be a most potent power of federal courts, but it is not a power explicitly stated within the Constitution. Rather, it is one the federal courts claimed for themselves as early as 1796 in the case of *Hylton v. United States.* Daniel Hylton, a Virginian, challenged the constitutionality of a 1794 federal tax on carriages. According to Hylton, the act violated a section of the Constitution mandating that direct taxes be apportioned on the basis of population. With only three justices participating, the Court upheld the act. Yet, by even considering it, the Court in effect used its authority to review an act of Congress.

It was not until 1803 in *Marbury v. Madison* that the Court invoked judicial review to strike down legislation deemed incompatible with the U.S. Constitution.[8] The dispute giving rise to the case, though, had begun more than two years earlier. It all started with the bitter election campaign of 1800 that culminated in the House of Representatives selecting Republican Thomas Jefferson to be president. When the Federalists lost both the presidential election and their majority in Congress, they took a number of steps to seize control of the third branch of government, the judiciary, before surrendering power to the Jeffersonians. Their first opportunity arose in late 1800 when the third chief justice of the United States, Federalist Oliver Ellsworth, resigned from office, allowing John Adams—not Jefferson—to name his replacement. Adams immediately offered the job to John Jay, who had served as the first chief justice but left to take the more prestigious post as governor of New York. When Jay refused to return to his former position, Adams turned to his secretary of state, John Marshall. Marshall, also an ardent Federalist, was confirmed by the Senate in January 1801, while continuing to hold his position as secretary of state. Next, the lame-duck Federalist Congress enacted the Judiciary Act of 1801. This created six new circuit courts and several district courts. These new courts, of course, necessitated the addition of judges and support staff (attorneys, marshals, and clerks). Accordingly, during his last six months in office Adams made more than two hundred nominations, with sixteen judgeships (the "midnight

---

[8] We derive this from Lee Epstein and Thomas G. Walker, *Constitutional Law for a Changing America: Institutional Powers and Constraints* (Washington, D.C.: CQ Press, 1992).

appointments") approved by the Senate during his final two weeks in office. Congress also reduced the size of the Supreme Court from six justices to five, effective upon the next resignation or death of a justice, in order to delay any Jefferson appointment.

Finally, the Federalist Congress passed the Organic Act, which authorized Adams to appoint forty-two justices of the peace for the District of Columbia. Interestingly, it was this final, seemingly innocuous action that set the stage for the dramatic case of *Marbury v. Madison*. In the confusion of the Adams adminis-tration's last days, at least four of these commissions were not delivered by the acting secretary of state Marshall. When the new administration came into office, James Madison, the new secretary of state, acting under orders from Jefferson, refused to deliver the commissions. As a result, in 1801 Marbury (and others who were denied their commissions) filed suit under section 13 of the Judiciary Act of 1789, requesting the U.S. Supreme Court to issue a writ of mandamus to Madison compelling him to deliver the commissions.

Thus, the volatile political climate subsequent to Jefferson's victory was coming to a climax. Marshall, now serving as chief justice, was perhaps in the most tenuous position of all. On the one hand, he had been a major supporter of the Federalist party, which now looked to him to "scold" the Jefferson administra-tion. On the other, Marshall wanted to avoid a confrontation between the Jeffer-son administration and the Supreme Court, which could end in disaster for the struggling nation. Trouble, in fact, was already brewing. *Marbury* was not handed down by the Court until two years after Marbury filed suit because the Jefferson-dominated Congress abolished the 1802 Term of the Court!

So how did Marshall get out of this political mess? He did so largely by cleverly framing his responses to the three questions he saw arising out of the dispute. First, did Marbury have a right to the commission? In Marshall's opinion, he did indeed. Once the commission was sealed the appointment process was complete; the delivery of it was not part of that process. Second, since Marbury had a right to the commission, did the law provide him with a remedy? Once again, Marshall responded positively: if somebody is legally wronged, the law provides a remedy. Finally, was a request for a writ of mandamus, filed in the U.S. Supreme Court, the proper remedy? To this, Marshall said no. Why? Because section 13 of the 1789 Judiciary Act was "repugnant" to the Constitution. In that legislation Congress gave the Supreme Court original jurisdiction to hear manda-mus cases, an addition of power that conflicted with the Constitution's grant of original jurisdiction in Article III. Marshall asserted that Congress could not change the Court's original jurisdiction and, as a result, the justices lacked the necessary authority to decide the dispute.

In so concluding, it might appear that Marshall, in fact, diminished the potential power of the federal judiciary. After all, he refused to allow Congress to enlarge the Court's original jurisdiction. But, by ruling in this way, Marshall greatly enhanced the power of the judiciary. He explicitly asserted that courts had the power not only to review acts of Congress, but to strike them down as well. How did Marshall justify this position? In his view,

> It is, emphatically, the province and duty of the judicial department, to say what the law is. Those who apply the rule to particular cases, must of necessity expound and interpret that rule.

Marshall went on to demonstrate that the nature of judicial power—"to say what the law is," as intended by those who framed the Constitution—must necessarily encompass the power to review acts of governmental officials to determine their compatibility with the Constitution. His point: if courts do not have this power, who does?

The Significance of Marbury v. Madison

Many scholars and legal analysts suggest that Marshall's opinion in *Marbury* was absolutely stunning, even brilliant. Consider the way he dealt with a most delicate political situation. By ruling against Marbury, Marshall avoided a potentially devastating clash with the new presidential administration; but, by asserting and exerting the power of judicial review, he informed Jefferson that the Court would play a major role in the American governmental system. So too, the decision itself helped to establish John Marshall's reputation as the greatest jurist in American history and to bring prestige to the institution itself. As we describe later in this chapter, prior to Marshall the Court was not a force in the new governmental system. The first two presidents had trouble even getting their preferred candidates to accept positions on the tribunal. *Marbury* changed that. It gave the Court a voice in the governmental system.

Relatedly, the opinion spoke to the future of the Supreme Court. *Marbury* firmly established the Court's authority to review *and* strike governmental actions that were incompatible with the Constitution. In Marshall's view, such authority, while not explicitly stated in the Constitution, was clearly intended by the Framers of that document. Was he correct? To be sure, his opinion makes a plausible argument, but some judges and scholars have suggested otherwise. Let us now consider their assertions on this and other issues arising from the Court's invocation of judicial review.

Debates over Judicial Review

Marbury explicitly gave the federal courts the power to review the actions of national institutions and actors. In later cases the Court assumed the same authority over state actions. What they did not do, and perhaps could not do, was put an end to the controversies surrounding judicial review. Though most Americans accept the fact that courts have this power, many legal analysts still debate whether they should. Let us, then, consider some of the theoretical debates surrounding judicial review, debates that political scientist David Adamany puts into five categories: Framers' intent, judicial restraint, democratic checks on the Court, public opinion, and protection of minority rights.[9]

FRAMERS' INTENT   The first, and perhaps oldest, debate is whether the Framers intended the federal courts to exercise judicial review. This was the major justification offered by Chief Justice Marshall and there is some historical evidence to support it. Most important is that the Framers had knowledge of judicial review. It had been exerted by English courts as early as 1610. Additionally, between 1776 and 1787, eight of the thirteen colonies incorporated judicial review into their constitutions. And, in fact, by 1789 various state courts had struck down eight acts passed by their legislatures as unconstitutional.

But this still leaves open the question of why the Framers left judicial review out of the Constitution. Given the experience of the state courts, their omission is even more perplexing. Some historians argue that they omitted it because Article III was a source of potential division at the Convention and the insertion of judicial review would have only heightened the differences. By the same token, however, many analysts claim that several factors point to the view that the Framers implicitly accepted the notion of judicial review. Over half the delegates to the Constitutional Convention approved of the concept, including those generally considered to be the most influential. And, as we have already noted, in *The Federalist* Hamilton adamantly defended the concept, arguing that one branch of government must safeguard the Constitution and that the courts would be in the best position to undertake that important responsibility.

Even with all of this evidence, there are still many who argue that the Framers did not intend for the courts to review acts of the other branches. As Adamany summarizes, "the Constitutional Convention rejected a proposed Council of Revision, including judges, to reject or revise laws that did not conform to the Constitution."[10] Even though some states adopted judicial review, their courts rarely exercised the power. And, "the outrage that followed some of those [state] decisions showed that judicial review was not widely accepted."[11] What, then, can we conclude about the intent of the Framers? Perhaps legal scholar Edward S. Corwin said it best: "The people who say the Framers intended it are talking nonsense, and the people who say they did not intend it are talking nonsense."[12]

JUDICIAL RESTRAINT   Another controversy surrounding judicial review involves the notion of "judicial restraint." That is, many legal analysts and justices have asserted that courts generally should defer to the elected institutions of

---

[9] Much of what follows relies on David Adamany, "The Supreme Court," in *The American Courts: A Critical Assessment,* John B. Gates and Charles A. Johnson, eds. (Washington, D.C.: CQ Press, 1991) and Epstein and Walker, *Constitutional Law for a Changing America.*

[10] Adamany, "The Supreme Court," 13.

[11] Ibid.

[12] Quoted in ibid.

government and avoid conflicts with those branches. The use of judicial review, of course, runs counter to this notion. Consider the case of *I.N.S. v. Chadha* (1983), in which the U.S. Supreme Court ruled unconstitutional a procedure called the legislative veto that was used by Congress to review and even nullify the actions of the executive branch. Congress, much to the disdain of some presidents, had written it into some two hundred laws. By even hearing *Chadha,* the Court placed itself squarely in the middle of an executive-legislative dispute. When it nullified the veto, the Court showed no deference to the wishes of the legislature. To this argument, supporters of judicial review point to Marshall's decision in *Marbury,* Hamilton's assertion in *The Federalist,* and so forth. They suggest the need for an umpire within the governmental system, one that will act neutrally and fairly in interpreting the constitutional strictures.

Again, the question of which posture is correct is one on which no concrete answer exists, only opinion. But what we do know is that most Supreme Court justices have not taken seriously the dictate of judicial restraint or, at the very least, have not let it significantly interfere in their voting. Even those who profess a basic commitment to judicial deference have tended to allow their attitudes and values to dictate decisional outcomes.[13]

DEMOCRATIC CHECKS   A third controversy involves what Adamany calls "democratic checks on the Court." According to one side of this debate, judicial review is defensible on the grounds that the Supreme Court, while lacking an explicit electoral connection, is subject to potential checks by the elected branches. That is, if the Court exercises judicial review in a way repugnant to the best interests of the people, Congress, the president, and even the states have a number of recourses. One or more of them can, for example,

- ▸ propose and ratify a constitutional amendment to overturn a decision
- ▸ change the size of the Court
- ▸ remove the Court's appellate jurisdiction
- ▸ use the nomination/confirmation process to alter the Court's membership

The problem with these checks, in the eyes of some analysts, is that most are rarely invoked. Only four amendments have explicitly overturned Court decisions; the Court's size has not been changed since 1869; only once has Congress removed the Court's appellate jurisdiction. And, despite the fact that we have seen increasing controversy over recent nominees to the Supreme Court, since the turn of the century the Senate has rejected only 7 percent of the fifty-six candidates on whom it has voted.

---

[13] See, for example, Harold Spaeth and Stuart Teger, "Activism and Restraint," in *Supreme Court Activism and Restraint,* Stephen Halpern and Charles Lamb, eds. (Lexington, Mass.: Lexington Books, 1982).

Nonetheless, we do not mean to imply that Congress, in particular, has no control over the federal courts and their decisions. We only have to consider the Senate's 1987 rejection of Robert Bork's nomination to the Court. To be sure, this was something of a rebuke to Ronald Reagan, the president who nominated Bork, but it also indicated the Senate's concern with the particular ideological direction a Court containing Robert Bork might take.

PUBLIC OPINION   A fourth debate surrounding judicial review concerns public opinion and the Court. It encompasses two related assertions. First, those who support judicial review argue that Court decisions are usually in harmony with public opinion, that is, even though the Court faces no real pressure to do so, it generally "follows the elections." Hence, Americans need not fear that the Court will abuse its power. Empirical evidence, though, is mixed. After conducting an extensive investigation of the relationship between public opinion and the Court, Thomas Marshall concluded that "the evidence suggests that the modern Court has been an essentially majoritarian institution. Where clear poll margins exist, three-fifths to two-thirds of Court rulings reflect the polls."[14] Yet, as he and others concede, the Court has at times handed down decisions well out of line with public preferences, such as its prohibition of prayer in school and of legislation outlawing flag burning.[15]

A second aspect of this particular controversy involves the "legitimacy-conferring" power of the Court. According to this view, when the Court reviews and *upholds* legislation, it plays the role of Republican schoolmaster, educating the public and conferring some measure of acceptance on governmental policies. Again, though, a great deal of evidence suggests that the Court does not and, more pointedly, cannot serve this function. Too few people actually know about any given Court decision and, even if they do, that does not necessarily mean they will shift their opinion to conform to the Court's.

ROLE OF THE COURT   A final controversy, and arguably the most hotly debated one, concerns the role the Supreme Court *should* play in our governmental system. Those who support judicial review assert that the Court must have this power if it is to fulfill its most important constitutional assignment: protector of minority rights. By their very nature as elected officials legislators and executives will reflect the interests of the majority. But those interests may promote actions that are blatantly unconstitutional. So that a majority cannot tyrannize a minority, it is necessary for the one branch of government that lacks an electoral connection to have the power of judicial review. This is an important argument, one whose veracity has been demonstrated many times throughout our history. Recall, for example, that when Southern legislatures enacted segrega-

---

[14] Thomas R. Marshall, *Public Opinion and the Supreme Court* (Boston: Unwin Hyman, 1989), 192.

[15] For an excellent review of this literature, see Caldeira, "Courts and Public Opinion."

tion laws, it was the U.S. Supreme Court that struck them down as violative of the Constitution.

The view of the Court as a protector of minority interests is not without its share of problems. First, it conflicts, at least in the opinion of some, with democratic theory. To these analysts, it is completely countermajoritarian for a Court composed of nonelected officials to strike laws passed by legislators who represent the people. The early New Deal period (especially 1935 and 1936)—when the Court kept striking down legislation aimed at alleviating the depression—is an oft-cited example of the dangers that can arise when the Court acts against the wishes of the people. Second, empirical evidence suggests that at times the Supreme Court has not used judicial review to protect the interests of disadvantaged minorities. Rather, according to Robert Dahl, many of the acts struck down by the Supreme Court before the 1960s were laws that harmed the privileged class, not politically powerless minorities.[16]

We see some of this in the most recent Court eras as well. For example, in *City of Richmond v. Croson* (1989) the justices considered a challenge to a plan devised by the city of Richmond to encourage minority businesses. In particular, the city mandated that those businesses to which it awarded construction contracts in turn subcontract at least 30 percent of the dollar amount of the contract to a minority business (those owned and managed by black, Hispanic, Asian, Eskimo, or Aleut citizens). The Supreme Court, however, struck down the plan; accordingly, it exerted the power of judicial review in a way that hindered, not supported, the interests of racial and ethnic minorities.

THE INSTITUTIONAL DEVELOPMENT OF THE COURT: A THUMBNAIL SKETCH

Taken together, Article III and *Marbury v. Madison* continue to provide the most important sources of the Court's powers. Nonetheless, since 1803, the Court and its roles within the legal system and governmental process have changed markedly. Some of this has occurred because of alterations in the structure of the American judiciary and in the interaction between the Court and the other political branches. These are subjects we consider in the last sections of this chapter. At least some of the changes, however, we can attribute to the Court itself. It has continued to develop, institutionally speaking, with different justices animating it over time. They have perceived and used their authority in varying ways, making for a rich judicial history.

In what follows we review the primary characteristics of six major Court eras and how each added to the Court's development. Below are explanations of two terms frequently used in discussions of the Court.

---

[16] Robert A. Dahl, "Decision-Making in a Democracy: The Supreme Court as a National Policy-Maker," *Journal of Public Law* 6 (Fall 1957): 279–295.

Supreme Court scholars often employ the terms *liberal* and *conservative* as shorthand ways to describe individual justices. Similarly, the Court itself can be classified as liberal or conservative depending upon the dominant political ideologies of the sitting justices and the nature of the decisions being rendered. While there has been some variation in the meaning of these concepts over time, conservative justices are those whose decisions tend to benefit the politically and economically advantaged classes. Conservative rulings give a preference to private property rights over the authority of the government to regulate the economy. Conservatives traditionally have a predisposition to favor states' rights on federalism questions and to be less supportive of expanded civil liberties and the rights of the criminally accused. Liberal justices, on the other hand, generally prefer legal change that works to benefit the disadvantaged classes. Liberals also have a greater faith in power exercised by the federal government rather than by the states. Liberal courts tend to give greater support to expanded civil liberties and the rights of the criminally accused. Over time the ideology of the Court majority has varied between liberal and conservative positions on major issues of legal and public policy.

The Least Significant Branch of Government (1790–1800)

Prior to the ascension of John Marshall, the Supreme Court was an impoverished institution, lacking prestige or significant authority. We can see this on a number of dimensions. First, while it was supposed to hold two sessions per year (in February and August), several were cancelled. The first session was a wash because only three of the six justices showed up in New York, the nation's first capital. When the Court moved to Philadelphia in 1791, the yellow fever epidemic forced it to cancel three more. And even when it did meet, it had very little business to conduct. Between 1791 and 1792, it heard no cases. Indeed, over the course of the entire decade it decided fewer than fifty cases—a big difference from today, when the justices receive five thousand petitions to review each year!

Another indication is that presidents had a difficult time convincing their favored nominees to accept positions and then to remain on the Court. One of George Washington's first nominees, Robert Harrison, declined an associate justiceship to take a more prestigious position as chancellor of Maryland. Even the nation's first two confirmed chief justices, John Jay and Oliver Ellsworth, were relatively apathetic about their Court duties. After his 1794 appointment as a special ambassador to England, Jay never returned to the Court. He later resigned to take another what he considered to be an influential position, the governorship of New York. Ellsworth also was far too enamored with his diplomatic work abroad (in France) to worry about the Court and resigned in 1800.

Why was it so difficult to find and retain justices? After all, today it is a distinct honor to serve on the Supreme Court of the United States. Part of the answer is that being a justice in the early years was arduous work. To be sure, the justices did not have a cumbersome workload, with so few cases coming to the Court. Yet they did have to attend to their business as circuit court judges (recall that, under the Judiciary Act, two Supreme Court justices sat on each circuit court), which meant traveling—by horseback—long distances on difficult paths to reach courthouses. Not surprisingly, the justices complained bitterly about this duty.

It also was true that the formative justices found themselves at the center of controversy quite early. Though they decided very few cases, at least one, *Chisholm v. Georgia* (1793), was the source of some outrage among the populace. When, in *Chisholm,* the Court allowed two citizens of South Carolina to sue the state of Georgia in federal court, supporters of state authority were angered. They thought it quite inappropriate for a sovereign state to be compelled to defend itself in a federal court when sued by citizens from another state. In response, Congress proposed and the states ratified the Eleventh Amendment to overturn the decision. Hence, on one of the few occasions when the Court actually reached an important decision, it was greeted by a hostile public.

Given all of this, it is not too surprising that the early Court played a minimal role in the new government. Indeed, perhaps John Jay said it best when he declined to accept President Adams's renomination for the chief justice position after Oliver Ellsworth resigned:

> The efforts repeatedly made to place the Judicial Department on a proper footing have proved fruitless. I left the bench perfectly convinced that under a system so defective, it would not obtain the energy, weight and dignity which are essential to its affording due support to the National Government, nor acquire the public confidence and respect which, as the last resort of the justice of the nation, it should possess.[17]

The Marshall Court Era (1801–1835)

When John Adams nominated John Marshall to be chief justice, he ushered in a completely new era in Court history. With Marshall at the helm, the Court sought to overcome its past and establish itself as an important institution within our governmental system. A big step toward this goal came in *Marbury v. Madison,* in which Marshall demonstrated to the powers-that-be that the Court would review their actions and strike down those incompatible with the Constitution. Another Marshall innovation was the eradication of the traditional *sertiatim* practice in which each justice wrote his own separate opinion in every case. The view of the new chief justice was that the Court needed to speak authoritatively and with one voice. To that end, he established the practice of a single "opinion of the court," which would encapsulate the views of the majority and would be systematically recorded and reported to the public.

---

[17] Elder Witt, *Congressional Quarterly's Guide to the U.S. Supreme Court,* 2nd ed. (Washington, D.C.: Congressional Quarterly, 1990), 8.

Even so, as Lawrence Baum wrote, the Marshall Court "was concerned with more than its own position. It addressed major issues of public policy as well."[18] True enough. Despite the fact that the business before the Court consisted largely of rather trivial private law disputes (maritime, property, contracts), it managed to hand down a number of significant opinions interpreting various aspects of the Constitution, such as nation-state relations and the powers of the other institutions. Importantly, Marshall Court opinions had a distinct trend. They lent solid support for the right to private property and the freedom of contract. But more importantly, Marshall's solid Federalist philosophy of preferring a strong national government over states' rights was branded onto the Constitution.

Although this era came to an end on July 6, 1835, with the death of John Marshall, his imprint on the Court remains ever so strong. As Elder Witt put it, "No one had done more than John Marshall to establish [the] enormous power [of federal judges] or to win the essential public respect for the still-young Supreme Court of the United States."[19] The same could be said of his effect on law. So many of his opinions remain "good law" today, forming the foundation for judicial interpretations of essential constitutional relationships.

The Taney and Civil War Court Eras (1836–1888)

Marshall has gone down in history as *the* greatest Supreme Court justice but, in the context of the day, he had many enemies, particularly among those who supported states' rights. They viewed Marshall's opinions as significant perversions of the careful balance of power between the states and the federal government set in the Constitution. But, of course, while Marshall was chief justice of the United States, it was his view of nation-state relations—not those of the states' rights advocates—that prevailed. That would change with Roger B. Taney's ascension to the chief justiceship.

On some scores, Marshall and Taney were not all that dissimilar. In particular, both were committed partisan activists.[20] The difference, of course, was that they were committed to significantly different conceptions of our government structure, particularly on federalism questions. Where Marshall was a Federalist, Taney was a Jacksonian Democrat, a full believer in those ideas espoused by Andrew Jackson, the president under whom he had served as attorney general, secretary of war and of the treasury, and who had appointed him chief justice. Where Marshall viewed the federal government as supreme, Taney (and Jackson) thought states' rights were not incompatible with those powers possessed by the national government. Had Taney been President Jackson's only appointment to the Court, he might not have been able to change the course of federal-state

---

[18] Lawrence Baum, *The Supreme Court,* 4th ed. (Washington, D.C.: CQ Press, 1992), 20.

[19] Quoted in Witt, *Guide to the Supreme Court,* 14.

[20] We adopt this discussion from Epstein and Walker, *Constitutional Law for a Changing America.*

relations, but that was not the case. Before his tenure was completed Jackson appointed six justices to the Court. Martin Van Buren followed with two additional justices of the same ideological stripe. By 1841, the balance of the Court was, like Taney, schooled in Jacksonian democracy. "It was," as Kent Newmyer noted, no longer "the Marshall Court. But, then again, it was not the age of Marshall."[21]

Despite this rather dramatic change in overall direction, the Court generally thrived under the leadership of Taney, at least until his opinion in the infamous 1857 case of *Dred Scott v. Sandford.* By holding that blacks had no real constitutional status, the Court firmly planted its feet in the states' rights, proslavery camp of the South. To make matters worse, *Dred Scott* could not have come at a worse time for nationalists. At that point the nation was on the verge of collapse. Taney's holding did little to settle the issues; it added fuel to the fire. Several years later, the logic of his *Dred Scott* ruling appeared in an even more attenuated form, when South Carolina issued its "Declaration of the Causes of Secession." President Lincoln, of course, presented precisely the opposite view—the Marshall approach to federal-state relations—in his 1861 inaugural address. But his words were insufficient to stop the outbreak of war. The *Dred Scott* decision and the war that followed left the Court at its weakest level since the pre-Marshall days, overshadowing the generally positive contributions of the Taney years.

In the immediate aftermath of the Civil War, the Court was led by chief justices Salmon Chase and Morrison Waite, who brought it back in line with the existing ruling regime. That is, the Court acceded (though not willingly) to congressional power over the defeated Southern region. And, with contentious regional issues settled by the war, the Court began to deal with a burgeoning caseload reflecting the many commercial and private law disputes the war had generated.

The Laissez-Faire *Court Era (1889–1937)*

With the Civil War behind it, the nation settled into the Industrial Revolution, characterized by the rapid expansion of business and industry throughout the United States. Not surprisingly, the Court's docket reflected the many economic questions such industrialization raised: Congress's authority to regulate commerce and the power of states to impose regulations on business, to name just two.

What was also not surprising was the Court's willingness to protect commercial interests from governmental attempts to regulate them. Between 1889 and 1933, seven of nine presidents were Republicans who advocated the advantages of a private market economy. These presidents, in turn, generally nominated justices who held similar views. As a result, activist Courts emerged, willing to strike down both state and federal laws seeking to regulate the powerful trusts

---

[21] R. Kent Newmyer, *The Supreme Court Under Marshall and Taney* (New York: Crowell, 1968), 94.

and holding companies of the day. During the 1920s, for example, the Court held more than 130 regulatory laws violative of various sections of the Constitution.[22] At the same time, though, the justices were perfectly willing to allow state control over civil rights policy, for one, ruling in the infamous case of *Plessy v. Ferguson* (1896) that "separate but equal" policies (those that segregated the races) were constitutional.

The Court's unwillingness to uphold regulations on businesses, in particular, came to a head in 1936–1937. By then, President Franklin Roosevelt, tired of seeing his New Deal legislation overturned by "holdover" (and old) justices, proposed a plan to appoint one new justice for every sitting member over the age of seventy. Although Roosevelt's "Court-packing" plan gathered insufficient congressional or public support for passage, in the end it may have contributed to a change in the Court's behavior. By 1937, the justices began to uphold New Deal laws that were not too different from those it had struck down the previous year. Some have termed this dramatic turn of events the "switch in time that saved nine."

The Roosevelt and Warren Court Eras (1937–1969)

After the famous "switch," the Court experienced a rapid turnover in membership as its older members retired. This gave Roosevelt the opportunity to appoint eight new justices. As a result, the newly composed Court continued upon the course charted in 1937, especially when it came to resolving disputes involving economic liberties.

Interestingly, too, the Court began to place greater emphasis on issues of civil rights, liberties, and justice. This new focus only sharpened with the appointment of Earl Warren to the chief justiceship in 1953. Although Warren, as a former California attorney general and as governor of the state, had been regarded as a moderate-conservative, he presided over what can only be described as a constitutional revolution, generated by a group of justices who were perhaps the most liberal in American history. A partial list of the more important Warren Court rulings includes: *Brown v. Board of Education* (1954), which overruled the "separate but equal" doctrine; *Baker v. Carr* (1962), which ultimately forced states to reapportion their legislative districts; *Griswold v. Connecticut* (1965), which created a constitutional right to privacy; and *Miranda v. Arizona* (1966), which required police to read suspects a set of warnings before interrogating them.

To be sure, these rulings were (and continue to be) important, but that does not mean they were particularly well regarded. In fact, many of the Warren Court's holdings were severely criticized. Initially, it was Congress that sought to stifle the Warren Court, but it was presidential nominee Richard Nixon in 1968 who was its loudest and most successful public critic. During his 1968 campaign

---

[22] Baum, *The Supreme Court,* 21.

and the early days of his presidency Nixon emphasized the theme of "law and order," claimed that the Supreme Court had gone too far in protecting the rights of the criminally accused, and pledged to appoint conservative "strict constructionists" to rebalance constitutional priorities. As he remarked in his August 1968 acceptance speech,

> And tonight it's time for some honest talk about the problem of order in the United States. Let us always respect, as I do, our courts and those who serve on them, but let us also recognize that some of our courts in their decisions have gone too far in weakening the peace forces as against the criminal forces in this country.

The Republican Court Era (1969–   )

After his electoral victory, President Nixon soon got the chance to fulfill his promise to restore law and order to American communities, as he appointed four justices to the Court. One of his earliest presidential acts was the nomination of Warren Burger to fill the chief justiceship vacated by Earl Warren. In Nixon's eyes, Burger was an ideal choice to lead a counterrevolution against the Warren Court's liberal jurisprudence. Prior to his elevation to the Supreme Court, Burger had been a judge on the U.S. Court of Appeals for the District of Columbia, where he was known to favor the government in cases of criminal law and procedure. When Burger took his seat, along with the later Nixon appointees William Rehnquist, Harry Blackmun, and Lewis Powell, the beginnings of a radically different Court era seemed imminent.

To be sure, the overall "conservatism" of the Court did increase. For example, the "new" Court was far less supportive of criminal rights than was Warren's (although it did not completely overturn any of the Warren Court's significant rulings, as some had expected). But the results of that ideological shift were not felt uniformly across all issues. It was the Burger Court that, among other innovations, legalized abortion, legitimated school busing, and provided women with heightened protection under the Fourteenth Amendment. As Stephen Wasby astutely observed:

> Perhaps because of the fanfare President Nixon made over his desire to change the Court's direction, the tendency of many commentators has been to *expect*—and from that to *see*—much change. . . . Starting from a presumption of *dis*continuity, they have tended to emphasize discontinuities with the Warren Court rulings. . . .
> A close look at what occurred through the 1973 Term does *not* produce such a picture. There has indeed been change. However, the importance of maintaining earlier rulings has been under-estimated, areas of noticeable continuity have been missed, and areas where the Burger Court has advanced along the paths first marked by Earl Warren and his brethren have

been set aside. Growth has been ignored, while the amount of erosion that has occurred has been played up.[23]

The Burger Court's *relatively* supportive attitude toward many disadvantaged interests (aside from the criminally accused) was not substantially interrupted by the 1975 resignation of the Court's most stalwart liberal, William Douglas, and the elevation of John Paul Stevens by President Gerald Ford. To the contrary, Stevens provided the Warren Court holdovers with important votes in many cases. His support for abortion rights, separation of church and state, and even the occasional criminal defendant kept the Burger Court from taking a full tilt to the right.

But this may no longer be the case. By 1992, Ronald Reagan and George Bush had appointed six of the Court's nine members, including the elevation of the Burger Court's most conservative member, William Rehnquist, to the chief justiceship. The counterrevolution that Nixon tried to launch may be in high gear. It is tempting to say that our most recent Republican president, George Bush, closed the book on the Warren era. The elevations of David Souter and Clarence Thomas have, in effect, exchanged the Court's last strong liberals, William Brennan and Thurgood Marshall, for justices who are substantially more conservative. The net result of these appointments has been to drive the Court further to the right. To date, the Rehnquist Court has already significantly narrowed the rights of the criminally accused, has been rather intolerant of governmentally imposed affirmative action programs, and has narrowed the abortion right created in *Roe v. Wade* (1973).

TODAY'S SUPREME COURT:
ITS ROLES IN THE AMERICAN LEGAL SYSTEM
AND IN THE GOVERNMENTAL PROCESS

As the discussion above makes clear, the Court has changed substantially over the past two hundred years. We can attribute some of this to the different justices who have served. But it is equally true that changes in the Court and in its roles have occurred as by-products of alterations in the structure of the American judiciary per se and in the relationship between it and the other political branches.

To put it succinctly, the U.S. Supreme Court has evolved as an important legal and political institution. As we describe below, it sits at the pinnacle of the American judicial system, presumably setting legal policy for all courts in the nation to follow. Nonetheless, as we shall see, it is also a political institution. It

---

[23] Stephen L. Wasby, *Continuity and Change* (Pacific Palisades, Calif.: Goodyear Publishing Co., 1976), 7–8.

interacts with the other branches of government to make decisions for the nation, decisions that quite often reflect the politics of the day.

The Pinnacle of the American Legal System

Though the 1789 Judiciary Act was the first major piece of congressional legislation relating to the courts, it was surely not the last. Since then Congress has enacted numerous laws concerning the federal judiciary; the states too have considerably altered the structure of their courts.

As we depict in Figure 1-1, those enactments have changed rather markedly our judicial system, or at the very least, its structure. Today, we can talk about our system as one that is dual, parallel, and three-tiered. It is dual because both the federal and state systems continue to coexist, each ruling on disputes falling under their particular purviews. This does not mean, however, that state courts never hear cases involving claims made under the U.S. Constitution, for example; or that federal courts necessarily shun cases arising out of state law. In fact, the Supreme Court can review cases involving federal questions on which state

FIGURE 1-1
The American Legal System

Federal Courts	State Courts
Highest Appellate Courts	
U. S. Supreme Court	State Supreme Court[a]
Intermediate Appellate Courts	
U.S. Courts of Appeals Court of Appeals for the Federal Circuit Temporary Emergency Court of Appeals	Courts of Appeals[b]
Trial Courts of General Jurisdiction	
U.S. District Courts	District Courts[c]
Trial Courts of Limited Jurisdiction	
Tax Court Rail Reorganization Court Claims Court Court of International Trade Court of Veterans Appeals	Examples include: Juvenile Court, Family Court, Small Claims Court, Justice of the Peace Court, Magistrate's Court, Traffic Court

[a]Sometimes called Supreme Judicial Court or Court of Appeals.
[b]These exist in about two-thirds of all states.
[c]Sometimes called circuit courts, courts of common pleas, superior courts.

supreme courts have ruled and can strike down state laws if they are incompatible with the Constitution. Similarly, many cases arising from state law and heard in state courts also contain federal law issues that must be resolved.

The case of *R.A.V. v. City of St. Paul, MN* (1992) provides an interesting example of the dual court system in action. It illustrates how a legal action can begin at the lowest levels of a state's judiciary and ultimately be decided by the federal Supreme Court. At issue here is an ordinance, enacted by the city of St. Paul, Minnesota, that prohibits certain kinds of "hate" expression. When R.A.V. (a seventeen-year-old high school dropout, Robert A. Viktora) allegedly burned a cross inside the fenced yard of the home of a black family living in the St. Paul area, the city charged R.A.V. with violating the ordinance. A state trial court judge, however, dismissed the charges against R.A.V., asserting that the ordinance violated freedom of expression guarantees contained in the First Amendment of the U.S. Constitution. The city appealed that decision to the Minnesota Supreme Court, which reversed the trial court's decision. It held that the ordinance was compatible with the First Amendment. In 1991, the Supreme Court of the United States agreed to review the Minnesota court's decision.

We refer to our system as a parallel and three-tiered one because we can map state and federal court hierarchies together. While differences exist among the states (recall that the Framers permitted each to retain and develop its own system), most today roughly parallel the federal system. As we can see in Figure 1-1, the bottom rungs of both consist of trial courts, the entry points into the system. At the middle of the ladder are appellate courts, those that upon request review the records of trial court proceedings. Finally, both have supreme courts, bodies that provide final answers to legal issues within their own domains. In the cross-burning case, for example, had the U.S. Supreme Court declined to review the Minnesota Supreme Court's ruling, the decision of the state court would have stood as the final judgment on the St. Paul ordinance.

While a supreme court sits atop each ladder, the U.S. Supreme Court plays a unique role—it is the apex of both state and federal court systems. Because it can hear cases (and ultimately overturn rulings) of state and federal court judges, it is presumably *the* authoritative legal body in the United States. In other words, when the Supreme Court speaks, the judiciary *should* listen. Whether or not it does is a question we take up in Chapter 6.

The Court and the Governmental Process

Though the Court is a legal body, it is a political institution as well. We see this on two levels: the Court is a key actor within the governmental process and its own processes are marked by politics. On the first dimension, we note several points of interaction between the Court and other governmental units and actors. The most obvious one is that the justices continue to exert their power to strike down laws and other government actions found to be in violation of the

federal Constitution. In Figure 1-2, we depict the number of cases in which the
Court struck down a federal, state, or local law. On the one hand, the data seem
to indicate that the Court has made frequent use of the power, striking down
more than 1,300 governmental acts since 1790. On the other, as Baum notes,
those represent a minute fraction of the laws enacted at various levels of our
governmental system. Between the 1790s and 1990s, for example, Congress

FIGURE 1-2

**Provisions of Federal, State, and Local Laws and Ordinances Held Unconstitutional by
the Supreme Court, 1786–1990**

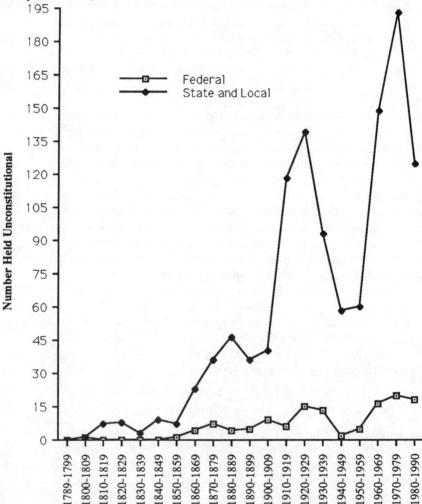

Source: Harold W. Stanley and Richard G. Niemi, *Vital Statistics on American Politics* (Washington,
D.C.: CQ Press, 1992), 306.

passed more than 60,000 laws, with the Court striking down far less than 1 percent.[24]

The more important question, then, may be one of significance: Does the Court tend to strike down important laws or relatively minor ones? Using the case of *Dred Scott v. Sandford* as illustrative, some argue that the Court does, in fact, often strike significant legislation. Undoubtedly, that was an opinion of major consequence. By ruling that Congress could not prohibit slavery in the territories and by striking down a law that had already been repealed (the Missouri Compromise), the Court fed into the growing divisions between the North and South, providing a major impetus for the Civil War. The decision also tarnished the prestige of the Court itself and the reputation of Chief Justice Roger Taney. But how representative is *Dred Scott*? Clearly, other Court opinions striking down governmental acts have neared it in importance. Those nullifying state abortion and segregation laws, the federal child labor acts, and many pieces of New Deal legislation were controversial and significant. Yet "a good many of the Court's decisions declaring measures unconstitutional, perhaps a majority, were unimportant to the policy goals of Congress and the president."[25] A similarly substantial portion of the state and local laws voided by the Court have been of relatively minor significance.

What, then, can we conclude about the Court's use of judicial review? On the whole, the record is rather murky. To be sure, judicial review is the Supreme Court's most significant check on the actions of other governmental officials. Yet, as Baum concludes, "While judicial review has helped the Court to play a major role in policy making, it certainly has not made the Court the dominant national policy maker."[26]

This, then, brings us to another point of interaction between the Court and the more political branches. Even when the justices do not strike down legislation, the simple act of reviewing laws can enmesh them in political controversy and can help set the agendas of other institutions. The 1989 case of *Webster v. Reproductive Health Services* provides a good example. In this instance, the Court reviewed a Missouri law that placed numerous restrictions on the right to obtain an abortion. When a majority of the justices agreed to uphold the legislation, they set into motion a national debate on the subject that continues to affect everything from the selection of future justices to the election of state legislators, governors, and members of Congress.

It is not only its rulings that define the Court as a political branch; political factors seep into virtually all aspects of the Court's operating procedures. A long line of scholarship demonstrates that political influences are now abundantly

---

[24] Baum, *The Supreme Court,* 185–191.

[25] Ibid., 186. For a list of federal laws struck down by the Court, see Witt, *Guide to the Supreme Court,* 1001–1009.

[26] Baum, *The Supreme Court,* 191.

present in the judiciary, and that the effect of this politicalization has touched virtually all aspects of the Court. Studies of judicial decision making—as we will describe in Chapter 5—have shown that judges frequently act as if their political attitudes dominate their decisions, rather than legal factors such as precedent. Students of the courts also have demonstrated that the political environment— encompassing factors such as party control of the government, public opinion, and the political setting—is at least sometimes associated with judicial out- comes. We also know that interest groups and other political actors regularly try to influence the Court's decisions, often with substantial success. We consider their role in Chapter 3. Finally, it is safe to say that the selection procedure by which presidents nominate and the Senate confirms is very much a political one. The Senate, for example, itself under pressure from organized interests and constituents, has pressed virtually all recent nominees to articulate their posi- tions on the "big" issues of our time. This is a subject we take up in the next chapter.

CONCLUSION

At the beginning of this chapter we noted that Americans have a great deal of confidence in the U.S. Supreme Court, but at the same time it is the branch of government about which they have the least amount of knowledge. Having read this chapter, perhaps now you can appreciate the confusion surrounding the Court. What began as a "legal" institution, with limited power and prestige, has now been transformed into a major political branch of government, one that wields great power in our system. Clearly, the Supreme Court is different from the other institutions of the national government. For example, its unique selec- tion and retention system sets it apart from the more political branches. Yet its history and decisions show that it may not be as different as some suppose. Political forces and influences do infiltrate its decisions, especially when the justices consider politically sensitive topics and rule on the Court's relationship with other institutions. It is this duality of role, as we shall see throughout this book, that makes the Court so intriguing and unusual.

ADDITIONAL READINGS

Abraham, Henry J. *The Judiciary: The Supreme Court in the Governmental Process,* 8th ed.
    (Dubuque, Iowa: Wm. C. Brown, 1991).
Baum, Lawrence. *The Supreme Court,* 4th ed. (Washington, D.C.: CQ Press, 1992).
McCloskey, Robert G. *The American Supreme Court* (Chicago: University of Chicago Press,
    1960).
O'Brien, David M. *Storm Center,* 2nd ed. (New York: W. W. Norton, 1990).

Rohde, David W., and Harold J. Spaeth. *Supreme Court Decision Making* (San Francisco: W. H. Freeman, 1976).

Segal, Jeffrey A. and Harold J. Spaeth. *The Supreme Court and the Attitudinal Modal* (New York: Cambridge University Press, 1990).

Wasby, Stephen L. *The Supreme Court in the Federal Judicial System,* 3rd ed. (Chicago: Nelson-Hall, 1988).

Witt, Elder. *Congressional Quarterly's Guide to the U.S. Supreme Court,* 2nd ed. (Washington, D.C.: CQ Press, 1990).

Two ✑

THE MEMBERS OF
THE COURT

S tudents new to the study of the Supreme Court often find the power and prestige of the institution so incredibly attractive as to prompt the question "Just what does it take to become a Supreme Court justice?" The correct answer is deceptively simple. There are only two requirements for obtaining a seat on the nation's highest court. Persons interested in becoming a justice must first find a president willing to appoint them and, second, a Senate willing to confirm them. The Constitution and federal laws impose no other formal qualifications. This differs markedly from Congress and the presidency. For those offices the Constitution requires candidates to meet formal age, residency, and citizenship qualifications.

The selection process, of course, is much more complicated than these simple formal requirements. The informal process imposes standards that do not appear in any statute book. For example, although there is no formal requirement that a potential justice be an attorney or even have legal training, a person without such minimal qualifications would have no chance of obtaining a seat on the Court. In this chapter we explore the Supreme Court selection process, examining the political forces that block the chances of some potential appointees and lead to the nomination and confirmation of others. We also review the characteristics of those individuals who have served on the nation's highest tribunal, and finish with a discussion of some of the important support personnel who assist the justices in completing their work.

THE SELECTION PROCESS

Some Supreme Court nominations, such as Ronald Reagan's 1987 selection of Robert Bork or George Bush's 1991 naming of Clarence Thomas, are very controversial and attract a great deal of publicity. Others, like Reagan's nomination of Anthony Kennedy in 1988, cause no more than a ripple of public awareness. Regardless of the level of controversy, however, each nomination must maneuver through a long and complicated political maze involving numerous points of scrutiny.

The Vacancy

There are, of course, a fixed and limited number of seats on the Supreme Court. The size of the Court is set by congressional statute and has varied over the nation's history.[1] Before the president can make an appointment to the Court a vacancy in one of those seats must occur.

THE SIZE OF THE COURT   In the Judiciary Act of 1789 Congress established six Court positions, five for the associate justices and one for a chief justice. During its first century the size of the Court was changed on several occasions, ranging from a low of five to a high of ten seats. Many of these changes were in response to the needs of an expanding judiciary as the nation grew westward. However, some changes have been the result of political maneuvering in Congress and have often reflected the quality of the legislature's relations with the executive branch. For example, in 1863 Congress increased the size of the Court from nine to ten in order to give President Lincoln an opportunity to appoint an additional justice who supported positions favorable to the Union. A reverse action was taken by the Republican-dominated legislature following the Civil War. To prohibit President Andrew Johnson, a Tennessee Democrat, from having any impact on the Court, Congress passed legislation allowing the number of justices to decrease to seven before the president would have an appointment. Congress nullified this statute as soon as Johnson's term expired. In 1869, during President Ulysses S. Grant's administration, the legislature reestablished nine as the size of the Court, and it has remained at that level ever since. The only serious twentieth-century attempt to alter the size occurred in 1937 when Franklin Roosevelt, frustrated with Court opposition to his New Deal economic policies, proposed his famous Court-packing plan, which provided that an additional justice be appointed for every sitting member over the age of seventy. Potentially this would have expanded the Court to fifteen justices. The plan, however, failed in Congress and signaled that the nation no longer found it acceptable to manipulate the Court's size for purely political purposes. Certainly, it is not likely that the current size of the Court will be altered in the foreseeable future.

WHEN VACANCIES OCCUR   Court vacancies do not happen on a regularly scheduled basis.[2] There is no fixed term for a Supreme Court justice. The Constitution stipulates that confirmed justices serve for terms of good behavior. Only through death, resignation, retirement, or impeachment does a vacancy occur. On average a justice leaves the Court every two years, but these depar-

---

[1] Stephen L. Wasby, *The Supreme Court in the Federal Judicial System,* 3rd ed. (Chicago: Nelson-Hall, 1988), 71–72.

[2] For a discussion of the occurrence of Supreme Court vacancies, see S. Sidney Ulmer, "Supreme Court Appointments as a Poisson Distribution," *American Journal of Political Science* 26 (February 1982): 111–116.

tures are not evenly distributed. Some presidents are fortunate to be able to replace a number of justices. In recent years, for example, Presidents Truman, Nixon, and Reagan each successfully nominated four justices and Eisenhower five. On the other hand, Franklin Roosevelt suffered through continued battles with the Court during his first term without a single Court vacancy to fill. His fortunes changed, however, when five vacancies occurred during his second term of office. Before he was done, Roosevelt named a total of nine justices. Not so lucky was Jimmy Carter, the only president to serve four or more years and not get a single opportunity to nominate a justice.

INVOLUNTARY TERMINATION   Justices may leave the Court of their own choice or involuntarily. Involuntary vacancies occur under two circumstances. The first is when a justice is removed by impeachment or resigns under threat of impeachment. The second occurs when a justice dies in office.

Removal by impeachment is the least likely cause of a Supreme Court vacancy. It would be an extraordinary event for the Congress to remove a justice from office. According to the Constitution, the House of Representatives has the sole power of charging a justice with the removable offenses of treason, bribery, or other high crimes and misdemeanors.[3] If the House impeaches a member of the Court on such grounds, a trial on the charges is held in the United States Senate. Two-thirds of the senators present must vote for a conviction in order to remove the justice from office.[4]

Although a small number of lower court judges have been impeached and convicted, no Supreme Court justice has ever been removed by the Congress. Samuel Chase, however, narrowly escaped this fate.[5] Justice Chase was appointed by President Washington in 1796. Among all of Washington's Federalist appointments to the Court, Chase was the most blatantly partisan. His behavior on the bench was sharply criticized by the Jeffersonians, and when they gained control of Congress following the 1800 elections it spelled trouble for the justice. By 1804, members of the House had assembled a series of charges against Chase. None of the charges involved actual crimes, but revolved instead around what the Jeffersonians perceived as lack of proper judicial temperament and the biased way the justice handled several politically charged cases. In March of 1804 the House passed a bill of impeachment pressing eight specific charges. The vote in favor of impeachment was 73–32, with the representatives dividing on straight party lines. The Senate trial was held the next year with the opponents of Justice Chase failing to gather the necessary two-thirds majority to remove him from office. He was acquitted on all eight counts.

---

[3] Article I, section 2.

[4] Article I, section 3.

[5] United States Senate, *The Trial of Samuel Chase,* 1805, 8th Congress, second session; Richard Lillich, "The Chase Impeachment," *American Journal of Legal History* 4 (1960): 49.

The Chase case precedent was an important one for the independence of the judiciary because the Senate concluded that the Constitution's impeachment provisions were reserved for behavior that constituted serious wrongdoing, perhaps even criminal behavior.[6] If the Congress had convicted Chase, it might have initiated a tradition of impeaching judges whenever their decisions or behavior were politically objectionable to the members of Congress.

The House of Representatives has not gone so far as to impeach any other member of the Court, but two twentieth-century justices found themselves targets of possible congressional action. On two separate occasions members of Congress called for the removal of William O. Douglas. In 1953 there were demands to investigate Douglas following his issuance of an order staying the execution of Ethel and Julius Rosenberg, who had been convicted of spying for the Soviet Union. Then in 1969 Minority Leader (and later President) Gerald Ford charged Douglas with several offenses including conflicts of interest and associations with Las Vegas gambling operations. Douglas survived both attacks. Not so fortunate was Justice Abe Fortas, who in 1969 was accused of ethical impropriety in taking fees from a foundation run by the family of a man who was indicted for violations of securities laws.[7] Members of the House initiated impeachment proceedings. Although Fortas maintained that he was innocent of any wrongdoing, the justice resigned from the Court rather than allow the impeachment process to continue.

Historically the single most common reason for the creation of a vacancy has been death, with 48 percent of the justices dying in office. This was especially the case prior to the twentieth century. In the years before 1900, two-thirds of the justices were struck down by death while still in active service. After 1900, death was responsible for only 30 percent of the justices leaving the Court. The death of a sitting justice has been rare in the contemporary period. The last justice to die in office was Robert Jackson, a Franklin Roosevelt appointee, who succumbed to a heart attack in 1954.

VOLUNTARY RETIREMENTS AND RESIGNATIONS   Slightly more than half of the justices have left by their own decision to step down. They have done so for many different reasons. Some have decided to pursue other opportunities. This was especially the case in the early years when service on the Court did not have the prestige it enjoys today. As we saw in the previous chapter, the first chief

---

[6] The standard used for the removal of federal judges can be observed in the case of the lower courts. In the 1980s Congress removed three federal judges. Two, District Judge Harry Claiborne of Nevada and District Judge Walter Nixon of Mississippi, were impeached after being convicted of criminal offenses, Claiborne of tax evasion and Nixon of perjury before a grand jury. Alcee Hastings, a federal district judge from Florida, was also removed. He had not been convicted of criminal charges. In fact, Hastings has been acquitted of bribery offenses. Nevertheless, the legislators found evidence of sufficient wrongdoing to agree that he should be removed.

[7] See Robert Shogan, *A Question of Judgment: The Fortas Case and the Struggle for the Supreme Court* (Indianapolis: Bobbs-Merrill, 1972).

justice, John Jay, left the Court in order to become governor of New York; and John Rutledge resigned in order to become chief justice of South Carolina. Occasionally this has also occurred in more recent times. Arthur Goldberg, for instance, resigned in 1965 to accept Lyndon Johnson's nomination to become ambassador to the United Nations.

Others did not find Court service to their liking. Disenchanted as a justice, John Clarke resigned in 1922 in order to devote his life to world peace and the success of the League of Nations. James Byrnes left in 1942, after having been appointed just the previous year, because he wanted to return to the world of active politics particularly at a time when the nation was at war. Charles Whittaker became a private citizen in 1962 after five years of service when he found the workload unbearable. Still others have left the Court for their own unique reasons. John Campbell, for example, resigned in 1861 to join the Confederacy, which he served as assistant secretary of war. Tom Clark stepped down in 1967 to allow President Lyndon Johnson to nominate his son, Ramsey, to be attorney general, thus removing any potential conflicts of interest.

The most common reason for voluntary termination of Court service, especially in recent years, has been advanced age or failing health. Justice Hugo Black and John Marshall Harlan retired in the summer of 1971. Black was eighty-five and Harlan seventy-two. Both were dead within the next three months. William O. Douglas retired in 1975, at seventy-seven years, bowing to the effects of a serious stroke. Between 1986 and 1991, Chief Justice Warren Burger and Associate Justices Lewis Powell, William Brennan, and Thurgood Marshall retired, with age (the youngest was Burger at seventy-nine years) and possible declining health a factor in each case. As Thurgood Marshall explained to the press upon retiring, "I'm old and I'm coming apart."

Age and health considerations may overcome the firm intentions of a justice to remain in office for political or policy reasons. The liberal Marshall, for example, had vowed to stay on the bench for as long as possible rather than allow the conservative Ronald Reagan or George Bush to name his replacement. Chief Justice William Howard Taft claimed, "As long as things continue as they are, and I am able to answer in my place, I must stay on the court in order to prevent the Bolsheviks from getting control."[8] Taft ultimately was forced to bow to age and health considerations, retiring in February of 1930. He died only a month later.

A factor in the increased voluntary terminations in this century has been the retirement benefits available to justices meeting the necessary service requirements. Under current law justices may retire on full salary if the sum of their age and years of service equals or exceeds eighty. Consequently, a justice seventy years of age with ten years of service or sixty-five with fifteen years on the bench may leave active duty with a full salary pension that includes any future salary increases

---

[8] See C. Herman Pritchett, *The Roosevelt Court* (New York: Macmillan, 1948), 18.

given to sitting justices. A justice meeting these requirements may leave the bench without suffering financial loss. This was not the case in the early years of the Court. Congress did not pass any judicial retirement statute until 1869. That law was enacted in part to encourage Justice Robert Grier, who suffered significant mental and physical decline, to retire. Prior to 1869, a justice leaving the Court, no matter the length of service, received no compensation. Of course, retirement benefits eligibility alone is not enough to encourage most justices to leave their prestigious positions, especially if they enjoy their work or prefer not to create a vacancy to be filled by a president of a different political ideology.[9]

The Nomination

When a vacancy occurs, the executive branch swings into action to identify potential nominees. The process is generally the same for all nominations, although when the position of chief justice becomes vacant the executive branch gives even greater care to the decision. Today the initial screening is done in the Justice Department. In fact, in recent administrations lists of preliminary candidates have been prepared in advance and held in reserve awaiting a Court vacancy. There is, of course, no shortage of candidates. The Justice Department and the White House are bombarded with suggestions. They come from almost every conceivable source: members of Congress, interest groups, bar association officials, political party influentials, and members of the judiciary. Sitting or former members of the Supreme Court have even advanced the candidacies of favored individuals. The most active in this regard was William Howard Taft, who served not only as president of the United States but later also as chief justice. Given his experience and status, he often had the ear of the sitting president when it came to judicial appointments. In 1991, a member of the United States Court of Appeals even published a letter in the *New York Times* urging President Bush to nominate one of his Second Circuit colleagues to the High Court.[10]

Justice Department officials may carry out the initial screening; they do so knowing what characteristics the president is seeking. Unlike nominations to the lower federal courts, in which the president's participation may be minimal, no Supreme Court nomination occurs without the chief executive's direct involvement. Supreme Court appointments are too important and the political ramifications too great for the president to delegate this authority to others. While there have been some systematic changes over time and differences from president to president, there are a number of common factors that chief executives consider.

LEGAL AND CHARACTER CONSIDERATIONS   No president wants to appoint to the Court an individual who is not competent to serve. No matter how politically

---

[9] For an analysis of the decision to step down, see Peverill Squire, "Politics and Personal Factors in Retirement from the United States Supreme Court," *Political Behavior* 10 (1988): 180–190.

[10] Jon O. Newman, "A Replacement for Thomas," *New York Times,* October 10, 1991, p. A27.

perfect an individual may be, the candidate must meet certain standards of legal expertise. Today this may include prominent legal education and some experience as a judge or legal practitioner. The nominee should have a reputation for intelligence and objectivity. Americans expect Supreme Court justices who are learned and scholarly, not appointees who are political hacks. When nominees lack a keen mind and a record of legal competence, they often find significant opposition during the confirmation process. Richard Nixon's nomination of G. Harrold Carswell in 1969 serves as an example.[11] Not only did Carswell run into serious difficulties caused by opposition from civil rights groups, but his record as a lower court jurist was called into question. He had one of the highest rates of having his rulings reversed by appeals courts. Carswell had demonstrated neither the intelligence nor the legal scholarship to warrant appointment to the world's most important court. Even Carswell's supporters had difficulty marshalling arguments on his behalf. Senator Roman Hruska (R-Neb.) impressed no one when he defended Carswell by saying: "Even if he were mediocre, there are a lot of mediocre judges and people and lawyers. They are entitled to a little representation, aren't they, and a little chance? We can't have all Brandeises and Frankfurters and Cardozos and stuff like that there."[12] The Senate responded by rejecting Carswell's nomination 45–51.

Similarly, the nominee should have ethical standards that are above question. This has especially been the case in the post-Watergate era. Judge Clement Haynsworth, a Nixon nominee in 1969, was ultimately defeated by the Senate in part because of conflict of interest charges. The executive branch goes to great lengths, including full investigations by the Federal Bureau of Investigation, to evaluate potential nominees for character or ethical deficiencies, knowing full well that if such traits exist they will ultimately be revealed by the press or in the Senate confirmation process. Such was the case in 1987 when Ronald Reagan announced his decision to nominate appeals court judge Douglas Ginsburg. The appointment was derailed even before the Senate formally received the nomination when press investigations turned up evidence of Ginsburg's use of marijuana years before. An even more spectacular reaction erupted in 1991 when charges of sexual harassment were made against Clarence Thomas.

PARTISAN AND IDEOLOGICAL CONSIDERATIONS   Perhaps more important than any other factor is the selection of a justice whose legal and political views are consistent with those of the president. Given that the Court will be interpreting the Constitution and federal laws and determining the validity of executive actions, a president would indeed be remiss to ignore this factor. When the chief executive miscalculates and elevates an individual who interprets the law at odds with the president's preferences, the impact can be substantial. Dwight Eisen-

---

[11] See Richard Harris, *Decision* (New York: Ballantine Books, 1971).
[12] Ibid., 117.

hower, for example, was forthright in expressing his disappointment in Earl Warren and William Brennan, whose nominations he branded the biggest mistakes of his presidential tenure.

The search for nominees with compatible political views, coupled with patronage considerations, usually leads to the selection of a nominee from the president's political party. The tradition of partisan selection was initiated by George Washington, whose eleven Court appointments were all Federalists. Over the course of history 90 percent of all justices appointed have been members of the president's party. In those few cases in which the president has selected a member of the opposition party, the nominee usually has been ideologically close to the president. Republican Theodore Roosevelt made this point in considering Democrat Horace Lurton for the Court, when he wrote to Henry Cabot Lodge, " . . . the *nominal* politics of the man has nothing to do with his actions on the bench. His *real* politics are all important."[13] For example, when conservative Republican Warren Harding nominated Democrat Pierce Butler, he could hardly have chosen someone whose ideology was closer to his own. Several of the cross-party nominations have been instances in which Republican presidents have selected Southern Democrats. Examples are President Taft's nominations of Horace Lurton of Tennessee and Joseph Lamar of Georgia, and Richard Nixon's selection of Lewis Powell of Virginia. However, on some occasions cross-party nominations have led to justices whose decisions ran in direct conflict with the president's political ideology. Herbert Hoover's nomination of Benjamin Cardozo and Eisenhower's selection of William Brennan are cases in point.

In recent years great attention has been placed on the Court appointments of Ronald Reagan and George Bush. Sharp attacks have been made on these presidents for placing too much attention on the ideological positions of their nominees. Critics have claimed that as a consequence of appointing only Republican conservatives, Reagan and Bush have robbed the Court of appropriate political balance. While the critics' description of the Reagan-Bush appointments is generally accurate, it should be remembered that presidents have always understood the significance of the political and legal philosophies of the members of the Supreme Court. Almost all of our chief executives have chosen their Court nominees with this as a dominant factor. For example, Abraham Lincoln named his justices with the notion that only individuals loyal to the president's view of the union would be considered. Certainly Franklin Roosevelt never considered appointing an individual to the Court who did not share a commitment to his liberal New Deal economic programs.

AGE   Undoubtedly the age of a potential nominee plays a role in the president's thinking. Because there is no set term of office, a justice may serve a

---

[13] Henry Cabot Lodge, *Selections from the Correspondence of Theodore Roosevelt and Henry Cabot Lodge,* 1884–1918 (New York: Charles Scribner's Sons, 1925), vol. 2, p. 228.

quarter century or more. In fact, Supreme Court nominations may well extend a president's influence far beyond his term of office. John Adams's last-minute nomination of John Marshall as chief justice, for example, allowed the philosophy of the Federalist party to continue having a meaningful role in government for the next thirty-five years, in spite of the fact that no Federalist candidate would ever again win the presidency and the party would never again control either house of Congress. A more recent example is Byron White, the most senior member of the Court as it entered the 1990s. White had been appointed seven presidencies earlier by John F. Kennedy.

In considering age, the president must walk a careful line. From the president's perspective nominees must be of sufficient age and experience to have well-established and firmly set political and legal philosophies. If the president is to select a relatively young candidate who will likely serve for decades, there can be little room for ideological miscalculations. Younger nominees may also spark opposition, as occurred when George Bush nominated the forty-three-year-old Clarence Thomas. Yet the president knows that selecting an older nominee will likely result in a shorter period of Court service. Historically, presidents have been most comfortable nominating justices who are in their mid-fifties, old enough to have a relatively predictable record, and yet young enough to expect a reasonably long tenure.

A nominee's opponents, as well as supporters, accept considerable risk if they ignore the age factor. When President Reagan nominated the conservative, combative, and scholarly Robert Bork in 1987, he touched off the most hotly contested nomination battle in modern history. Democratic politicians and liberal interest groups opposed the nomination with great vigor and ultimately secured Bork's defeat. President Reagan responded by nominating federal appeals court judge Anthony Kennedy to fill the vacancy. Kennedy received Senate approval by a unanimous vote. In some ways, however, the liberals' victory was a hollow one. They had defeated the sixty-year-old Bork and in his place received the fifty-two-year-old Kennedy. Justice Kennedy's voting record has been easily as conservative as the liberal forces feared Bork's would be, and given their age differences there is every reason to expect that Kennedy's tenure will be much longer than Bork's would have been.

GEOGRAPHICAL REPRESENTATION   During our nation's first century, geography played a major role in the nomination process.[14] National politics revolved around sectional concerns. There was an expectation that each region of the nation deserved representation on the Court. For many years appointments were informally tied to the judicial circuits, with one justice appointed from each. Consequently, it was usually the case that a justice who left the Court would be replaced by a nominee from the same section of the country. It would have

---

[14] See Henry J. Abraham, *Justices and Presidents,* 2nd ed. (New York: Oxford University Press, 1985).

been politically unthinkable to leave a region unrepresented. On several occasions otherwise qualified and well-positioned candidates were denied nomination for failure to meet the geographical requirements.

In more recent decades the importance of the geographical factor has greatly diminished. When Lewis Powell retired in 1987 he left the Court without a Southerner for the first time since Reconstruction. In spite of this, the next five nominations (Bork, Ginsburg, Kennedy, Scalia, and Souter) went to candidates from other regions. This situation was rectified only in 1991 when Clarence Thomas of Georgia was selected to fill Thurgood Marshall's seat, and in that case Thomas's geographical origin was not a significant factor. During this same period, four of the nine sitting justices were from the Far West (Rehnquist, O'Connor, White, and Kennedy), with two (Rehnquist and O'Connor) from the relatively small state of Arizona. In the early periods of our history, a second justice from even a large state such as New York would have raised serious questions.

This is not to say that geography totally vanished from the selection scene during the last half of the twentieth century. In fact, President Richard Nixon, in order to gain political support from the South, pledged to nominate a Southerner to the Court. He attempted to make good on this promise with his first opportunity to select an associate justice. Unfortunately for Southern interests, Nixon failed to gain confirmation for either Clement Haynsworth of South Carolina or G. Harrold Carswell of Florida. Finally he turned to a Northerner, Harry Blackmun of Minnesota, to fill that position in 1970. Southerners had to wait an additional year before Nixon successfully appointed Lewis Powell, Jr., of Virginia. Powell's nomination did not add to the South's representation, however, since he replaced retiring justice Hugo Black of Alabama.

REPRESENTATION FOR RELIGIOUS, RACIAL, AND GENDER GROUPS   Closely related to geographical representation are considerations given to various demographic groups. The earliest example of this were presidential actions to ensure that the Catholic and Jewish populations had representation on the Court. Beginning in 1894 with the appointment of Edward White and continuing to the present time, there has been Catholic representation on the Court, with the exception of the period 1949–1956.[15] Similarly, from 1916 to 1969 there was at least one Jewish justice. These appointments were important for political reasons. Presidents wanted to attract the support of these religious groups, and recognizing one of their number for a place on the high court was one way to do so. But the "seat" concept also had a limiting effect. Once the religious seat was filled, appointing a second representative from that group was often politically

---

[15] Roger Taney was actually the first Catholic justice, but when he died in 1864 there was no expectation that a Catholic would be appointed to replace him. It was thirty years before the next Catholic was chosen.

difficult. This was the situation President Hoover faced when he nominated Benjamin Cardozo while Louis Brandeis still served.

For both of these religious groups, the idea of a designated "seat" has lost most of its political power. In part this has coincided with a breakdown in the political cohesiveness of these populations. When Justice Abe Fortas resigned in 1969, Richard Nixon ignored the practice of replacing him with another Jew. The next Jewish nomination did not occur until Reagan's unsuccessful selection of Douglas Ginsburg in 1987, but Ginsburg's religious or ethnic background had little to do with his selection. The Catholic seat has also lost its status, but its diminished recognition has manifested itself in the opposite fashion. In 1988, with Anthony Kennedy's confirmation, three Catholic justices served on the Court (Justices Scalia and Brennan were the other two). Clearly factors other than religious affiliation were responsible for the nominations of Kennedy and Scalia with Brennan already on the Court; so too was religion absent in the 1991 naming of Clarence Thomas, who had a Catholic upbringing. Consequently, for both groups it no longer appears politically necessary that they be represented on the Supreme Court, nor does their representation appear to be limited to one or a maximum of two justices.

The concept of representation for certain demographic groups, however, did not die with the decline in the importance of religious affiliation. What has changed are the particular groups that now are considered by many to deserve representation. Thurgood Marshall's 1967 appointment as the first black justice and Clarence Thomas's selection to succeed him reflect the recognition of both Democratic and Republican parties that the nation's black population should have a place on the country's top court. Ronald Reagan's naming of Sandra Day O'Connor in 1981 as the first woman to serve as a justice undoubtedly establishes a permanent female presence on the bench. With their numbers increasing in both politics and the legal profession, it is very doubtful that the Court will ever go long without having women and blacks among its members. A similar phenomenon is soon likely to emerge with respect to the nation's Hispanic population. The inclusion of members of various demographic groups not only is politically important but also adds to the legitimacy of the Court.

POLITICAL PAYOFFS AND PERSONAL FRIENDSHIPS   Historically, presidents have tended to select individuals with whom they have had considerable previous contact. About half the justices who have served on the Court personally knew the man who appointed them. Many were close political allies or had delivered some crucial political support for the president along the way. Some presidents have placed a great deal of importance on appointing justices they knew. Harry Truman's four Supreme Court appointments, for example, were all chosen from among those individuals with whom he personally associated while serving in the Senate or the executive branch. Similarly, Franklin Roosevelt selected nominees who had established their political or personal loyalties to him. Lyndon

Johnson nominated his close friend Abe Fortas in 1965 and then unsuccessfully attempted to elevate him to the chief justiceship in 1968. When John Kennedy nominated Byron White, he selected a man he had known as a youth and had served with in the navy, to say nothing of White's service in Kennedy's presidential campaign and in the Justice Department.

In more recent years the personal factor has declined. None of the Supreme Court appointments made during the Nixon, Ford, Reagan, and Bush presidencies can be described as the selection of a close personal associate. In some cases, the president had no previous contact with the future justice at all. Instead, recent presidents have increasingly relied on the recommendations of trusted advisers and thorough investigations to establish the ideological and political credentials of potential nominees. Having a political ally who has the president's ear can often be the determining factor. It is clear, for example, that David Souter's 1990 rise from almost total obscurity to the Supreme Court was due to the urging of John Sununu, President Bush's chief of staff and Souter's former mentor in New Hampshire.

The Confirmation Process

In Article II, section 2, the Constitution requires that presidential appointments to the Supreme Court be made "by and with the Advice and Consent of the Senate." Although this means that the president's choice must receive favorable votes from a majority of those voting in the Senate, the Constitution tells us little else about the role of the Senate in the confirmation process.[16]

THE ROLE OF THE SENATE   It should not be surprising that whenever the president makes a controversial nomination there is substantial debate over the proper function of the Senate. Two positions are normally articulated. The first is that the appointment of Supreme Court justices is essentially the domain of the president. The role of the Senate should be a limited one, only to ensure that the president does not nominate a clearly unqualified candidate. Proponents of this position generally feel that the Senate should do no more than establish the basic credentials of the nominee. Legislators should not base their decisions on a nominee's political or legal philosophy. It is enough to determine that the candidate has sufficient legal qualifications, judicial temperament, and ethical standards. The opposing view holds that the Senate should take an activist approach to Court nominations.[17] This position interprets the Advice and Consent Clause as giving the legislature a meaningful and coequal role in the selection of Supreme Court justices. The Senate should not be a rubber stamp for the presi-

[16] Paul A. Freund, "Appointment of Justices: Some Historical Perspectives," *Harvard Law Review* 101 (April 1988): 1146–1163.

[17] Henry Paul Monaghan, "The Confirmation Process: Law or Politics?" *Harvard Law Review* 101 (April 1988): 1202–1212.

dent, but should inquire with diligence into every aspect of a nominee's credentials, including political and legal philosophies. As early as 1795, when the Senate rejected Washington's nomination of John Rutledge to be chief justice, the legislature served notice that it was not going to give in to the president's choice every time. Furthermore, proponents of this position argue that the Senate has every right to reject a nominee whose views are at odds with those of the legislature.

As in many areas of political life, the position senators take on this fundamental question depends largely on their political relationship with the president. A senator of the president's political party almost invariably argues that the legislative role in the appointment process should be limited and that the president should be given great latitude to appoint a justice of his own choosing. On the other hand, the opposition party usually advances the position that the Senate should be an active and independent evaluator of a prospective justice's suitability for the Court.

The confirmation process is played out against this rather vague constitutional backdrop to advice and consent. In the beginning, and for most of our history, the procedures for confirmation involved few individuals outside the president and the members of the Senate. Over time, however, the process has become much more complex, involving protracted investigations and hearings as well as the participation of various organized interests outside the Senate. What was a relatively private process during most of our history has evolved into a fully public and politicized event.[18]

The Senate assigns primary responsibility for evaluating Supreme Court nominees to its Committee on the Judiciary. This committee currently consists of fourteen senators. Its partisan makeup roughly reflects the party divisions in the Senate as a whole. The committee is normally chaired by the senior member of the majority party. As a preliminary matter, the committee requests nominees to submit detailed information about their backgrounds, educations, families, and positions in the public and private sector. Copies of all the nominees' writings, speeches, and other public pronouncements are also requested. In recent years the demand for records and supplementary materials has exploded. In the case of the 1991 Clarence Thomas nomination, 30,000 pages of documentation were requested by the Senate committee even before the public hearings began. The committee staff then studies the information and may well request additional data or carry out further investigation at the direction of the senators. The process of studying a nominee's background today normally takes about two months, after which the Senate schedules hearings to consider the nomination.

INTEREST GROUP INVOLVEMENT   During the period between the president's announcement of his choice and the Senate hearings on the nominee, numerous

---

[18] Nina Totenberg, "The Confirmation Process and the Public: To Know or Not to Know," *Harvard Law Review* 101 (April 1988): 1213–1229.

other individuals and groups initiate studies into the qualifications of the candidate. These usually involve groups representing interests that may be affected by the decisions of the Court and have a stake in who is appointed. Based upon their analyses of the nominee, these groups will later express support for or opposition to confirmation.

The most regular and best organized of the groups participating in this process is the American Bar Association.[19] The ABA is the nation's largest organization of attorneys and it has a long history of expressing its evaluation of nominees for the judiciary. Prior to World War II this expression of opinion was unsystematic and irregular. In 1946, however, the ABA created its Committee on the Federal Judiciary, whose role is to investigate and make recommendations on nominations to the federal courts. The establishment of the committee gave the ABA a continuing body to examine nominations systematically and issue recommendations in the name of the organized bar. Because of the ABA's expertise in legal matters and its rather large and influential membership, the recommendations of the committee are taken seriously.

Presidents have varied as to the amount of consideration they give to ABA evaluations. At certain times during the Eisenhower, Nixon, and Ford administrations, the ABA was given a list of candidates under consideration for Supreme Court appointment before the president made his final choice. The president would then take the ABA evaluations into account in making the final decision. For the most part, however, this process did not work well, especially when the ABA was critical of individuals favored by the president. In most cases, therefore, the ABA has not had prenomination access to lists of potential nominees. Instead it has been more common for the Committee on the Federal Judiciary to do its investigations only after the president has announced his choice for a particular seat.

The ABA has used several different rating systems over the years. Today it assigns a nominee one of three ratings: Well Qualified, Qualified, and Not Qualified. Over time the ABA committee generally has been supportive of nominees for the Court, and when it grants a candidate its highest rating by unanimous vote, confirmation prospects are undoubtedly boosted. On the other hand, when the committee gives a low rating or is split on the nominee's abilities it can be a signal that the president's choice may have confirmation difficulties.

Legal organizations other than the ABA are also frequently active in the confirmation process. These are associations of lawyers with specialized interests, such as civil rights attorneys, or those whose memberships consist primarily of minorities or women. In addition, legal scholars, either independently or through their professional groups, often study a nominee and submit a report to the Senate.

Other interest groups have become increasingly active in the confirmation

---

[19] Joel B. Grossman, *Lawyers and Judges: The ABA and the Politics of Judicial Selection* (New York: John Wiley, 1965).

process. A coalition of labor and civil rights groups, for example, mounted a successful campaign to defeat the nomination of John Parker in 1930. Again, in 1969 and 1970, civil rights organizations and labor unions joined to block the confirmations of Clement Haynsworth and G. Harrold Carswell. In the 1980s and 1990s the array of groups active in confirmation politics and the level of their participation have grown tremendously. The confirmation hearings of Robert Bork and Clarence Thomas, for example, attracted the involvement of civil rights groups, women's groups, abortion rights supporters and opponents, environmental groups, and good government associations. Interest groups, of course, are much more concerned with promoting the status of their members or the cause they seek to advance than with judicial process itself. Consequently their arguments tend to focus on the policy positions of the nominees rather than on their legal craftsmanship.

The 1987 battle over the confirmation of Robert Bork attracted the most interest group participation to date. Because Bork was perceived by many as a conservative extremist, groups supporting liberal causes reacted immediately when his nomination was announced. Bork himself credits the interest group campaign against him, which he claims to have been orchestrated by Edward Kennedy and other liberal senators, as the primary factor in his defeat.[20] The groups that mobilized, either officially or through the actions of their leaders, were numerous: People for the American Way, Southern Christian Leadership Conference, AFL-CIO, Women's Legal Defense Fund, Leadership Conference on Civil Rights, Alliance for Justice, NAACP, National Abortion Rights Action League, American Civil Liberties Union, Planned Parenthood, and others. These organizations spent significant amounts of money lobbying the Senate directly and even explicitly threatening some senators with electoral reprisals if the legislators did not vote as urged by the groups. They also executed a public opinion campaign to convince the electorate to oppose the Bork nomination. Among other tactics, the People for the American Way produced and repeatedly showed a sixty-second television commercial, with actor Gregory Peck as the off-camera narrator, branding Bork as an enemy of American liberties.

Senator Kennedy gave powerful support to the charges made against Bork. In one often-quoted speech he declared:

> Robert Bork's America is a land in which women would be forced into back-alley abortions, blacks would sit at segregated lunch counters, rogue police could break down citizens' doors in midnight raids, schoolchildren could not be taught about evolution, writers and artists would be censored at the whim of government, and the doors of the Federal courts would be shut on the fingers of millions of citizens for whom the judiciary is often the only protector of the individual rights that are the heart of our democracy.[21]

---

[20] See Robert H. Bork, *The Tempting of America* (New York: Simon and Schuster, 1990), esp. part III.

[21] Speech on Senate floor, July 1, 1987.

Whether these charges were true or not, the campaign to label Bork a dangerous ultraconservative succeeded and the nominee was defeated. The Bork incident demonstrates how much the confirmation process has moved away from a rather simple matter of the Senate advising the president and has instead evolved into a full-fledged national political event.

COMMITTEE HEARINGS   When an appropriate amount of investigation has been completed, the Senate Judiciary Committee begins its formal public hearings. The purpose of these hearings is for the members of the committee to question the nominee directly as well as to hear from other parties and groups that have views on the confirmation issue. The hearings give the senators an opportunity to probe publicly into the qualifications and views of the nominee. The public nature of the process is important, for it allows the press and the general citizenry to observe the nominee under questioning. How the public evaluates the nominee as a future Supreme Court justice often affects how the individual senators will vote on confirmation. In the Clarence Thomas confirmation battle the fact that public opinion polls indicated that the majority of the American people believed his denial of sexual harassment allegations undoubtedly saved his nomination.

Today we take these hearings for granted. We expect to see excerpts of the hearings on the television news and read press accounts of how the nominee performed. It should be kept in mind, however, that public hearings are a relatively modern phenomenon. During most of the history of the Court, the Senate considered nominations without such public proceedings. Until 1929, the Senate met in closed executive session to take up the issue of Supreme Court confirmations. The Senate, by a two-thirds vote, could open the sessions to the public, but this was rare. However, the senators took this action when considering the nomination of Louis Brandeis in 1916 and again with the nomination of Harlan Fiske Stone in 1925.

Nominees for the Court historically have not appeared before the committee and allowed themselves to be questioned. The first nominee to do so was Harlan Fiske Stone. When his nomination ran into some difficulties on the Senate floor and the committee was asked to reconsider the issue, Stone volunteered to appear. Stone's adept handling of questions posed by his opponents led to his ultimate confirmation by a 71–6 vote. Six years later in 1939, Felix Frankfurter offered to be available to the committee at their call, but his presence was not requested.

In spite of these precedents, the custom of nominees appearing before the committee was not yet firmly established. As late as 1949, for example, Sherman Minton refused a Senate request to appear, claiming that his years as a United States senator and federal judge provided a more than ample record upon which the senators could exercise their judgment. Such a refusal would be unheard of today. The Senate and the people generally expect nominees to appear and answer questions. The 1991 confirmation hearings exploring the sexual harassment charges against Clarence Thomas, for example, were not only televised in their entirety but received exceptionally high ratings, attracting more viewers than the major league baseball playoffs.

There is, however, disagreement as to the appropriate scope of questioning. Clearly, senators cannot demand that nominees commit themselves as to how they will vote on specific cases or issues likely to come before the Court. For a nominee to do so would be to prejudge cases and to compromise objectivity in order to obtain confirmation. Judges, however, can be asked questions pertaining to their judicial philosophies and modes of constitutional interpretation. Over the past quarter century senators, especially those opposing a particular candidate, have attempted to expose the nominee's views on political, social, and legal issues as fully as possible. Nominees successful in the confirmation process have been those able to dodge such questioning on the grounds that it calls for views on issues that might come before the Court. Box 2-1 provides some excerpts from Sandra Day O'Connor's handling of questions on the abortion issue. Her example was followed by subsequent nominees with equal success.

Robert Bork, however, took a different approach. His long scholarly career with numerous published articles, public addresses, and lectures left a voluminous paper trail regarding his views on controversial legal issues. Given this record, Bork could hardly avoid responding to questions. In addition, Bork's personality was not such as to allow him to avoid intellectual debate on legal questions, particularly when confronted by a committee dominated by Democratic senators. For several days, Bork fielded questions from the committee, rarely refusing to respond. His strategy was not successful. With his views fully exposed, Bork's nomination was given a negative recommendation by the committee and suffered defeat on the Senate floor. Subsequent nominees learned from this experience and followed the much safer course of refusing to answer controversial questions of legal policy, much to the frustration of the opposition senators.

In probable response to the grilling of Bork, Presidents Reagan and Bush offered candidates for the Court with little record of scholarly publication and no evidence of asserting challenging or controversial views.[22] Without an extensive record to probe, opposition senators had little ammunition with which to attack the nominees. For example, David Souter, in spite of his years as a state attorney general and judge, had engaged in almost no scholarly writing and had decided few controversial cases. This lack of a paper trail and the fact that he was so adept at avoiding tough questions posed by the committee earned him the title of the "stealth nominee." From the president's perspective it may be advantageous to nominate candidates who are difficult to challenge. Yet there is a negative consequence as well. By selecting only those who do not have extensive written records of scholarly achievement and have not articulated positions on

---

[22] Bush's nomination of Clarence Thomas is a possible exception to this trend.

difficult legal and political issues, presidents may well be ignoring the calibre of a person who carries the greatest potential for being a truly outstanding justice.

After questioning the nominee and hearing from other interested parties wishing to express their views, the Judiciary Committee issues a recommendation to the full Senate. This recommendation carries considerable weight. No nominee to the Supreme Court has been confirmed after receiving a negative recommendation from the committee. The only justice to be confirmed with less than a positive recommendation was Clarence Thomas, over whom the committee was divided 7–7.

FLOOR ACTION   The final stage of the process is Senate floor action. The nomination is debated in open session by the senators. For the most part this stage is much less important than the committee deliberations. Arguments made on the floor change few votes. By this time the positions of most senators have already been decided. The speeches and debate do little more than fill out the record of arguments for and against confirmation. During this time, of course, supporters and opponents do have an opportunity to exert some influence on senators who may be undecided. If the vote is expected to be close, political pressure can be very intense. This pressure is generated by the administration in support of the nominee as well as from outside interest groups, especially those with significant memberships in the senators' home states. Senators, for example, will undoubtedly pay keen attention to the views expressed by organized labor or civil rights groups if large numbers of their constituents are union members or racial minorities. In this respect, providing "advice and consent" for a nomination to the Supreme Court becomes one more political issue upon which senators must take a stand. And the stand they take may influence how some voters will react to them at reelection time.

In the final analysis the Senate votes, with a simple majority required for confirmation. In absolute terms, nominees fair reasonably well in this process. Only about 20 percent of those formally nominated by the president have been rejected by the Senate. Table 2-1 provides information on those nominees who have suffered Senate rejection. Yet in absolute terms this figure is quite high. In fact, Supreme Court nominees have suffered the highest rejection rate of any office requiring Senate confirmation. By comparison, for example, the Senate has rejected only twelve cabinet appointments during the nation's entire history—and fully half of those occurred during the turbulent administration of John Tyler in the 1840s.[23]

While on the surface it might seem reasonable that the confirmation decision would be based exclusively on an evaluation of a nominee's qualifications, research has demonstrated that political and institutional factors play an influen-

---

[23] Harold W. Stanley and Richard G. Niemi, *Vital Statistics on American Politics,* 3rd ed. (Washington, D.C.: CQ Press, 1992), 278.

Box 2-1

THE O'CONNOR CONFIRMATION HEARINGS
AND THE ISSUE OF ABORTION

On September 9–10, 1981, Sandra Day O'Connor, President Reagan's nominee to the Supreme Court, appeared before the Senate Judiciary Committee. Although the hearings covered a wide variety of subjects, the issue of abortion was central. Conservative senators in particular were concerned that the nominee might support *Roe v. Wade* and the right of women to obtain abortions with few legal restraints. Although O'Connor stated that she opposed abortion as a personal value in her own life, she artfully dodged questions that sought to identify her position on abortion as a matter of legal and public policy. O'Connor's successful strategy was later followed by conservative nominees who avoided similar questioning by liberal senators. Appearing below are excerpts from the O'Connor hearings that are representative of her responses to the questions on abortion.

Senator Strom Thurmond (R-SC): Judge O'Connor, there has been much discussion regarding your views on the subject of abortion. Would you discuss your philosophy on abortion . . .?

O'Connor: Very well. May I preface my response by saying that the personal views and philosophies, in my view, of a Supreme Court Justice and indeed any judge should be set aside insofar as it is possible to do that in resolving matters that come before the Court.

Issues that come before the Court should be resolved based on the facts of that particular case or matter and on the law applicable to those facts, and any constitutional principles applicable to those facts. They should not be based on the personal views and ideology of the judge. . . .

Senator Dennis DeConcini (D-Ariz): Returning to the subject—and I am sure it probably will never end—of abortion. . . . I wonder if you could share with us . . . your personal philosophy or feeling as to abortion so the record would be clear today.

O'Connor: O.K., Senator. Again let me preface a comment by saying that my personal views and beliefs in this area and in other areas have no place in the resolution of any legal issues that will come before the Court.

Senator Jeremiah Denton (R-Ala): In your personal view where do you feel abortion is not offensive . . .?

O'Connor: I am "over the hill." I am not going to be pregnant any more, so it is perhaps easy for me to speak. . . . Where you draw the line [between legally permissible and impermissible abortions] as a

> matter of public policy is really the task of the legislator to deter-
> mine.... These are things that the legislator must decide.
> *Senator John East (R-NC):* ... if I may have your response to [the
> dissenting opinions in *Roe v. Wade*]?
> *O'Connor:* Senator East, with all respect, it does seem inappropriate to
> me to either endorse or criticize a specific case or a specific opinion
> in a case handed down by those judges now sitting and in a matter
> which may well be revisited in the Court in the not too distant
> future.
> *Senator East:* I can appreciate you cannot promise anything; I can ap-
> preciate you could not comment upon pending cases; but when we
> are told that there cannot be comment upon previous cases and
> previous doctrines of substance, I query as one lowly freshman Sena-
> tor whether we are able really to get our teeth into anything.

tial role in the process. [24] A key element is the political and power relationships between the president and the Senate. The influences here manifest themselves in a number of ways, but two are dominant.

First, a nominee is much more likely to be confirmed if the White House and the Senate are controlled by the same political party. Under these circumstances the Senate majority and the president are likely to have similar policy prefer- ences and share views of the type of justice who should be appointed. The Senate also has a stake in the success of the president and there are few political or power struggles between the two. The opposite is the case when the two are dominated by different partisan interests. Here not only do the two institutions have different political philosophies and policy goals, but there is a natural and continuing power struggle as well. Overall, when the president enjoys the same partisan affiliation as a majority of the Senate, Supreme Court nominees are confirmed in excess of 90 percent of the time. When the two institutions have opposing partisan loyalties, the president's success rate drops to about 60 per- cent. The last three formal rejections (Haynsworth, Carswell, and Bork) were all cases of a Republican president and a Democratic Senate. Clearly, if the presi- dent's party is not in control of the Senate or if its majority is weak, the president must select his nominee with great care.

Second, a nominee will be much more likely to be confirmed if the president is politically powerful relative to the Senate. For example, presidents are the least politically powerful during the last year of their four-year term, a period during which the future control of the White House is uncertain. Supreme Court nomina- tions made during this portion of a president's tenure have relatively low rates of

---

[24] For a discussion of these factors, see Jeffrey Segal, "Senate Confirmation of Supreme Court Justices: Partisan and Institutional Politics," *Journal of Politics* 49 (November 1987): 998–1015.

TABLE 2-1
Supreme Court Nominations Rejected by the Senate

Nominee	Year	President/Party	Senate Party Majority	Outcome/Vote
William Paterson*	1793	Washington (Fed)	Federalist	Withdrawn
John Rutledge**	1795	Washington (Fed)	Federalist	Rejected (10–14)
Alexander Wolcott	1811	Madison (D-R)	Demo-Rep	Rejected (9–24)
John Crittenden	1828	J.Q. Adams (D-R)	Democratic	Postponed
Roger Taney*	1835	Jackson (Dem)	Democratic	Postponed (24–21)
John Spencer	1844	Tyler (Whig)	Whig	Rejected (21–26)
Reuben Walworth	1844	Tyler (Whig)	Whig	Withdrawn
Edward King	1844	Tyler (Whig)	Whig	Postponed
Edward King	1844	Tyler (Whig)	Whig	Withdrawn
John Read	1845	Tyler (Whig)	Whig	No action
George Woodward	1845	Polk (Dem)	Democratic	Rejected (20–29)
Edward Bradford	1852	Fillmore (Whig)	Democratic	No action
George Badger	1853	Fillmore (Whig)	Democratic	Postponed
William Micou	1853	Fillmore (Whig)	Democratic	No action
Jeremiah Black	1861	Buchanan (Dem)	Democratic	Rejected (25–26)
Henry Stanbery	1866	Johnson (Dem)	Republican	No action
Ebenezer Hoar	1869	Grant (Rep)	Republican	Rejected (24–33)
George Williams**	1873	Grant (Rep)	Republican	Withdrawn
Caleb Cushing**	1874	Grant (Rep)	Republican	Withdrawn
Stanley Matthews*	1881	Hayes (Rep)	Democratic	No action
William Hornblower	1893	Cleveland (Dem)	Democratic	Rejected (24–30)
Wheeler Peckham	1894	Cleveland (Dem)	Democratic	Rejected (32–41)
John Parker	1930	Hoover (Rep)	Republican	Rejected (39–41)
Abe Fortas**	1968	Johnson (Dem)	Democratic	Withdrawn
Homer Thornberry	1968	Johnson (Dem)	Democratic	No action
Clement Haynsworth	1969	Nixon (Rep)	Democratic	Rejected (45–55)
G. Harrold Carswell	1970	Nixon (Rep)	Democratic	Rejected (45–51)
Robert Bork	1987	Reagan (Rep)	Democratic	Rejected (42–58)
Douglas Ginsburg	1987	Reagan (Rep)	Democratic	Withdrawn before formal submission

*Nominee later confirmed.
**Nomination for Chief Justice.

success, with only slightly more than half receiving confirmation. Similarly, presidents who are not elected (e.g., assume the office upon the death of the elected president) also have low levels of political power. This is reflected in the success of their Supreme Court nominees, who are confirmed at a rate only slightly exceeding 50 percent. The most notorious example of this occurred during President Tyler's administration. Vice President Tyler assumed the presidency following the death of William Henry Harrison. Tyler's tenure lasted almost four full years and during this time he made six nominations to the Court but only one (Samuel Nelson) was confirmed by the Senate. In addition, as the general balance of power between the executive and legislative branches shifts over time, the prospects for confirmation also shift. During the period from Theodore Roosevelt to John

Kennedy, for example, when presidential power was generally high relative to Congress, only one Supreme Court nominee was rejected by the Senate. That occurred in 1930 when the Senate declined to confirm Judge John Parker. Responsibility for Parker's defeat is usually assigned to opposition from organized labor and other interests, but it is also true that President Hoover was in a weak position as the nation plummeted into its deepest economic depression.

At the level of the individual senator's vote on confirmation other factors come into play.[25] Clearly, responsible senators look first to a nominee's qualifications. A prospective justice with unquestionable legal skills, judicial temperament, and ethical standards will likely receive a senator's favorable vote even if the legislator and nominee differ ideologically. This situation actually occurs with relative frequency. Between 1954 and 1992, for example, recorded or voice votes were taken on twenty-four Supreme Court nominations, with eleven receiving formal, recorded opposition from no members of the Senate. On the other hand, a senator will likely vote to reject a nominee with proven ethical gaps or low competence levels even if the two are ideological soulmates.

There remains, however, a large number of nominations where the choice is not clear-cut. In these instances, predicting the votes of individual senators is somewhat difficult, but certain factors have been identified as being important in the legislator's decision-making process. Considerations of ideological preference and electoral politics play a significant role. The closer the nominee's ideology is to the senator's the more likely the legislator will vote in favor of confirmation. This is simply a matter of a senator preferring a justice whose ideological values and policy preferences are similar to those favored by the legislator. Additionally, the senator is likely to take into account his constituency's interests and preferences. Undoubtedly a vote for or against a nominee is a political action that might well affect the senator's reelection chances. When there is significant constituent opinion on the confirmation question, particularly if it is accentuated by mobilized interest group activity, the senator will likely be pulled in that direction. All things being equal, a senator will prefer a nominee who supports those legal interpretations that are likely to lead to decisions and policies beneficial to the home state voters.

Generally speaking, the confirmation process has worked relatively well over time. The tension between the executive and legislative branches balances out and provides the necessary checks and balances that were intended by the Framers. More recently, however, the process has been subject to critical attack for becoming too politicized, with senators paying more attention to interest groups and their own reelection prospects than to the needs of the Court and the legal qualifications of the nominees. So too, it has been argued, that the participants in this process have excessively focused on ideology. The public's reaction

---

[25] See, for example, Charles M. Cameron, Albert D. Cover, and Jeffrey A. Segal, "Senate Voting on Supreme Court Nominees: A Neoinstitutional Model," *American Political Science Review* 84 (June 1990): 525–534.

to the 1991 Clarence Thomas confirmation battle, with its nationally televised hearings filled with sexually oriented language and vicious attacks launched against those on both sides, was overwhelmingly negative and lowered the prestige of the Senate and the Court. However, the bottom line remains that a president who avoids hostile relationships with the Senate and selects legally and ethically competent nominees without extreme legal or political views will enjoy high levels of success in securing positive confirmation votes.

CHARACTERISTICS OF SUPREME COURT JUSTICES

Although the Constitution sets no formal qualifications for being a Supreme Court justice, the demands of the selection process are such that individuals with certain backgrounds and experiences are favored. In spite of the fact that the nation's history now spans some two hundred years and we have developed from a small, agrarian country to a large, industrialized one, the profile of the typical Supreme Court justice has changed only modestly over time. In this section we review the background characteristics of those who have survived the appointment process to become members of the Court, examining patterns of both stability and change from John Jay through Clarence Thomas.[26] Table 2-2 on page 52 provides a statistical illustration of the backgrounds of the 106 individuals who have served on the Court.

Family Origins

As might be expected of those who have held a nation's highest judicial office, justices of the Supreme Court have tended to come from socially and economically advantaged families. In fact, fewer than 20 percent of the justices can be said to have come from lower socioeconomic class origins. This was especially true in the Court's earliest years. The justices selected during the Federalist and Jeffersonian periods were drawn from the nation's most important and politically active families. This is indeed understandable given the nation's relatively small population, the scarcity of formal opportunities for higher education, and the lack of a large and well-developed legal profession. Being reared in an economically secure and politically active family provides the child with a head start that others do not enjoy. The record of preference for those from higher socioeconomic class families continued well into the twentieth century, with a slight modification during the Jacksonian era. Since the New Deal period, however, there has been an increase in the presence on the Court of those with more common backgrounds. This has been due largely to the expanded opportunities for education and political advancement. Modern era justices such as William Douglas, Hugo Black, Earl Warren, Warren Burger, and Thurgood Marshall clearly had humble beginnings.

---

[26] For a discussion of the historical patterns in the backgrounds of Supreme Court justices, see chapter 3 in John R. Schmidhauser, *Judges and Justices* (Boston: Little, Brown, 1979).

TABLE 2-2

Characteristics of 106 Supreme Court Justices: John Jay through Clarence Thomas

	No. of Justices
Place of Birth	
Rural	27
Small town/city	49
Large city/metropolis	30
Region	
East	38
South and Border	35
Midwest	24
West	9
Religion	
Protestant	86
Catholic	11
Jewish	5
Other/Unknown	4
Ethnic Background	
British Isles	88
Other European	16
African	2
Sex	
Male	105
Female	1
Political Party	
Federalist	13
Democratic-Republican	7
Whig	1
Republican	42
Democrat	42
Independent	1
College:	
Private study/tutors	12
College of Average Standing	32
Prestigious College	62
Legal Education	
Self-taught	2
Apprenticeship	43
Law School of Average Standing	15
Prestigious Law School	46
Primary Level of Prior Government/Political Service	
Federal	57
State	37
Other/Nonpolitical	12
Prior Judicial Experience	
Five years or more	47
Less than five years	18
None	41
Age at Appointment	
30–39	4

TABLE 2-2
Continued

40–49	27
50–59	59
60–69	16
Position When Appointed	
Private Practice	25
Federal Judge	25
State Judge	21
Cabinet	14
Congress	8
Justice Department (not Attorney General)	4
Governor	3
Professor	2
Other	4
Years of Service on Court (excluding justices sitting in 1992)	
1–4	11
5–9	23
10–19	29
20–29	23
30–36	11

Clarence Thomas, joining the Court in 1991, came from a family that faced severe poverty. Yet the majority, even in contemporary times, were born into middle or upper class family settings.

About two-thirds of the justices were also born into families with members who were very active in politics, and most had relatives who were engaged in some aspect of the legal profession. Several had close relations who were judges on important state and local courts. And others even had family connections to the Supreme Court itself. Justices Lucius Q. C. Lamar (1888–1893) and Joseph R. Lamar (1910–1916), for example, were cousins; John Marshall Harlan's (1877–1911) grandson who shared the same name served on the Court from 1955 to 1971; and the service of David Brewer (1889–1910) actually overlapped for a time with that of his uncle Stephen Field (1863–1897). During his second term, Grover Cleveland nominated two brothers to the Supreme Court, Wheeler and Rufus Peckham. The Senate rejected Wheeler in 1894, but confirmed Rufus the following year. High social and economic status coupled with early socialization into the tradition of government service and the law provide fertile conditions for future Supreme Court justices.

All but six of the justices were born in the United States. Three of those, as might be expected, were among Washington's appointees. James Wilson (1789–1798) was born in Scotland, James Iredell (1790–1799) in England, and William Paterson (1793–1806) in Ireland. David Brewer (1889–1910) was born the son of a Congregationalist missionary in what is now Turkey. Two twentieth-century jurists were also born abroad. George Sutherland (1922–1938) was born in

England but his family immigrated to the United States when he was still an infant. Felix Frankfurter (1939–1962) was born in Vienna, Austria, but moved to the United States with his parents at the age of twelve.

The future justices spent their early years in an environment typical of that experienced by advantaged families of the times. In the early years of the Court most of the justices were born in rural areas or in small towns. This was consistent with the tendency of political power in the United States to be exercised by the landed gentry. Over time, as more people moved to the cities and political power followed them, we find increasing numbers of justices to have been reared in more urban environments.

Families with British ancestry have produced the most justices. Given the peoples who founded this nation and the immigration patterns over the years, it is not surprising that roughly 80 percent of our justices have come from English, Scottish, and Irish backgrounds. Another 15 percent of the justices can trace their roots back to some other European origin, and two justices have enjoyed an African heritage. There has yet to be an appointee with an Asian or Latin American background. However, members of these ethnic groups have become increasingly involved in the legal profession and now hold important lower court judgeships. It is undoubtedly only a matter of time before one of their number joins the Court.

Consistent with the nation's history, almost all of our justices were exposed to religious traditions during their youths and most remained loyal to their affiliations. The collective religious blend of the Court has been overwhelmingly Protestant. Most commonly the justices have been affiliated with the "high status" denominations such as the Episcopal and Presbyterian churches. In this area, Supreme Court justices are similar to other political elites in American history. The first Roman Catholic was Chief Justice Roger Brooke Taney (1836–1864) from Maryland. After Taney died it was thirty years before the next Catholic was chosen, Edward White of Louisiana. White's tenure (1894–1921), first as an associate justice and then as chief, began the Catholic seat tradition discussed earlier. By the 1990s, nine Catholics had served on the Court. The first Jewish justice was Louis Brandeis, appointed in 1916. Brandeis was later followed by four other justices with Jewish backgrounds.

Education and Early Careers

As a group, the justices reflect the benefits of educational opportunity. In America's early years, of course, higher education was available only to the more affluent families, if it was available at all. A large percentage of the nation's early political leaders did not attend college in any formal sense. Many were self-taught or relied on tutors. The backgrounds of the early justices reflect this historical phenomenon. Of President Washington's appointments, John Rutledge, Thomas Johnson, and Samuel Chase did not attend college. Because higher education for so long was not available to the lower economic classes, we see justices without college degrees serving on the Court even into the twentieth century. For example, James Byrnes (1941–1942), Robert Jackson (1941–1954), and Charles Whittaker (1957–1962) did not attend any college. Others, such as Hugo Black (1937–1971), attended for only a year or so. On the other hand, over half the justices attended elite, highly rated colleges and were given access to the best undergraduate educations the nation had to offer.

The legal training of the justices reflects the same historical pattern. In the early years access to a formal law school education was extremely limited due to the scarcity of such institutions. In fact, the most accepted way to obtain a legal education was to "read the law" in an apprenticeship with an established attorney. When sufficient knowledge of the law had been acquired, aspiring lawyers would present themselves for examination to be admitted to the bar. The first individual appointed to the Supreme Court who attended an established American law school was Levi Woodbury (1846–1851), the thirtieth justice. Woodbury attended Tapping Reeve Law School in Connecticut, but only for a short period of time. For the most part he learned his legal craft from private study. The first graduate of an American law school to serve on the Court was Benjamin Curtis (1851–1857), who graduated from Harvard in 1832. Although access to law school educations became quite widespread in the twentieth century, it was not until Charles Whittaker replaced Stanley Reed in 1957 that the entire Court held earned law degrees.

As a group, our Supreme Court justices have received first-rate legal educations. During the period in which apprenticeship was the norm, the backgrounds of the justices reveal that they commonly studied under the nation's most influential lawyers. Later, when law school became the norm, we find the future justices attending the nation's most elite law schools.

Almost all of the justices began their careers in the private practice of law. Some, like Justice Lewis Powell, remained in private practice for all of their pre-Court years. The majority, however, became involved in active politics in one form or another. Many, such as William Howard Taft and Earl Warren, made politics and government service a full-time vocation and did not practice law for long periods of time. A few in the more modern period were fortunate enough to win coveted clerkships with a Supreme Court justice. William Rehnquist clerked for Robert Jackson, Byron White for Fred Vinson, and John Paul Stevens for Wiley Rutledge. Others used their legal talents as government attorneys. Several, for example, served as the nation's attorney general or solicitor general, and many others spent part of their careers with the Justice Department. Still another career route to the Supreme Court has been legal scholarship. Significant numbers of our justices have served as law professors at some point in their careers. William Douglas (Columbia, Yale), Felix Frankfurter (Harvard), Owen Roberts (Pennsylvania), and Antonin Scalia (Chicago) are examples of justices who held full-time professorships at distinguished law schools. Still others were law school deans, such as Harlan Fiske Stone (Columbia), Horace Lurton (Vanderbilt), and Wiley Rutledge (Washington University and Iowa). At one point in the mid-1940s a majority of the Court had spent a considerable portion of their earlier careers as professors of law.

Nomination Factors

Regardless of their educational and career paths, all of those who obtained seats on the Supreme Court had positioned themselves to become the president's choice. Many times this was simply a matter of being in the right place at the right time. When a vacancy occurs a successful nominee must be of the right political party, from the right region, with the right background, and possess the right ideological and political credentials. The prospective justice must also have sufficient political allies to convince the president to make the nomination and the Senate to confirm. Obviously, a great deal of luck is involved, but certain patterns are present.

As we noted in the preceding section on the nomination process, age can be an important factor in a president's choice. Four justices were appointed while they were still in their thirties, all during the Court's first twenty-five years. The youngest were Joseph Story and William Johnson, both thirty-two. While such justices have the advantage of a long life expectancy (both Story and Johnson served for more than three decades), it is no longer likely that any individual so young will have had sufficient experience or accomplishments to merit such a high appointment. Clarence Thomas's 1991 elevation at the age of forty-three is an exception to recent trends. Nor will a president likely select an individual of advanced age. Only sixteen justices were over the age of sixty when appointed, the most recent being Lewis Powell in 1971 at the age of sixty-four. The most preferred age group historically has been candidates in their fifties. Over half of the successful nominees have been in this group.

It is also instructive to determine where presidents look when they are faced with the task of selecting a Supreme Court justice. Examining the last positions held by the justices prior to their nomination gives us a good indication of the kinds of immediate past experiences presidents have seen as appropriate for grooming an individual to be a good judge. Here we find some significant changes over time. In the Court's first century it was common for presidents to search for Supreme Court justices among the nation's private practitioners or state court judges. This phenomenon is understandable. In the nation's formative years, the legal profession was relatively small and the more prominent members easily identified. Lawyers engaged in litigation on important constitutional matters were the giants of the profession. Law schools had not yet developed to the point of producing sufficient numbers of legal scholars. Most court cases, even the more important ones, were heard in state courts. The lower federal courts remained relatively weak and of less importance than their state counterparts. When nineteenth-century presidents looked for the nation's great jurists they naturally thought of the highest courts in the states.

The twentieth-century presidents have largely turned away from selecting private practitioners and state court judges. A few exceptions to this changing pattern, however, have occurred. Lewis Powell, for example, was engaged in private practice in his Richmond, Virginia, law firm in 1971 when nominated by Richard Nixon, and Sandra Day O'Connor sat on an Arizona state appeals court when named by Ronald Reagan in 1981.

More commonly, however, twentieth-century presidents have looked to the ranks of politicians and lower federal court judges to find their nominees. In addition, there have been distinct differences according to the party of the president. Five Democratic presidents of this century (Wilson, Roosevelt, Truman, Kennedy, and Johnson) appointed nineteen justices. Of this number, none came from the ranks of state court judges and only two (Brandeis and Fortas) from private practice. Instead, Democratic presidents have selected individuals in federal legislative or executive politics. Seven held positions in the Justice Department (including four attorneys general), three others held other posts in the executive branch, and three were U.S. senators. Only three were drawn from the federal bench (and one of those, Sherman Minton, was a former U.S. senator) and one (Felix Frankfurter) was a law professor.

Republican presidents show a much different pattern. Republican presidents in this century appointed thirty-one Supreme Court justices through 1991. Relatively few of them came from active political positions (two governors, Earl Warren and Charles Evans Hughes, and three from the Justice Department, Harlan Fiske Stone, William Moody, and William Rehnquist). In addition, one professor and four from private practice were selected. But fully two-thirds of the Republican appointees came from the ranks of the judiciary (fifteen from the lower federal courts, five from the state courts, and one from the International Court of Justice). All five of the Reagan and Bush appointees were sitting judges when nominated. The tendency of the Republicans to select those serving in the lower courts is even stronger when we consider the individuals chosen by the president but not confirmed. In the Republican case, all five unsuccessful nominees in this century (Parker, Haynsworth, Carswell, Bork, and Ginsburg) were sitting federal judges when nominated.

Assuming these patterns continue, there are lessons to be learned by those who want to join the Supreme Court. Republican aspirants should position themselves in a lower federal court judgeship, particularly at the court of appeals level. From this vantage point opinions in real court cases can be written and, if well reasoned and ideologically correct, they may catch the eye of the president's advisers. Advice for Democrats must be offered with more caution. There has not been a successful appointment by a Democratic president since Lyndon Johnson's nomination of Thurgood Marshall in 1967, and we do not know if the patterns of the past would be applicable today. However, Democratic hopefuls should position themselves in partisan political offices. It would be advantageous to be a U.S. senator, for example, or to hold one of the three or four top posts in the Justice Department. From these offices Supreme Court aspirants can demonstrate their political loyalties and ideological reliability. Of course, all of this advice for would-be Supreme Court justices is much easier said than done.

The more recent tendencies of presidents (and especially Republican presidents) to select individuals from the lower courts brings up the often argued question of the importance of prior judicial service. Should Supreme Court justices have some experience as a lower court judge before assuming their duties on the nation's highest court? It surprises many that more than half of the Court's justices had less than five years of prior judicial experience, and 38 percent had never sat on a court at all before accepting the robes of a justice. Even more astounding is that some of history's most influential justices were those with no prior experience as a judge of any kind—John Marshall, Roger Brooke Taney, Louis Brandeis, Harlan Fiske Stone, Charles Evans Hughes, William O. Douglas, and Earl Warren among them. Perhaps with its docket so filled with questions of political and social significance and generally lacking the technical legal questions common in the lower courts, successful service on the Supreme Court does not necessarily require years of prior judicial experience.

Once on the Court, of course, the justices may serve for as long as good health and commitment to the position remain. Their tenures have been lengthy. Only eleven justices served less than five years. Four of those resigned prior to 1804, during the Court's infancy. Four others died or were unable to continue for health reasons. Only three in modern times left the Court after serving such a short period of time. James Byrnes resigned in 1942 after little more than a year because he missed the partisan political world, Arthur Goldberg left in 1965 to represent the United States at the United Nations, and Abe Fortas was forced to leave in 1967 under ethical scandal. At the other extreme, eleven justices served more than thirty years. The record is held by William O. Douglas, who graced the Court for more than thirty-six years. Two-thirds of the justices had tenures of more than a decade. Almost all remained on the bench after their appointing president and his administration left office, making those nominated to the Supreme Court the longest lasting of the president's executive choices.

The Rehnquist Court

As the Supreme Court entered 1992, the justices generally reflected the collective portrait of those who had served previously. Table 2-3 summarizes their backgrounds. The ages of the justices ranged from forty-three to eighty-three, with an average of sixty-three years. Byron White was the most senior in length of service with a thirty-year tenure on the Court. A third of the justices had been serving for fewer than five years. In terms of age and length of service, the Rehnquist Court of the early 1990s was certainly not significantly out of line with Courts of the past.

The backgrounds of the justices also generally reflected historical patterns, with some important deviations. Eight of the nine justices were Republicans,

TABLE 2-3
The Rehnquist Court, 1992

Justice	Year Born	Year Appointed	Political Party	Appointing President	Home State	College	Law School	Religion	Position When Appointed	Years of Prior Judicial Experience
Rehnquist, William	1924	1971 1986*	Rep.	Nixon Reagan*	Arizona	Stanford	Stanford	Lutheran	Ass't. U.S. Atty. Gen.	0
White, Byron	1917	1962	Dem.	Kennedy	Colorado	Colorado	Yale	Episcopalian	Deputy U.S. Atty. Gen.	0
Blackmun, Harry	1908	1970	Rep.	Nixon	Minnesota	Harvard	Harvard	Methodist	U.S. Appeals Court Judge	11
Stevens, John	1920	1975	Rep.	Ford	Illinois	Chicago	Northwestern	Nondenominational Protestant	U.S. Appeals Court Judge	5
O'Connor, Sandra Day	1930	1981	Rep.	Reagan	Arizona	Stanford	Stanford	Episcopalian	State Appeals Court Judge	6
Scalia, Antonin	1936	1986	Rep.	Reagan	D.C.	Georgetown	Harvard	Catholic	U.S. Appeals Court Judge	4
Kennedy, Anthony	1936	1988	Rep.	Reagan	California	Stanford	Harvard	Catholic	U.S. Appeals Court Judge	12
Souter, David	1939	1990	Rep.	Bush	New Hampshire	Harvard	Harvard	Episcopalian	U.S. Appeals Court Judge	12
Thomas, Clarence	1948	1991	Rep.	Bush	Georgia	Holy Cross	Yale	Catholic	U.S. Appeals Court Judge	1

*Appointment as chief justice.

appointed by Republican presidents. While this domination of the institution by the members of a single party is not common, it is certainly not without precedent. For example, in the 1940s the Democrats controlled the Court by a similar margin, as did the Republicans in the 1880s. And, of course, the early Court was entirely Federalist. The geographical representation of the current justices deviated a bit from the historic norms, reflecting the weakening of the regional factor in the appointment process. As noted earlier, having four justices from the Western states is unprecedented. It is also highly unusual for there to be no justice from the mid-Atlantic states (although Justice Scalia was born in New Jersey). Historically, over a quarter of all the justices have been from that region. In years past it would have been unthinkable for the states of New York, Pennsylvania, and Maryland to be without representation. Similarly, the presence of three justices who were raised in the Catholic Church never occurred before the late 1980s. Although with Clarence Thomas, the Court certainly had an individual who grew up in very humble surroundings, most of the Rehnquist justices were born into economically comfortable families.

The Court remains dominated by whites, males, and those with northern European ethnic ancestry. Clarence Thomas, of course, is the only black member of the Court, and Sandra Day O'Connor the sole woman. Antonin Scalia, son of an immigrant, is the first Italian-American to sit on the Court.

The educational backgrounds and career experiences of the Rehnquist Court justices are also in line with the institution's history. Except for Byron White's University of Colorado degree, all of the justices attended private, and mostly prestigious, undergraduate schools. Their collective law school experiences are even more elitist. All nine attended law schools normally rated among the nation's most prestigious. Four were educated at Harvard, and two each at Yale and Stanford. In spite of the vastly expanded opportunities to achieve legal educations, being trained at a traditionally elite law school clearly is an advantage to later obtaining a coveted position on the Court.

Most of the justices spent a portion of their early careers in private practice and were engaged in some form of political or government service. As a group, however, they have a modest degree of real political experience. None of the Rehnquist justices previously served as a cabinet official or as a member of Congress. Only Sandra Day O'Connor has held a nonjudicial elective office (Arizona state legislator). Three of the justices spent time in a federal administrative post. William Rehnquist and Byron White served in the Justice Department, and Clarence Thomas headed the Equal Employment Opportunity Commission. David Souter and Sandra Day O'Connor spent their early careers in state government. Justices Blackmun, Stevens, Kennedy, and Scalia were primarily engaged in private practice or teaching the law before being appointed to the lower federal courts. Three of the nine spent more than a decade as a lower court judge, and all but Rehnquist and White had some prior judicial experience. Six of the justices were members of the United States Courts of Appeals when nominated, reflecting the increasing tendency of presidents to elevate individuals who are sitting on the nation's second highest court.

SUPPORT PERSONNEL

The Supreme Court historically has prided itself as being the one important government institution in which the actual officeholders do the most significant work themselves. Unlike members of Congress or the executive branch where decision makers are surrounded by large staffs that do a great portion of the institution's work, the nine justices make their decisions in a closed room without others present. Of course, no government body that receives four to five thousand case filings a year can function effectively without some measure of supporting personnel. Yet the staff that runs the Supreme Court is small and the focus remains on the nine justices.

Administrative Staff

About three to four hundred people are employed by the Court, with most performing the administrative duties that are necessary to keep the institution running effectively. In addition to certain specialized positions (the administrative assistant to the chief justice, a public information officer, and a curator), there are individuals and offices that provide important administrative assistance, furnishing the justices with the resources they need and keeping the facilities working and the paperwork flowing.

THE CLERK OF THE COURT   In 1790, the justices authorized the appointment of a Supreme Court clerk. It was the first of the Court's administrative positions. In the beginning the clerk took care of whatever tasks the justices assigned, but the primary purpose of the office was to handle the Court's paperwork and record keeping. The clerk received the formal appeals, provided records to the justices, informed attorneys of the Court's rules, and kept case files. For the first century the clerk's office was supported exclusively from the filing fees paid by litigants. Now the office and the salary of its employees are funded through the normal federal budgetary process and the filing fees are assigned to the U.S. Treasury.

The clerk of the court remains responsible for maintaining the Court's records and ensuring that the enormous flow of paperwork is handled efficiently. The office receives all appeals, petitions, and motions, and administers the Court's schedule and dockets. The office distributes all necessary filings and supporting records to the individual justices. The clerk is also the main link between lawyers and the justices. The office informs attorneys about Court rules, notifies lawyers about appearance schedules, and informs counsel when the justices have taken action on a relevant case. The effective functioning of the clerk's office means that the justices need concentrate only on their decision-making tasks and not on time-consuming administrative matters.

THE MARSHAL   In 1867 Congress authorized the justices to appoint a marshal. In the beginning this office was primarily responsible for maintaining order when the Court was in session. Prior to 1867, the justices borrowed the services of the marshal of the District of Columbia courts to provide the necessary security.

Since the appointment of the first Supreme Court marshal, the duties of the office have grown considerably. First, the marshal remains in charge of Court security. This function extends now to the entire building and grounds, and includes the administration of a small police force. Second, the marshal serves as the supervisor of the Court's physical facilities and grounds, including cleaning, repair, and maintenance. Third, the marshal's office handles the Court's fiscal affairs, paying bills, issuing salaries, and purchasing equipment and supplies. Because of its varied functions, the marshal's office employs some two hundred workers, making it the largest office in the institution.

REPORTER OF DECISIONS   The reporter of decisions was a position that began informally. Beginning in 1790, Alexander Dallas, a Philadelphia lawyer and later secretary of the treasury under Madison, simply began publishing the texts of the Court's early opinions. He did this on his own without official recognition by the Court. The custom of a private individual taking on this duty continued for many years. The reporter was compensated by the sale of the reports. Beginning in 1817, Congress appropriated a partial salary for the job, but the reporter continued to receive some compensation from sales.

Today the reporter is a full-time employee of the Court, but the duties of the office remain similar to what they were at the beginning. Now the reporter is in charge of constructing the official record of decisions and opinions. These are published in the *United States Reports,* the official compilation of the Court's actions. The reporter, however, does more than simply reprint the opinions drafted by the justices. Among the tasks of the job are to check all references and citations for accuracy, enforce a uniform style, find errors of fact or omission, and make the necessary technical corrections before the opinions are printed in the official record.

LIBRARIAN   Although it is said that the heart of any legal operation is its law library, the Court did not have one of its own until well into its history. At first, the justices had no official access to law books other than their personal copies and it was not until 1812 that the justices were given permission to use the Library of Congress. Beginning in 1832, however, Congress authorized the Court to begin building its own library collection, provided that members of Congress had access to the holdings. Even today the rules of the Supreme Court stipulate that senators and representatives have user privileges. Given the sparse nature of its holdings there was no need for a special officer to handle the collection, so this responsibility was given to the marshal. By the late 1800s, the collection had expanded to the point that a professional librarian was needed to maintain it and manage its growth. The position of Court librarian was established in 1887, but was not made independent of the marshal's office until the 1940s. Today the librarian oversees a collection of over 300,000 items as well as computer-based bibliographic and data files that constitute the foundation of the justices' and law clerks' research activities.

Legal Staff

In addition to the Court employees who are devoted to administrative services, there are a small number of staff positions dedicated to assisting the Court with its legal work. Most of these individuals are attached to the offices of the justices. Others work for the Court as an institution.

THE LAW CLERKS   Of all the supporting personnel employed by the Court, only the law clerks join the justices in contributing to the decisions and opinions reached. The clerks work in the offices of the individual justices. They are considered to be confidential assistants to the justices and conduct their activities outside the public's eye. Because of this fact, there is little general knowledge about the law clerks and often misconceptions arise about their role.[27]

During the Court's first century there were no law clerks. The justices completed all of the legal work themselves without assistance. As the caseload grew in number and complexity, the justices began urging Congress to appropriate money for legal assistants. When no financing was forthcoming, Justice Horace Gray used his own personal funds in 1882 to hire the first clerk. Gray's clerk, a recent law school graduate, served the justice more as a personal servant than as a legal assistant. In 1886 Congress first allocated money for the hiring of a clerk for each of the justices.

The justices are now authorized to hire four law clerks each, although some prefer to work with just three. The clerks are hired by the individual justices, usually from the ranks of outstanding recent graduates of the nation's better law schools. The justices use their own criteria to select these assistants. Obviously their intellectual and educational qualifications are of primary importance. Some justices have preferred to select clerks from their own former law schools or from their own home regions. Many of the clerks in recent years have already served a year as a clerk for a lower court judge. It is customary for the law clerks to serve for just one year, but some of the justices have experimented with keeping a clerk for an additional period of time.

The clerks function at the discretion of the justices, and their duties differ a

---

[27] J. Harvie Wilkinson III, *Serving Justice* (New York: Charterhouse, 1974).

bit from office to office. The most common task of the law clerks is to screen certiorari applications (requests for the Court to accept an appeal for a full hearing) and to prepare memoranda summarizing their contents. As we shall see in the next chapter, these petitions stream into the Court in large numbers. The screening function of the law clerks is indispensable because no justice could keep pace with these submissions without assistance. Some of the justices now pool their clerks and share the certiorari memoranda produced by them. The law clerks also act as research assistants for the justices, writing reports on various legal questions. In most offices, the justices allow the law clerks to participate in opinion writing. This may extend to writing first drafts consistent with instructions provided by the justice, or critiquing the justice's drafts and helping in the revision process.

Periodically, criticism has been raised over the influence of the clerks. There have been fears expressed that the clerks may be too involved in matters that affect case and opinion outcomes, especially in the offices of justices who have developed health problems or have slowed because of age. These fears are generally groundless. The tradition of annual turnover hardly allows the opportunity for any clerk to exert undue influence. Instead, law clerks provide meaningful assistance to the justices but work only under direct supervision. Because of their recent experiences in law school, they also bring to the Court knowledge of the most recent advances in legal theory and scholarship. This can be a major contribution to the justices, who serve in an institution somewhat isolated from the world outside Washington.

THE LEGAL OFFICE   In 1973, the Court responded to its own needs for legal representation by creating the office of legal counsel. The two attorneys who staff this office act as house counsel for the Court. Unlike the law clerks, the attorneys in the legal office are employed with the understanding that they will remain for at least four years. They represent the Court in any legal matters that involve the institution. They also advise the other Court officers on questions of legal procedure and compliance with various federal statutes. On occasion they may handle unusual legal matters or emergencies that involve the Court as a whole or the individual justices in their official capacities. In addition, the office of legal counsel may represent the Court on pending legislation in which the Court has an interest.

CONCLUSION

The work of the Supreme Court depends almost exclusively on its justices. It is one of the few units of the federal government where the actual officeholders do the work and make the decisions. Because of the power they exercise, a position on the Supreme Court is highly coveted and often the source of conflict between the president and the Senate. There are no formal qualifications for sitting on the

Court. Any person nominated by the president and confirmed by the Senate may serve. Informally, however, the process demands that successful candidates have strong legal qualifications and be of good character. In addition, considerations of regional representation, party affiliation, religious and ethnic background, age, and ideology frequently come into play.

Reaching the Supreme Court requires a demanding confirmation process. Those selected by the president undergo investigations by the Federal Bureau of Investigation, the American Bar Association, the Senate, the press, and a host of private organizations and interest groups. In recent years the process has become more ideologically charged, more public, and increasingly drawn into Senate electoral politics.

Historically the justices have been chosen from the nation's political and economic elite, generally representing those classes and groups that are influential in American politics. Because access to high quality educational opportunities and political connections are generally required to reach this level of the judiciary, representatives of the lower socioeconomic groups have had a much lower chance of sitting on the Court. Similarly, women and those from racial and ethnic minority groups have had low levels of Court representation. While diversity on the Court has increased markedly since the 1930s, the Court remains dominated by those from the politically and economically advantaged sectors of our society.

ADDITIONAL READINGS

Abraham, Henry. *Justices and Presidents,* 2nd ed. (New York: Oxford University Press, 1985).

Blaustein, Albert P., and Roy M. Mersky. *The First One Hundred Justices* (Hamden, Conn.: Shoe String Press, 1978).

Cameron, Charles M., Albert D. Cover, and Jeffrey A. Segal. "Senate Voting on Supreme Court Nominees: A Neoinstitutional Model," *American Political Science Review* 84 (June 1990): 525–534.

Chase, Harold W. *Federal Judges: The Appointing Process* (Minneapolis: University of Minnesota Press, 1972).

Danelski, David J. *A Supreme Court Justice Is Appointed* (New York: Random House, 1964).

Ewing, C. A. M. *The Judges of the Supreme Court, 1789–1937* (Minneapolis: University of Minnesota Press, 1938).

Grossman, Joel B. *Lawyers and Judges: The ABA and the Politics of Judicial Selection* (New York: John Wiley, 1965).

Schmidhauser, John R. *Judges and Justices: The Federal Appellate Judiciary* (Boston: Little, Brown, 1979).

Simon, James. *In His Own Image* (New York: David McKay, 1973).

Squire, Peverill. "Politics and Personal Factors in Retirement from the United States Supreme Court," *Political Behavior* 10 (1988): 180–190.

Three ❧

THE CASES

O
ne of the major characteristics separating legal from political institutions is the degree of freedom members have to set their own agendas. If, for example, members of Congress wanted to enact legislation outlawing restrictions on racist or sexist speech, they could simply propose it to their respective chambers. If Chief Justice Rehnquist wanted to issue a legal ruling against such ordinances, he would not be able to do so with such ease. He would have to wait for the issue of hate speech to present itself in a case appealed to the Supreme Court. In short, while politicians can initiate whatever policy proposals they see fit, federal judges and justices are far more constrained. Traditional legal doctrine simply prohibits them from issuing any decision in the absence of a formal request to do so.

Yet, a major question we address in this chapter is whether this handicaps the Court. That is, just because different rules operate for the judiciary than for legislatures or executives, does that necessarily mean that the Court lacks the ability to structure its own agenda? To answer this, we need to think about both the Court's workload and those procedures it follows to select the cases it will decide.

After reading material on these subjects, we think that you will find that while the justices may lack the complete freedom enjoyed by legislators, they do, in fact, have a great deal of discretion over "deciding what to decide." Some of the factors guiding the Court's agenda setting are just as political as those determining what issues a member of Congress will or will not raise. Seen in this light, the case selection process provides yet another example of the Court's role as both a legal and political institution.

THE CASELOAD

During its 1990 term nearly 5,000 cases arrived at the Supreme Court's doorstep. If you think that this is an unusually high number of requests, especially in light of the fact that the justices heard and decided, with written opinions, only 129 of those cases, you would be correct. As we illustrate in Figure 3-1, the number of

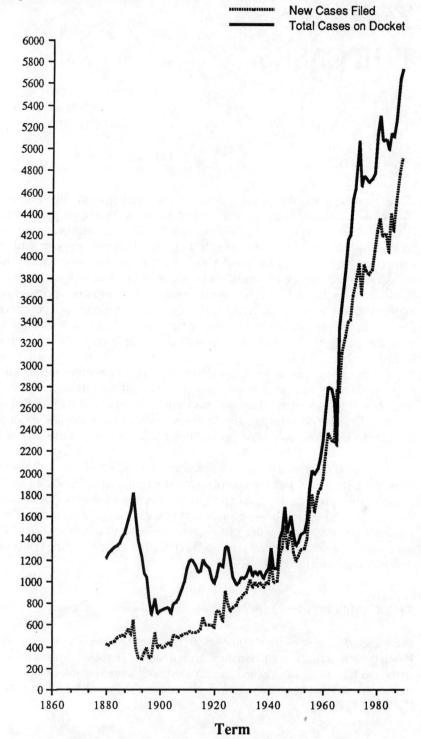

FIGURE 3-1
The Supreme Court's Workload

.... New Cases Filed
——— Total Cases on Docket

requests for review have increased rather dramatically over the century, even though the number of cases the Court formally decides each year has not witnessed a similar increase. In the 1890s, around 1,800 litigants wanted the justices to hear their cases; today, that figure hovers between 4,000 and 5,000. This is even more astonishing in light of the Court's entire history. Though we lack truly accurate data on the Court's caseload in the 1800s, we know that "not a single case was filed during the Court's first two terms, and only five were filed in 1793."[1] No wonder John Jay, the nation's first chief justice, "spent much of his tenure abroad on diplomatic assignments"![2]

The growth of the Court's caseload naturally leads to several questions. How do cases get to the Supreme Court? What kinds of cases come to the Court? What factors account for the caseload growth? What sorts of problems, if any, does it create for the justices? And what bearing does it have on the institution?

How Do Cases Get to the Court: Jurisdiction and the Routes of Appeal

As we already noted, in recent years 4,000 to 5,000 parties ask the Court to hear and decide their cases. How do these cases get to the Court? An extremely small percentage of them invoke the Court's original jurisdiction and come directly to the Court. The original jurisdiction cases are those that have not been heard by any other court. Article III of the Constitution authorizes suits involving ambassadors and those to which a state is a party to be heard by the Supreme Court on original jurisdiction. The Court, however, does not have exclusive jurisdiction over all such cases. Congressional legislation allows the lower courts to exercise concurrent authority over most cases meeting the original jurisdiction requirements. Consequently, the Supreme Court normally accepts only those cases in which one state is suing another. The rest it refers back down to the lower courts for an initial ruling. The most common such case heard by the Court involves one state suing another over a disputed boundary. In recent years the Court has decided between one and five original jurisdiction cases per year. In the next chapter we will discuss the procedures the Court uses to decide these uncommon cases.

Most cases reach the Court under its appellate jurisdiction, which means that another court—federal or state—has already rendered a decision and one of the parties is asking the Supreme Court to review that decision. In invoking the Court's appellate jurisdiction, litigants can take one of three routes, depending on the nature of their dispute: appeal as a matter of right, certification, and certiorari.

Cases coming to the Court on appeal as a matter of right (normally referred to simply as "on appeal") must be accepted by the Court for a decision. These cases

---

[1] David W. Neubauer, *Judicial Process* (Pacific Grove, Calif.: Brooks/Cole, 1991), 387.

[2] Ibid.

contain issues that Congress has determined are so important that a ruling by the Supreme Court is necessary. Prior to 1988, federal statute placed in this category cases in which the lower court ruled that a state or federal law is unconstitutional or in which a state court upheld a state statute that had been challenged as being in violation of the U.S. Constitution. Although the Supreme Court was obliged to decide such cases, many of these appeals did not present particularly important issues and the justices often found ways to deal with them more expediently. As William McLauchlan reports, between 1971 and 1983 the justices either did not even consider or issued summary decisions (a shorthand ruling) in 75 percent of appeals cases.[3] At the Court's urging, Congress virtually eliminated mandatory appeals in 1988. Now the Court is legally obliged to decide only those few cases appealed from special three-judge district courts. The balance of the cases arriving under the Court's appellate jurisdiction—those from state courts and federal courts of appeals—are left to the Court's discretion. The justices can decide whether or not they want to hear and decide them formally.

A second route to the Court, and one rarely used, is certification. Under the Court's appellate jurisdiction (and by an act of Congress), lower appellate courts can file writs of certification, asking the justices to respond to questions aimed at "clarifying" federal law. Only judges may use this route, so it is hardly surprising that very few cases actually come to the Court in this way. The justices may accept a question certified to them or may dismiss it.

The third and most common way litigants ask the Court to review their cases is through a request for a writ of *certiorari*, from the Latin meaning "to be informed." In a petition for a writ of certiorari, the litigants desiring Supreme Court review ask the Court, literally, to become "informed" about their cases by requesting the lower court to send up the record. The vast majority of those 4,000 or so cases that arrive at the Court each year come as requests for certiorari. The Court has virtually complete discretion to determine which of those requests it will grant. In fact, it responds favorably to only about 5 percent of such petitions. When the Court grants a petition for certiorari, it means that the justices have decided to give the case a full review. If the petition is denied, as most are, the Court will not review the case and the decision of the lower court remains in force. Because the certiorari process is the normal route by which contemporary appeals are accepted for review, the remainder of this chapter deals primarily with cases that arrive at the Supreme Court by this mechanism.

What Kinds of Cases Come to the Court?

Now that we know something about how cases get to the Court, we need to consider what kinds of disputes parties ask the justices to resolve. This, as you

---

[3] William P. McLauchlan, "The Business of the United States Supreme Court, 1971–1983: An Analysis of Supply and Demand," paper presented at the 1986 annual meeting of the Midwest Political Science Association.

might suspect, is relatively difficult to study. To identify substantive areas of the Court's workload, researchers must examine the thousands of petitions arriving at the Court each term. One scholar, William McLauchlan, did just that for the period between 1971 and 1983. In particular, he placed incoming cases into eight categories. We summarize the results of his study in Figure 3-2.

What can we learn from the data presented in Figure 3-2? First and most obvious is that almost one-third of Supreme Court filings involve cases of criminal law and procedure. This, as McLauchlan writes, is not unexpected "given the development of criminal procedural rights during the Warren Court era, and the various efforts to get those protections altered (limited or expanded) by the Burger Court."[4] Moreover, prisoners file the bulk of these petitions. Since many are indigents (and, thus, do not have to pay normal fees or follow other Court rules, which govern the filing of petitions), they really do not have much to lose by attempting to obtain Supreme Court review.

Cases of criminal law and procedure, while accounting for a large portion of total filings, remained stable—perhaps even evincing a slight decrease—over the decade. Where we see increases is in the "public law" category, which includes litigation involving civil rights and discrimination, consumerism, education, and family and children. In 1971, such cases composed about 13 percent of the docket; by 1983, that figure had doubled. Again, we can only speculate, but it seems reasonable to assume that litigants are increasingly looking to the Court to set policy on important social issues because other institutions will not do so. This is a subject to which we will return later in the volume.

McLauchlan's other areas collectively compose a rather small, but constant, portion of the total filings. Each year, the Court continues to receive a certain number of cases involving the judicial process (e.g., legal procedure and the profession), labor (e.g., employer-employee relations and work conditions), and state/local matters (e.g., streets and highways). What is interesting, though, is that traditional "common law" cases, such as torts, property, and estates, continue to appear in the Court's workload. "While," as the study's author notes, "the Supreme Court is no longer primarily a common law court—rather dealing with statutory provisions and constitutional issues—it still faces some demand from litigants for resolution of such issues."[5]

Accounting for the Growth of the Court's Caseload

Whether they come to the Court through its original or appellate jurisdiction, or involve issues of criminal law and procedure or torts, we do know—as Figure 3-1 shows—that the number of cases has increased dramatically over the past century. How do analysts explain the growth of the Court's caseload? In general, they point to four contributing sources. The first is societal demand.

---

[4] Ibid., p. 10.

[5] Ibid., p. 13.

FIGURE 3-2
Proportion of Supreme Court Filings by Case Type, 1971–1983

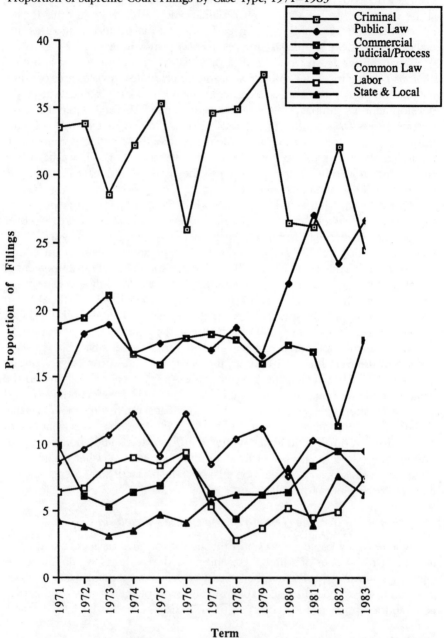

Source: William P. McLauchlan, "The Business of the United States Supreme Court, 1971–1983: An Analysis of Supply and Demand," paper presented at the 1986 meeting of the Midwest Political Science Association, Chicago, 47.

Simply stated, as the population of the United States has increased, there are more people available to initiate litigation at trial and to appeal those decisions up the judicial ladder. Indeed, if we drew a population line and superimposed it on Figure 3-1, it would roughly parallel the growth in the Court's caseload.

Still, increasing population levels provide only a partial explanation. To complete the picture, we must look at how Congress, interest groups, and even the Court itself have contributed. The role of Congress is rather obvious. The more laws it enacts, the more fodder for litigation, with some legislation providing more than others. A prime example is the 1964 Criminal Justice Act in which Congress provided to persons convicted of federal crimes a cost-free appellate review. As one author contends, "This legislation, rather than the 'liberal' opinions of the Warren Court, caused a 345 percent increase in federal criminal law cases in the Supreme Court—and the 'explosive growth' of the federal criminal docket of the Supreme Court accounts for over fifty percent of the total growth of the Supreme Court's docket in recent years."[6] Another way Congress has encouraged litigation is by providing for awards of attorneys' fees in certain kinds of cases. Prior to the 1960s, winning parties could not collect attorneys' fees from their opponents; today, Congress has enacted scores of statutes that provide for that possibility. Finally, laws creating increased rights for minorities, women, consumers, and so forth have inevitably encouraged litigation aimed at their enforcement. Especially noteworthy is the Civil Rights Act of 1964, a comprehensive law outlawing discrimination on the basis of race, color, sex, national origin, and religion in a wide array of contexts.

Interest groups also have contributed. While Congress has passed laws, such as the Civil Rights Act, it is often interest groups that seek judicial enforcement and interpretation of them. We lack data on the number of cases submitted per term by organizations, but the Court considers petitions filed by civil rights and liberties groups (e.g., NAACP Legal Defense Fund), labor organizations (e.g., the AFL-CIO), and the environmentally concerned (e.g., the Environmental Defense Fund), not to mention the other three hundred or so organizations that regularly participate in litigation. These groups—as we shall describe later—often view the Court as an amenable arena in which to achieve their objectives and, thus, press their claims there. In so doing, they often have "transformed" social problems into legal ones.[7] Abortion provides a good example. Prior to the 1970s, abortion policy was a matter largely controlled by state legislatures. When the pro-choice movement was unable to convince most state legislatures to liberalize their laws, it turned the issue into a legal one, challenging restrictive legislation in Court.

Finally, as the abortion example suggests, the Court itself has contributed. By hearing and resolving the initial abortion case, *Roe v. Wade* (1973), the justices

---

[6] Howard Ball, *Courts and Politics* 2nd ed. (Englewood Cliffs, N.J.: Prentice-Hall, 1987), 122–123.

[7] Stephen L. Wasby, *The Supreme Court in the Federal Judicial System* 3rd ed. (Chicago: Nelson-Hall, 1988), 191.

"opened the window" on this area of law, encouraging others to bring their challenges into court.[8] This is what happened on an even larger scale during the Warren Court era. Its expansion of the rights of criminal defendants and "its willingness to waive its ordinary requirements for paupers"[9] led to dramatic increases in the numbers of *in forma pauperis petitions,* those unpaid petitions usually filed by prisoners. In the 1950s, about 500 of these petitions from indigents were filed per year; during the 1970s and 1980s, about 2,000, or half the Court's filings.

Is the Caseload Increase a Problem?

That the Court's caseload, at least in absolute figures, has increased and that the factors enumerated above contributed to that growth is not in dispute. What has been the subject of debate is whether the increase is "bad." Some justices have suggested that it has not had any appreciable effect; former justice William Douglas once remarked that "no Justice of this Court need work more than four days a week to carry his burden" and "if anything" the justices are "underworked, not overworked."[10] Certain considerations support Douglas's assertion. For example, despite the increasing number of cases filed, the justices actually hear and formally decide about the same number of cases year in and year out. So there may be more appeals brought to the Court, but once the justices decide which cases they want to hear their workload has remained constant.

Still, many other justices throughout history have argued that the Court's increasing caseload has had a major and negative effect. It would not be an exaggeration to say that "concerns about the ability of the Supreme Court to handle rapidly rising case loads are nearly as old as the Court itself."[11] Beginning in the nineteenth century, justices pressured Congress to eliminate their circuit-riding duty and, since then, others have fought for reforms of many different types. Especially vocal "lobbyists" have been the two most recent chief justices, Burger and Rehnquist. In response to charges that the annual number of cases fully decided had not increased markedly between 1935 and the present, Rehnquist argued that "the great difference is in the percentage of cases we are able to review as compared to those which we are asked to review. In 1935, there were roughly 800 petitions for certiorari, so that by granting and hearing 150 of them we reviewed somewhere between 15 and 20 percent of the cases . . . but for the past ten years, the petitions for certiorari have numbered more than 4,000; by granting review and deciding only 150 of those . . . we grant review in

---

[8] See Richard L. Pacelle, Jr., *The Transformation of the Supreme Court's Agenda* (Boulder, Colo.: Westview Press, 1991).

[9] Lawrence Baum, *The Supreme Court,* 4th ed. (Washington, D.C.: CQ Press, 1992), 112.

[10] Quoted in Wasby, *The Supreme Court in the Federal Judicial System,* 195.

[11] Neubauer, *Judicial Process,* 387.

less than five percent of the cases in which it is asked."[12] In other words, the chief justice was pointing out the obvious: the old threat, "I'll take you all the way to the Supreme Court," is indeed a hollow one. Given the Court's selectivity, only a tiny proportion of cases make it that far. In addition, Rehnquist, Burger, and some scholars have expressed concerns about the quality of the Court's work. As Rehnquist asserted, the push to meet docket demands may have a negative effect on other aspects of the justices' work: "It is essential that [the Court] have the necessary time for careful deliberation and reasoned decision of the very important types of cases which are the staple of its business."[13]

How has Congress responded to pressure to alleviate the Court's caseload "problem"? Historically, it has taken one of two approaches. The first is to give the Court greater discretion over the kinds of cases it hears and decides. It has continually chipped away at the Court's mandatory appellate jurisdiction. We shall consider this in greater detail in the next section. The second is to thicken the judiciary itself by adding judges, clerks, and even courts. The most important example of this was the Court of Appeals Act of 1891, which created the intermediate federal appellate court structure that remains largely intact today. The addition of these courts of appeals, initially, had "a dramatic impact on the caseload of the Supreme Court."[14] Because these new courts heard appeals from the district courts that previously would have gone to the Supreme Court, the Court's caseload declined from 1,816 filings in 1890, to 379 in 1891, to 275 in 1892. But, as we know, this act—in the long run—did not alleviate the problem. In fact, there are even some who argue that adding lower courts and judges actually had (and continues to have) the effect of increasing filings. Under their logic, the more lower federal court judges deciding cases, the more potential appeals that can be generated up to the Supreme Court. The growth in the number of filings seems to lend this some support.

Over the past two decades, Congress has considered more novel solutions. The first was put forth in 1972 by a group created by Chief Justice Burger (and convened by the Federal Judicial Center), the "Study Group on the Caseload of the Supreme Court." Headed by Harvard law professor Paul A. Freund, the group argued that "if the Court could be relieved of the burden of having to select its cases for review, the justices presumably would be able to do a more thorough job on the cases they decided on the merits."[15] Accordingly, it proposed the creation of a National Court of Appeals. This new court would be staffed on a rotating basis by current court of appeals judges and would function as a gatekeeper for the Supreme Court. It would screen cases, deny review to those petitions that had no

---

[12] Quoted in Elder Witt, *Congressional Quarterly's Guide to the U.S. Supreme Court,* 2nd ed. (Washington, D.C.: CQ Press, 1990), 740–741.

[13] Quoted in Wasby, *The Supreme Court in the Federal Judiciary System,* 195.

[14] Witt, *CQ's Guide to the U.S. Supreme Court,* 740.

[15] Sheldon Goldman and Thomas P. Jahnige, *The Federal Courts as a Political System,* 3rd ed. (New York: Harper and Row, 1985), 106.

merit, and refer those it found meritorious to the Supreme Court for full consideration. The group's plan, however, was never adopted, largely because several justices opposed it. An especially loud critic was former chief justice Earl Warren, who thought the proposed court would be "a political device that would hamper the Court from enforcing basic constitutional rights."[16] So, too, some questioned the constitutionality of creating a court whose powers would overlap with those of the Supreme Court. They argued that such a court would violate the language of Article III, which reads: "The judicial Power . . . shall be vested in *one* supreme Court . . ." (emphasis added).

Around the same time that the Freund group made its recommendation, a congressional commission, (the Commission on Revision of the Federal Court Appellate System) headed by Senator Roman Hruska, also took up the caseload problem. In 1975, it too issued a report recommending the creation of a National Court of Appeals. The Hruska Commission's court, however, would have different functions than that proposed by the Freund group: it would "decide cases of lesser importance referred to it by the Supreme Court."[17] Congress seriously considered this proposal until it received word from the Justice Department that the new court would add "expense and delay to the process without appreciably relieving the caseload burden."[18]

Through the remainder of the 1970s, the caseload issue had all but disappeared, only to reemerge in 1982. After the 1981 Term (which contained an unprecedented number of cases on the docket), Justice John Paul Stevens delivered a speech in which he revealed that he personally read only about 20 percent of all certiorari petitions; that he left the balance to his clerks.[19] Shortly thereafter other members of the Court spoke out, returning the caseload issue to the fore. This, in turn, served to renew Chief Justice Burger's intent to convince Congress to take some action. In 1983, he came up with yet another proposal: the creation of a temporary court, later referred to as the Intercircuit Tribunal of the United States Courts of Appeals, which would be composed of U.S. court of appeals judges and would resolve points of law over which two or more federal appellate courts disagreed. Legislation was introduced in Congress, but again no concrete action was taken. Disagreement ensued over who would appoint judges to the new court (the chief justice of the United States, court of appeals judges, or the president). Moreover, many even questioned whether the proposed reform would actually help alleviate the Court's workload. In fact, some scholars argued that "the amount of unresolved intercircuit conflict with which the new court is supposed to deal may be overestimated."[20]

---

[16] Ibid.

[17] Witt, *CQ's Guide to the U.S. Supreme Court,* 741.

[18] Goldman and Jahnige, *The Federal Court as a Political System,* 106.

[19] Ibid., 107.

[20] Neubauer, *Judicial Process,* 390.

What Effect Has the Increase Had on the Institution?

Despite pleas from our last two chief justices, Congress has not seriously sought to rectify the caseload problem, if indeed one exists. As a result, the number of filings has remained high, though—as of now—rather stable. Undoubtedly, justices will continue to assert that this situation negatively affects the overall quality of their work. Yet, at the same time, it also has increased the power of the Court.

At the beginning of this chapter we noted that a significant constraint on the Court is its inability to generate policies on any issues its members so desire; that, unlike members of Congress, the justices must wait for cases to come to them. Its burgeoning caseload, though, in part serves to offset this constraint. It is probably true that virtually any issue striking the fancy of the justices is represented among the 4,000 to 5,000 filings the Court receives each year. Just consider the range of issues represented on the 1991 docket: environmental protection, hate speech laws, standing to sue, abortion, school desegregation, affirmative action, and criminal law and procedure. The Court's docket, in short, represents a microcosm of those issues on society's agenda at almost any given time.

Theoretically, then, the Court has almost complete discretion to select those cases it wants to hear and decide from the large number filed. In the next section, we consider some of the factors that affect the Court's decision to deny or grant review. For now, though, it is important for us to understand just how the justices gained control over selecting what cases would be placed on their plenary docket (the cases the Court plans to hear and formally decide). Prior to 1891, the justices had almost no control over their appellate docket. They were forced to handle appeals coming from the lower federal courts. This burden was largely removed after 1891 when Congress created the court of appeals system that serves as an intermediate level court between the district courts and the Supreme Court.

Since then, Congress has passed legislation designed to give the Court greater latitude in dealing with its workload, the most important being the Judiciary Act of 1925. Even with the federal courts of appeals acting as a buffer, prior to 1925 the "Supreme Court had to decide almost all of the cases that came its way; its [appellate] jurisdiction was almost entirely 'obligatory'."[21] After intense lobbying from Chief Justice (and former president of the United States) William Howard Taft and others, Congress alleviated that situation by giving the Court "the power to refuse to decide on the merits of the cases on its docket."[22] In so doing, it transformed the Court's primary responsibilities. No longer would it be an error correction body, merely reviewing virtually all cases that came to it.

---

[21] Gregory A. Caldeira and John R. Wright, "The Discuss List: Agenda Building in the Supreme Court," *Law and Society Review* 24 (1990): 809.

[22] Ibid.

Now it would be a court of discretionary jurisdiction, able to pick and choose those cases it deemed most significant.[23]

The 1925 legislation gave the Court its primary authority to control its own docket. This legislation not only provided much needed workload relief, but the Court now could reject trivial appeals and concentrate on cases of significance. As the case filings continued to grow through the mid-1900s, however, the Court once again felt the workload pinch and the justices began to argue that their discretionary jurisdiction needed to be expanded. After all, even under the 1925 legislation there were significant numbers of appeals that the Court was obliged to hear, and the Court found it increasingly necessary to handle these cases using abbreviated procedures. Finally, in 1988 Congress provided the Court with what it wanted. Almost all cases were removed from the mandatory jurisdiction category and placed under the Court's discretionary powers.[24]

AN OVERVIEW OF THE CASE SELECTION PROCESS

As we indicated above, the Court's burgeoning caseload presents something of a mixed blessing. On the one hand, with 4,000 to 5,000 cases pouring into the Court each term, one of the most arduous tasks faced by the justices is determining the 150 or so they will formally decide. One author estimates that to do so, the justices must read over 375,000 pages of briefs and other memoranda.[25] On the other, the huge amount of discretion frees the Court from one of the major constraints on judicial bodies: that they lack control over their own agendas. To the contrary, because of the latitude granted, case selection has become one of the most significant tasks the justices perform. As political scientist H. W. Perry notes, "Setting the agenda defines and orders alternatives, and scholars have long noted that outcomes—for example, legislation, an executive action, or a judicial opinion—are dependent upon the availability and ordering of alternatives."[26]

It is, therefore, not surprising that numerous scholars have studied the Court's case selection process. Some have conducted contextual, descriptive investigations, interviewing key participants (e.g., justices and law clerks); others have developed models to explain the Court's behavior, evaluating (through statistical analyses) the Court's past record of denying or granting certiorari. From these we can deduce two sets of factors that affect the selection decision, factors that reflect the dual roles of the Court: procedural/legal ones and those that are more political in nature. In what follows, we consider both and their

---

[23] Neubauer, *Judicial Process,* 57.

[24] See Lynn Weisberg, "New Law Eliminates Supreme Court's Mandatory Jurisdiction," *Judicature* 72 (1988): 138.

[25] David M. O'Brien, *Storm Center,* 2nd ed. (New York: W. W. Norton, 1990), 218.

[26] H. W. Perry, Jr., "Agenda Setting and Case Selection," in *The American Courts: A Critical Assessment,* John B. Gates and Charles A. Johnson, eds. (Washington, D.C.: CQ Press, 1991), 235.

relative influences on the Court. But before we do so, we provide an overview of the case selection process itself.

The original pool of 4,000 to 5,000 petitions faces several "checkpoints" along the way, checkpoints that significantly reduce the amount of time that the Court, acting as a collegial body, spends on deciding what to decide. The staff members in the office of the Supreme Court Clerk perform the first. When petitions for certiorari arrive, the clerk's office examines each to make sure that they are in reasonably proper form; that is, that they meet the rather precise Court rules. For example, briefs filed by nonindigents must have pages 6⅛ by 9¼ inches with typed matter 4⅛ by 7⅛ inches and must be printed in clear type (never smaller than 11-point) adequately leaded; and the paper must be opaque and unglazed.[27] But because petitions filed by "paupers" need not conform to that and other standards, "petitions on the docket vary from elegantly printed and bound documents, of which multiple copies are submitted to the Court, to single sheets of prison stationery scribbled in pencil and filled with grammatical and spelling errors."[28]

Once the clerk's office conducts its prescreening, it gives all acceptable petitions a docket number and forwards copies to the offices (called "chambers") of the individual justices. At that point, each justice reviews the petitions, making independent decisions about which cases she or he feels worthy or unworthy of a full hearing. In so doing, most justices rely heavily on their law clerks to assist them. Some have their clerks read and summarize all the petitions; others use the "certiorari pool system" in which clerks from different chambers collaborate in reading and then writing memoranda on the petitions. In either case, the justices use their clerks' reports as a basis to make case selection decisions.

In all of this the chief justice has a special role, serving as yet another checkpoint for the petitions. Several days before the full Court meets to make case selection decisions, the chief justice circulates a "discuss list," containing those cases he feels worthy of full Court consideration; any justice may add cases to (but not subtract them from) this list. Only those cases contained on this list are discussed by the justices in conference—the rest are automatically denied review.

Given the significance of the discuss list, it is somewhat interesting that scholars have not paid much attention to it, focusing instead on the actual decision to grant or deny certiorari. Recent research by Caldeira and Wright, however, makes a strong case for considering its importance.[29] For one thing,

---

[27] Supreme Court Rule 33(1).

[28] Witt, *CQ's Guide to the U.S. Supreme Court,* 738.

[29] Doris Marie Provine's *Case Selection in the United States Supreme Court* (Chicago: University of Chicago Press, 1980) also considered special lists used by the justices. For the time period she was examining, though, the chief justice maintained a "dead list" composed of cases the Court *was not* planning to consider.

only about 20 to 30 percent of those cases filed actually make it to the discuss list; the balance are never even discussed by the justices! Apparently, this reflects "widespread agreement" among the members of the Court "on the frivolousness" of the vast majority of petitions filed.[30] If this is so, then we might question whether, in fact, the case selection process is as burdensome as some have suggested. More important perhaps is that Caldeira and Wright demonstrated that there are systematic reasons why some cases make it onto the discuss list and other do not. Among the most important ones are whether the U.S. government was the petitioning party, real conflict over a point of law existed in the lower courts, or an interest group filed an amicus curiae (friend of the court) brief. Since these and several other factors also affect the actual certiorari decision, we shall consider them more fully in the next section. Suffice it to say for now that because of the discuss list and the other "prescreening" devices, by the time the full Court meets, its task has become considerably lighter.

Because the Court's conferences are attended only by the justices and held in private, we do not know precisely what transpires and can offer only a rough picture based on comments by the justices and scholarly assessments. These sources tell us that the discussion of each petition begins with the chief justice presenting a short summary of the facts. The associate justices, who sit at a rectangular table in order of seniority, then comment on each petition, again with the most senior justice speaking first and the newest member, last. In so doing, the associates usually provide some indication of how they will vote. But, given the large number of petitions of which the Court must dispose during the course of the term, it is hardly surprising that "most cases receive very brief discussion in conference, and ordinarily justices simply state the positions that they have reached individually before the conference."[31]

By tradition, the Court grants certiorari to those cases receiving the affirmative vote of at least four justices, the so-called rule of four. They place those and the ones rejected on a "certified orders list," which they release to the public. For those cases rejected, the lower court decision stands. For cases granted certiorari, the clerk of the court informs participating attorneys, who then have specified time limits in which to turn in their written legal arguments ("briefs"), and the case is scheduled for oral argument.

PROCEDURAL AND LEGAL CONSIDERATIONS AFFECTING THE CASE SELECTION DECISION

This is how the certiorari process works. Let us now consider the more intriguing issue, centering on those factors—procedural/legal and political—that affect

---

[30] Caldeira and Wright, "The Discuss List: Agenda Building in the Supreme Court," 813.

[31] Baum, *The Supreme Court,* 100.

the justices' decisions. As we shall see, procedural and legal considerations tend to act as constraints on the kinds of cases the Court can hear. If a case meets these "legalistic" criteria, then the Court has virtually complete discretion to determine whether or not it will grant review. It is at this stage that "politics" creeps into the decision-making process.[32]

Procedural Considerations[33]

Article III—or at least the Court's interpretation of it—places constraints on the ability of federal tribunals generally, and the Supreme Court in particular, to hear and decide cases. Two are particularly important for the review decision: the case must be appropriate for judicial resolution (*justiciability*); and the appropriate person must be bringing the case (*standing*). Unless these procedural criteria are met, the Court—at least theoretically—will deny review. Below, we describe both "doctrines of access" in more detail.

JUSTICIABILITY   According to Article III, judicial power of the federal courts is restricted to "cases" and "controversies." Taken together, these words mean that a litigation must be justiciable—appropriate or suitable for a federal court to hear and resolve. As Chief Justice Earl Warren asserted, "cases" and "controversies"

> are two complementary but somewhat different limitations. In part those words limit the business of the federal courts to questions presented in an adversary context and in a form historically viewed as capable of resolution through the judicial process. And in part those words define the role assigned to the judiciary in a tripartite allocation of power to assure that the federal courts will not intrude into areas committed to the other branches of government. Justiciability is the term of art employed to give expression in this dual limitation placed upon federal courts by the case-and-controversy doctrine.[34]

Though Warren also suggested that "justiciability is itself a concept of uncertain meaning and scope," he did elucidate several characteristics of a suit that would render it nonjusticiable.

First, federal courts will not issue *advisory opinions*. They will not render advice in hypothetical suits because if litigation is abstract, it possesses no real controversy. The language of the Constitution does not prohibit advisory opinions, but quite early on, the Court read the "case" or "controversy" restriction to prohibit it from rendering them. In July of 1793, Secretary of State Thomas Jefferson on behalf of President Washington asked the justices if they would be

---

[32] We adopt this framework from Perry, "Agenda Setting and Case Selection."

[33] We adopt this from Lee Epstein and Thomas G. Walker, *Constitutional Law for a Changing America: Institutional Powers and Constraints* (Washington, D.C.: CQ Press, 1992).

[34] *Flast v. Cohen,* 392 U.S. 83 (1968).

willing to address questions concerning the appropriate role America should play in the ongoing English-French war. Less than a month later in a letter to the president the justices denied the request:

> The three departments of government [being] in certain respects checks upon each other, and our being judges of a court in the last resort, are considerations which afford strong arguments against the propriety of our extrajudicially deciding the questions alluded to, especially as the power given by the Constitution to the President, of calling on the heads of departments for opinions, seems to have been *purposely* as well as expressly united to the *executive* departments.

With these words, the justices set important precedent regarding advisory opinions: issuing them would violate the separation of powers principle embedded in the Constitution. And, in fact, the subject has reemerged only a few times in our history—in the 1930s, for example, when President Roosevelt considered a proposal that would require the Court to issue advisory opinions on the constitutionality of federal laws. Yet, according to one source, "that plan was soon abandoned, partly because of its obvious unconstitutionality."[35]

Nonetheless, scholars still debate the Court's 1793 letter to President Washington. Some agree with the justices' logic. But others assert that more institutional, and even political, concerns were at work; perhaps the Court sought to avoid being "thrust" into disputes "too early and too often."[36] So too, it is true that courts in some states do issue advisory opinions and, thus, do not view them as violating principles of justiciability. Whatever the reason, all subsequent Supreme Courts have followed that 1793 precedent: requests for advisory opinions present nonjusticiable disputes.

A second corollary of justiciability is *collusion*. That is, the Court will not decide cases in which the litigants

▶ desire the same outcome,

▶ evince no real adversity between them, or

▶ are merely testing the law.

Why the Court deems collusive suits nonjusticiable is well illustrated in *Muskrat v. United States* (1911). At issue here were several congressional laws involving land distribution and appropriations to native Americans. To determine whether these laws were constitutional, Congress authorized David Muskrat and other native Americans to challenge them in court. When the dispute reached the U.S. Supreme Court, it dismissed it. As Justice Day wrote,

---

[35] For a discussion of this, see Gerald D. Gunther, *Constitutional Law*, 11th ed. (Mineola, N.Y.: Foundation Press, 1985), 1536.

[36] Gunther, *Constitutional Law*, 11th ed., 1537.

Th[e] attempt to obtain a judicial declaration of the validity of the act of Congress is not presented in a "case" or "controversy," to which, under the Constitution of the United States, the judicial power alone extends. It is true the United States is made a defendant to this action, but it has no interest adverse to the claimants. The object is not to assert a property right as against the Government, or to demand compensation for alleged wrongs because of action upon its part. The whole purpose of the law is to determine the constitutional validity of this class of legislation, in a suit not arising between parties concerning a property right necessarily involved in the decision in question, but in a proceeding against the Government in its sovereign capacity, and concerning which the only judgment required is to settle the doubtful character of the legislation in question.

Despite the rather definitive nature of this ruling, the concept of collusion has been interpreted in varying ways by different Courts. In other words, though the *Muskrat* case remains good precedent, the Court has not always followed it. To the contrary, as C. Herman Pritchett has noted, "several significant pieces of constitutional litigation" were the result of collusive suits.[37] For example, in *Pollock v. Farmers' Loan and Trust Co.* (1895), the Court struck down as unconstitutional a federal income tax. The litigants in this dispute—a bank and a stockholder in the bank—both wanted the same outcome: the demise of the tax. By the same token, it is true that the Court has decided many disputes brought by interest groups to "test" the constitutionality of specific pieces of legislation, including *Hammer v. Dagenhart* (1918), in which a business-oriented organization—the Executive Committee of Southern Cotton Manufacturers—designed litigation directed at overturning a federal child labor act. Why the Court decided these cases, but not *Muskrat,* is certainly open to debate. The general point, though, is a simple one: collusion is a rather slippery concept, open to interpretation. Accordingly, political considerations may affect the Court's interpretative process.

A third characteristic of a nonjusticiable dispute is *mootness.* In general, the Court will not decide cases in which the controversy itself is no longer live by the time it reaches its doorstep. *DeFunis v. Odegaard* (1974) provides one example. After being rejected for admission to the University of Washington Law School, Marco DeFunis brought suit against the school, alleging that it had engaged in reverse discrimination (i.e., it rejected him, while accepting statistically less-qualified minority students). In 1971, a trial court found merit in his claim and ordered that the university admit him. While DeFunis was in his second year of law school, the state's high court reversed the trial judge's ruling. He then appealed to the U.S. Supreme Court. By that time, he had registered for his final quarter in school. In a *per curiam* opinion,[38] the Court refused to rule on the merits of DeFunis's claim, asserting that it was moot:

---

[37] Pritchett, *The American Constitution* (New York: McGraw-Hill, 1959), 144.

[38] A *per curiam* opinion is a short statement issued by the Court as a whole rather than authored by an identified justice.

Because [DeFunis] will complete his law school studies at the end of the term for which he has now registered regardless of any decision this Court might reach on the merits of this litigation, we conclude that the Court cannot, consistently with the limitations of Art. III of the Constitution, consider the substantive constitutional issues tendered by the parties.

Related to the concepts of advisory opinions and mootness is that of *ripeness*. Under existing Court interpretations a case is nonjusticiable if the controversy is premature—has insufficiently gelled—for review. *International Longshoreman's Union v. Boyd* (1954) provides one illustration. In 1952, Congress passed a law mandating that all aliens seeking admission into the United States from Alaska be "examined" as if they were entering from a foreign country. Believing that the law *might* affect seasonal American laborers working in Alaska temporarily, a union challenged the law. Writing for the Court, though, Justice Felix Frankfurter dismissed the suit. In his view,

> That is not a lawsuit to enforce a right; it is an endeavor to obtain a court's assurance that a statute does not govern hypothetical situations that may or may not make the challenged statute applicable. Determination of the . . . constitutionality of the legislation in advance of its immediate adverse effect in the context of a concrete case involves too remote and abstract an inquiry for the proper exercise of the judicial function.

The Court's opinions in *DeFunis* and *International Longshoreman's Union* seem to suggest that the rules governing mootness and ripeness are virtually set in stone. To the contrary: like collusion, we find the same inconsistencies emerging with the concepts of mootness and ripeness. For example, determining whether or not a case is "dead" is more elusive than the *DeFunis* opinion characterized it. Consider *Roe v. Wade* (1973), in which the Court legalized abortions performed during the first two trimesters of pregnancy. Norma McCorvey (a/k/a Roe) was pregnant at the time the suit was filed in 1970. When the Court handed down the decision in 1973, she had given birth to that baby. Nonetheless, the justices did not declare the dispute moot.

The Court offered several justifications for differentiating *Roe* from *DeFunis*.[39] Likewise, we could think of reasons to explain its decision to decide some cases in which the parties colluded, but not others.[40] But the point is this: the elements

---

[39] For example, the Court noted that:
- DeFunis brought suit on behalf of himself; *Roe* was a class action.
- DeFunis had been admitted to law school so he would "never again be required to run the gauntlet"; Roe could become pregnant again, that is, pregnancy is a situation capable of repetition or recurrence.

[40] Witt, *CQ's Guide to the U.S. Supreme Court,* provides a reasonable explanation: "The Court's decision to hear or dismiss such a test case usually turns on whether it presents an actual conflict of legal rights. . . ." In other words, the Court might overlook some element of "collusion" if the suit presents a real controversy or the potential for one.

separating a moot or a premature dispute from one that is not, while important to the Court's case selection decisions, are open to interpretation by different justices and Courts, with the inevitable political factors seeping into the decision.

A final type of nonjusticiable suit is one that involves a *political question.* According to Chief Justice Marshall in *Marbury v. Madison:*

> The province of the court is, solely, to decide on the rights of individuals, not to inquire how the executive, or executive officers, perform duties in which they have a discretion. Questions, in their nature political, or which are, by the constitution and laws, submitted to the executive, can never be made in this court.

In other words, there is a class of questions, even if they are constitutional in nature, that the Court will not address because they are better "solved" by other branches of government. Consequently, had Michael Dukakis asked the Court to declare him president because he was a better candidate in 1988 than George Bush, the justices would not have heard the suit; nor would the Court decide a challenge by congressional Democrats claiming that President Bush should not have vetoed an unemployment benefits bill. Neither of these two questions presents an issue appropriate for the courts. The first is properly decided by the electorate and the second is a matter of presidential discretion. Both are political questions, not legal ones.

Once again, though, differentiating political questions from those that are justiciable is not necessarily a task free from political and other considerations. As noted above, the justices would not decide a challenge by Democrats to a presidential veto; yet they have taken cases involving questions of political gerrymandering (purposefully drawing the boundary lines of legislative districts to advantage one political interest over others), even though some analysts have argued that these are inherently political.

In sum, there are at least five characteristics of a dispute that would make it nonjusticiable. Presumably, then, if a case possessed one of these the Court would deny review. As we have seen throughout this section, however, the problem is that these elements of justiciability are not as clear as many analysts would like. In short, while it is important that we understand those elements that separate a justiciable from a nonjusticiable dispute because they can influence the Court's case selection decisions, it can be difficult to predict whether the Court will, in fact, deny or grant review on the basis of these particular procedural criteria.

STANDING TO SUE   Another access doctrine is standing. If the party bringing the litigation is not the appropriate one, the Court will not grant review. Put in somewhat different terms, "not every person with the money to bring a lawsuit is entitled to litigate the legality or constitutionality of government action in the federal courts."[41] Rather, as Justice William Brennan noted, Article III requires that litigants demonstrate "such a personal stake in the outcome of the controversy as to assure that concrete adverseness which sharpens the presentation of issues upon which the court so largely depends for illumination of difficult constitutional questions."[42]

In many private disputes, it is not difficult for litigants to demonstrate such a personal stake or injury. Where the issue gets a bit trickier is in those suits that involve parties wishing to challenge some governmental action on the grounds that they are taxpayers. Such claims raise an important question: Does the mere fact that one is a taxpayer provide a sufficiently personal stake to challenge a governmental program, sufficient enough to meet the "standing" requirement?

The Court initially addressed this question in the case of *Frothingham v. Mellon* (1923), in which it outlined a very restrictive approach to standing:

> The party . . . must be able to show not only that the statute is invalid but that he has sustained or is immediately in danger of sustaining some direct injury as the result of its enforcement, and not merely that he suffers in some indefinite way in common with people generally.

For the next forty years, *Frothingham* served as a major bar to taxpayer suits. Unless litigants could demonstrate that a government program injured them or threatened to do so—beyond the mere expenditure of tax dollars—the Court would deny review. In *Flast v. Cohen* (1968) though, the Warren Court substantially relaxed that rule. It held that if taxpayers can indicate a logical link between their status and the legislation, and one between their status and a specific constitutional infringement, then they may have standing.

In theory, this appears to be a relatively straightforward standard; in practice, though, it is open to a significant amount of interpretation. In fact, though the Burger and now Rehnquist Courts have not overruled *Flast,* they have significantly "limited and narrowed the requirements litigants must meet" in order to have standing to sue.[43] Some now suggest that recent interpretation of the doctrine governing standing resembles *Frothingham* more than it does *Flast.* This may be an overstatement, but it is true that, like the elements of justiciability, standing is open to interpretation. In particular, some allege that courts have used the standing doctrine as a way to achieve their more political or ideological goals. Seen in this light, it is not all that surprising that the Warren Court expanded standing requirements and the Burger Court contracted them. As one author put it, the former saw "the judiciary as an instrument for correcting or preventing wrongs and injustices"; the latter "articulated a more restrictive role of the judiciary."[44]

---

[41] Pritchett, *The American Constitution,* 145.

[42] *Baker v. Carr,* 369 U.S. 189 (1962).

[43] Neubauer, *Judicial Process,* 376.

[44] Ibid.

Does this mean we should disregard standing and other procedural constraints as too "politically charged" to be of any real value in understanding the case acceptance decision? On the one hand, we must question the extent to which doctrines of access are real restraints on the Court or are actually political constraints open to interpretation. On the other, as H. W. Perry has argued, "procedural issues are crucial for understanding why certain cases are accepted and why others are not. . . . Though the Supreme Court is capable of modifying its restrictions—or, as it does sometimes, ignoring them without satisfactory explanation—it generally takes such barriers to review quite seriously." He also asserts, quite reasonably, that "it is the presumption of justices that if an issue is important, it will come back in another case, so there is no need to take a case that is jurisprudentially unsound."[45]

Legal/Technical Criteria

Debates over whether procedural criteria actually affect the Court's certiorari decision will undoubtedly continue. What we can say for sure is that even if these procedural criteria "serve as preliminary screening devices by which some cases are eliminated," it is true that "most cases meet these criteria, and the Court must use others to choose among them."[46] These include "legal factors," some of which the Court has encapsulated in its Rule 17 governing the certiorari decision-making process:

1. A review on writ of certiorari is not a matter of right, but of judicial discretion, and will be granted only when there are special and important reasons therefor. The following, while neither controlling nor fully measuring the Court's discretion, indicate the character of reasons that will be considered.

a. When a federal court of appeals has rendered a decision in conflict with the decision of another federal court of appeals on the same matter; or has decided a federal question in a way in conflict with a state court of last resort; or has so far departed from the accepted and usual course of judicial proceedings, or so far sanctioned such a departure by a lower court, as to call for an exercise of this Court's power of supervision.

b. When a state court of last resort has decided a federal question in a way in conflict with the decision of another state court of last resort or of a federal court of appeals.

c. When a state court or a federal court of appeals has decided an important question of federal law which has not been, but should be, settled by this Court, or has decided a federal question in a way in conflict with applicable decisions of this Court.

---

45 Perry, "Agenda Setting and Case Selection," 241–242.

46 Baum, *The Supreme Court*, 103.

To some degree, as H. W. Perry points out, this rule is tautological: "What makes a case important enough to be certworthy is a case [the justices] consider important enough to be certworthy."[47] Still, the Court does seem to follow at least parts of Rule 17. For example, virtually all studies of the certiorari process indicate that the existence of conflictual rulings among federal courts or between federal and state courts—a key concern of Rule 17—is an important consideration. As S. Sidney Ulmer asserted: "In making up its plenary case agenda, the Court is significantly responsive to the legal-systemic variable—conflict. . . . "[48]

Even so, scholars have faced something of a challenge in identifying whether "conflict" actually exists in a given case. One obvious route to establishing its presence is to examine the briefs of petitioning attorneys and see whether they claim the existence of legal conflict. The problem with this is, as Ulmer notes, that "attorneys have good reasons to believe that the presence of conflict enhances the probability of discretionary review." As a result, they tend to "pad" or "puff" up their claims.[49] To get around this, researchers must go back to lower court rulings to determine whether, in fact, a genuine conflict does exist.

Identifying the presence of conflict, though, is just the first step; scholars have also contemplated various ways of defining the term. Some have simply followed the dictates of Rule 17; others have taken a more rigorous approach. For example, in their study of the certiorari decision-making process, Caldeira and Wright[50] included three distinct measures of conflict:

1. A disagreement between a lower court and an appellate court (i.e., did the appellate court reverse the lower court?)
2. A conflict *alleged* by the petitioning attorney in one or more of the following situations:
   a. conflict between two state supreme courts
   b. conflict between two federal circuit courts
   c. conflict with U.S. Supreme Court precedent
   d. conflict between a state court and a federal court
3. A conflict *actually* existing in situations a–d noted above.

Intriguingly, they find that all three types of conflict increase the probability that the Court will grant review; however, the existence of actual conflict is far and away the most significant of the conflict variables. If actual conflict is present in a case, a 33 percent chance exists that the Court will grant review—as compared with the usual certiorari rate of about 5 percent.

---

[47] Perry, "Agenda Setting and Case Selection," 237.

[48] S. Sidney Ulmer, "The Supreme Court's Certiorari Decisions: Conflict as a Predictive Variable," *American Political Science Review* 78 (1984): 910.

[49] Ibid., 904.

[50] Gregory A. Caldeira and John R. Wright, "Organized Interests and Agenda Setting in the U.S. Supreme Court," *American Political Science Review* 82 (1988): 1109–1127.

What then can we conclude about legal/technical constraints on the Court's certiorari process? To be sure, the Court does seem to follow the dictates of Rule 17. In particular, the presence of "actual conflict" in a given case will substantially increase the likelihood of review. Yet, as Caldeira and Wright explain, Rule 17 is not all that helpful in understanding "how the Court makes gatekeeping decisions." Like procedural criteria, Rule 17 may act as a constraint on decision making. The Court, for example, may use the existence of actual conflict as a threshold—cases that do not possess conflict *may be* rejected; but that does not mean that cases with conflict are *necessarily* accepted. As a result, legal criteria—while important—do not provide a full explanation of the certiorari decision.

POLITICAL INFLUENCES ON THE CASE SELECTION DECISION

Since most scholars agree that procedural and legal factors may act as constraints on the Court's behavior but do not necessarily further our understanding of what occurs if a case meets those criteria, they have looked elsewhere. In particular, analysts have identified a number of *political* pressures that come to bear on the Court's case selection process. We consider four: the solicitor general as a participant, interest group involvement, the substantive issue, and the ideology of the Supreme Court and its members.

The Solicitor General

Although scholars disagree over the importance of some factors explaining the certiorari decision, there is virtual unanimity when it comes to the U.S. solicitor general's role. Simply stated, when the solicitor general—the attorney who represents the United States government before the Supreme Court—files a petition, the Court is "significantly more likely to grant certiorari than under other circumstances."[51] Just consider that the Court accepts about 70 to 80 percent of those cases in which the federal government is the petitioning party, compared with its usual rate of about 5 percent!

How can we account for this astonishing degree of success? Scholars have posited a number of reasons. For one, the Court is certainly cognizant of the solicitor general's special role. Although they are presidential appointees whose decisions will reflect the administration's philosophy, solicitors general are nonetheless supposed to represent the interests of the United States. And, given the Court's position as the highest in the United States, these are interests it can hardly ignore. Second, it is also true that the justices have come to rely on the solicitor general to act as a prescreening device; that is, they expect the solicitor general to examine carefully those cases that the government could appeal and

---

[51] Ibid., 1115.

bring only important ones to their attention. Finally, because solicitors general are involved in so much Supreme Court litigation, they possess a great deal of knowledge about the Court that other litigants do not have. They are, as such, "repeat players," who know the "rules of the game" and can use them to their advantage. Put more concretely, solicitors general know how to structure their petitions to attract the attention and interest of the justices.

As our discussion above suggests, most research has focused on how and why the solicitor general has been so successful in obtaining Supreme Court review. More recently, though, some scholars have argued that the same factors that tend to explain the solicitor general's incredible review rate also might apply to other attorneys, particularly those who appear often before the Court and have accrued "repeat player" status. For example, in her study of the Legal Services Program, which was established by the federal government to provide legal care to the poor, Susan Lawrence reports that it had "an exceptional 64 percent review rate."[52]

Her research, coupled with the remarks of some of the justices indicating that they do tend to favor certain attorneys over others, suggests that we may need to consider the role of parties other than the solicitor general in the case selection process. Perhaps with more research we will be able to understand better which parties are successful and why.

Interest Groups

Although we often tend to conceptualize the Supreme Court as a "legal institution," immune from political pressures, this is hardly the case. Even so, it is hard to imagine that interest groups—the most political of all agents—could actually affect the Court, arguably the least political of all branches. But research establishes beyond a doubt that they do, in fact, have a great deal of influence on the justices at the certiorari stage through the filing of amicus curiae briefs.[53]

As we shall describe in Chapter 5, research focusing on amicus curiae briefs has primarily examined their importance at the plenary review stage. This focus reflects the fact that most organized groups wait until after the Supreme Court has announced its intention to hear a given case before filing a friend of the court brief. For many groups this seems to be a logical way to proceed; after all, why should they waste precious resources on filing a brief in a case that the Court probably would not agree to hear? A study by Caldeira and Wright, however, indicates that this assumption may be quite misplaced. These researchers found that amicus curiae briefs filed at the certiorari stage (i.e., before the Court made its selection decision) and in favor of certiorari significantly increase the chances that the Court will take the case. And, the more the merrier! As Caldeira

---

[52] Susan E. Lawrence, *The Poor in Court* (Princeton, N.J.: Princeton University Press, 1990), 96.

[53] Caldeira and Wright, "Organized Interests and Agenda Setting in the Supreme Court." The discussion that follows comes from this work.

and Wright put it, "Not only does [an amicus] brief in favor of certiorari significantly improve the chances of a case being accepted, but two, three, and four
briefs improve the chances even more." Another interesting finding of their
study was that even when a brief is filed *in opposition to* granting certiorari, it
only serves to have the opposite effect, increasing—not decreasing—the probability that the Court will hear the case.

What can we make of these findings? Most important is this: though the
justices may not be "strongly influenced" by the arguments contained in these
briefs (if they were, why could briefs in opposition to certiorari have the opposite effect?), they do seem to use them as "cues." In other words, because interest
group briefs filed at the certiorari stage are somewhat uncommon (about 8
percent of all petitions are accompanied by amicus curiae briefs), they serve to
single out a case, to draw the justices' attention. In other words, if major organizations are sufficiently interested in an appeal to file briefs in support of Court
review, then the petition for certiorari is probably worth the justices' serious
examination.

Even so, it may be too soon to conclude that the briefs themselves are no
more than red flags for the justices. Even if the justices do not always personally
read the briefs, the groups filing them have distinct substantive interests, and the
justices clearly respond to those concerns if only by the mere act of granting
review. This is particularly important since, as we illustrate in Table 3-1, we know
that certain kinds of interests are more likely than others to file briefs at the case
acceptance stage. What we see is that organizations with economic concerns—
corporations, business, trade and professional associations—are far more active
than most charitable and community groups or even citizen/public interest/
advocacy organizations. More research is needed to assess systematically the
impact this may have on the composition of the Court's plenary docket. Nonetheless, it is clear that "economic interests . . . have considerably greater input into
the Court's selection of cases" than do most other kinds of groups.[54]

Issue Area

As the above discussion indicates, scholars agree that the presence of the
U.S. government and of amicus curiae briefs significantly increase the likelihood
of Supreme Court review. In contrast, they tend to disagree over whether the
particular type of legal issue presented in the petitions makes much of a difference. Early studies suggested that if a petition contained a civil liberties issue, the
Court was more likely to grant it. But more recent work casts considerable doubt
on whether case type has any real impact. In his study of certiorari decisions
made by the Vinson, Warren, and Burger Courts, Ulmer concluded that "civil
liberty and economic issues make trivial contributions" to the certiorari deci-

---

[54] Gregory A. Caldeira and John R. Wright, "Amici Curiae before the Supreme Court: Who Participates, When, and How Much?" *Journal of Politics* 52 (August, 1990), 803.

TABLE 3-1
Amici Briefs Filed at the Case Selection Stage by
Group Type, 1982 Term

Type of Amicus	No. Cases	No. Briefs
Individual	6	7
Corporation	26	29
Government		
United States	59	59
State	46	88
County	8	9
Municipality	10	16
Other	4	5
Charitable/Community	9	9
Public interest law firm	16	18
Citizen/Public interest/Advocacy	35	43
Business, trade, professional	77	110
Union	12	12
Peak association	16	17
Other	21	25

Source: Gregory A. Caldeira and John R. Wright, "Amici Curiae Before the Supreme Court: Who Participates, When, and How Much?"
Journal of Politics 52 (August 1990): 796.

sion, at least compared with other factors (e.g., conflict, solicitor general participation).[55] Likewise, of all the factors Caldeira and Wright considered (e.g.,
amicus curiae briefs, conflict, solicitor general participation), the only one that
had no appreciable affect on the Court was case type.

With recent evidence pointing against the importance of case type, should
we then dismiss it as a factor in the Court's case selection process? We think that
would be premature for a number of reasons. First, scholars have been "madden-
ingly inconsistent" in the way they have defined particular issue areas.[56] Hence, it
is rather unclear whether case type truly does not matter or if that conclusion
reflects problems in the research process. Second, analysts have tended to lump
together many different kinds of cases into overarching categories. A "civil liberties" category, for example, might contain cases as diverse as religious liberty,
criminal rights, and privacy. It may be then that the Court is more prone to take,
say, religious liberty cases rather than ones involving criminal law. But because
analysts often use such broad categorizations, we cannot know for sure. Finally,
as we describe below, while case type may not be important to the *Court's*
ultimate decision, it can be a factor in explaining the certiorari votes of individual justices.

---

[55] Ulmer, "The Supreme Court's Certiorari Decisions," 908.

[56] Neubauer, *Judicial Process,* 386.

Ideology of the Justices and the Court

Does the ideology of justices affect their votes on certiorari petitions? We have strong reasons to suspect that it does. For one, the justices of the moderately conservative Burger Court were far more likely to grant review to cases in which the lower court reached a liberal decision so that they could reverse it. This behavior was especially prevalent in civil liberties cases: if the court below had ruled in favor of the rights claim, then the Supreme Court was significantly more likely to take the case. Such a tendency will probably continue into the Rehnquist Court era; indeed, according to the present chief justice, "the most common reason members of our Court vote to grant certiorari is that they doubt the correctness of the decision of the lower court."[57] And, of course, as Baum suggested, "justices' evaluations of lower court decisions are based largely on their ideological positions."[58]

Many scholars argue that votes at the case selection stage are often "related to votes on the merits."[59] So, for example, those justices on the Rehnquist Court who would vote to hear a civil liberties case in which the lower court reached a liberal decision would most likely reverse the lower court after giving the appeal a full review on the merits. The opposite perhaps held true for the Warren Court: the justices would have been more likely to take a lower court case reaching a conservative outcome and then reverse on the merits.

Finally, and particularly important given the strongly conservative ideological makeup of the current Court, justices may engage in strategic voting behavior at the certiorari stage. That is, not only are certiorari votes "related to the votes on the merits, but calculations of likely outcomes on the merits drive the cert. vote."[60] In other words, justices try to think about the long-term implications of their certiorari vote: if they vote to grant a particular petition, what would be the odds of their position "winning" at the merits stage? Undoubtedly, some of this calculation does go on. One justice explained his certiorari "calculus" to Perry in this way: "I might think the Nebraska Supreme Court made a horrible decision, but I wouldn't want to take the case, for if we take the case and affirm it, then it would become a precedent."[61] For those justices of the Rehnquist Court who know they will often find themselves in the minority—that is, the liberals—such advance planning may be particularly important to avoid the creation of a vast body of conservative precedent. Still, it is important to recognize that "many decisions on cert. are made without any

---

57 Quoted in Baum, 105.

58 Ibid., 105.

59 Perry, "Agenda Setting and Case Selection," 239.

60 Ibid.

61 Quoted in Baum, *The Supreme Court,* 106.

inclination to calculate an expected outcome on the merits."[62] Sometimes, for example, a justice may feel so strongly about a particular issue that he or she will vote to grant review without any regard for what might happen at the merits stage. We only have to consider Justice Thurgood Marshall's votes in capital punishment cases to see the truth in this. Despite the fact that the majority of justices with whom he sat believed the death penalty to be a constitutional form of punishment, he dissented from virtually every denial of certiorari in petitions raising such claims. To be sure, Marshall recognized that the Court would never adopt his views on the merits, yet he believed so strongly that he felt compelled to put them forth.

CONCLUSION

At the beginning of this chapter, we suggested that one of the things distinguishing legal from political institutions is the constraint existing on the ability of members to set their own agenda. While members of Congress, for example, can propose any sort of legislation they desire, justices do not have that luxury. They must wait for cases to come to them. Still, we asked you to consider this question: Just because different rules operate for the judiciary than for legislative and executive branches, does that necessarily mean that the Court lacks the ability to structure its own agenda?

How can we now answer that question? We think any response will necessarily be mixed, reflecting the dual roles played by the Supreme Court. On the one side, the Court simply is not as free as the more political institutions to set its own agenda. It is, after all, a legal institution bound and restricted by those norms and rules governing the exercise of judicial power. The Court, for example, probably would not agree to review a case in which the parties clearly lacked standing, or the dispute itself had become moot. Moreover, we know—as their own rules suggest—that the justices are far more prone to grant review in disputes over which some disagreement exists in the lower courts. On the other side, to what extent do these legal and procedural considerations actually constrain the Court's ability to set its agenda? Given the enormous variety of cases coming into the Court each year, coupled with the fact that most do meet the minimal legal criteria, it is only reasonable to suggest that the justices enjoy a good deal of latitude. What's more, very political factors seem to affect that discretionary process. Case selection, then, provides yet another example of the Supreme Court acting as both a legal and a political institution.

---

[62] Perry, "Agenda Setting and Case Selection," 240.

ADDITIONAL READINGS

Caldeira, Gregory A., and John R. Wright. "Organized Interests and Agenda Setting in the U.S. Supreme Court," *American Political Science Review* 82 (December 1988): 1109–1127.

Casper, Gerhard, and Richard Posner. *The Workload of the Supreme Court* (Chicago: American Bar Foundation, 1976).

Lawrence, Susan E. *The Poor in Court: The Legal Services Program and Supreme Court Decision Making* (Princeton: Princeton University Press, 1990).

McLauchlan, William P. *Federal Court Caseloads* (New York: Praeger, 1984).

Pacelle, Richard L., Jr., *The Transformation of the Supreme Court's Agenda* (Boulder, Colo.: Westview Press, 1991).

Perry, H. W., Jr., *Deciding to Decide: Agenda Setting in the United States Supreme Court* (Cambridge: Harvard University Press, 1991).

Provine, Doris Marie. *Case Selection in the United States Supreme Court* (Chicago: University of Chicago Press, 1980).

Four ✑

THE SUPREME COURT DECIDES

A t the very heart of the Supreme Court is its decision-making function. For more than two centuries the justices have followed tradition-rich procedures to arrive at solutions to disputes that have presented some of the most important issues of a self-governing people. The justices discuss and decide cases in closed conference, outside the view of the public or the press. Only the final outcomes are issued and aside from formal written opinions the justices do not explain or defend their decisions after they are announced. Because this process seems to be at odds with the exercise of political power in a democracy, it is important to understand how the Court goes about its work and to remove some of the mystery that shrouds it.

The Supreme Court undergoes constant change. Justices come and go. Dominant legal philosophies give way to new theories of the law. The variety of cases making up the Court's docket is in a perpetual state of evolution as the conditions and problems of society change. But what has remained relatively constant is the way in which the Court processes cases and arrives at decisions. While there have certainly been some modifications in the process designed to facilitate efficiency, the basic decision-making procedures have resisted fundamental change. The justices have demonstrated a dogged loyalty to traditional methods of arriving at their decisions.

We first turn our attention to the various stages in the formal decision-making process, explaining the movement of an appeal from its acceptance by the Court through the final announcement of its resolution. In the next chapter we examine the factors, both legal and extralegal, that play a role in the decision making of the individual justices.

THE SCHEDULE AND DOCKET

In the Supreme Court's first several years the justices assembled for a relatively short period of time to hear appeals that had been filed since the Court's last session. In some years there were no cases to decide and in others the Court had to sit for only a few days to handle its workload. Most of the justices' time was spent riding circuit, hearing cases as lower court judges around the country. After the appointment of John Marshall as chief justice, however, the work of the Court began to change. Cases increased in number and importance, and the time necessary for the justices to deal with this expanded role increased as well. The expansion of the Court's role and workload has continued into the contemporary period.

Organizing the Term

Today the Court is presented many more cases than it can possibly give full review. In spite of this demand, the justices have remained loyal to the practice of formally meeting for only a portion of the year. The period in which the justices are in residence and hearing cases is called an "annual term." Since 1917 the justices have opened their annual term on the first Monday in October. The Court then stays in regular session until late June or early July. During the late summer months the justices do not formally sit. The organization of the annual term is illustrated in Box 4-1.

The justices divide their annual term into two-week segments. During the first two weeks of the term the justices sit in open court, usually three days a week, to hear oral arguments in cases scheduled for a full hearing. This is followed by a two-week period in which the justices do not sit publicly, but devote their time to other tasks—keeping up with writ of certiorari petitions, studying briefs, writing opinions, and so forth. The pattern of alternating two weeks of public sittings and two weeks of recess continues through April or sometimes into May, when the Court completes hearing oral arguments in all of the cases scheduled for a full hearing that term. During the final two months of the term the justices meet in open session usually only to announce their decisions on cases argued earlier in the year. As conditions merit, of course, the justices are free to alter the schedule.

During the summer months when the Court is not in formal session, the justices may spend some time on vacation, but the summer is also devoted to study, reflection, and preparation for the coming term. Some attention must be given to handling emergency matters. For example, the justices may be presented a petition for a stay of execution to give a condemned prisoner an opportunity to file a legal action challenging the death sentence. Such emergency matters are normally handled by a single justice who is empowered to issue temporary orders arising from a particular circuit. In addition, of course, the stream of writ of certiorari applications does not stop and these must be studied as well.

On occasion, the Court has also had to extend its regular session or schedule a special meeting during summer months in order to resolve a particularly important case that cannot wait until the justices reconvene in October. For example, in 1974 the justices extended their term into the summer recess period in order to hear President Richard Nixon's argument that executive privilege allowed him to

---

Box 4-1

THE SUPREME COURT'S ANNUAL TERM

Activity	Time
Start of the term	First Monday in October
Oral argument cycle	October–April, Mondays, Tuesdays, Wednesdays in two-week sessions.
Recess cycle	October–April, two or more weeks following oral argument sessions; Christmas, Easter.
Conferences	Wednesday afternoons following Monday oral arguments (Court discusses the cases argued Monday).
	Fridays following Tuesday, Wednesday oral arguments (Court discusses cases argued Tuesday and Wednesday; certiorari petitions).
	Fridays before two-week oral argument periods.
Opinion announcement	Throughout the term, with bulk coming in late spring/early summer.
Summer recess	Late June/early July through end of September.
Initial conference	Late September prior to opening of new term (resolve old business, consider certiorari petitions filed over the summer recess).

---

refuse to comply with court orders that he provide prosecutors with documents and tape recordings relevant to the Watergate investigations. The survival of Nixon's presidency rested on the resolution of this case, and it was clear that a decision could not be postponed until the beginning of the Court's regular session in October. The justices unanimously ruled against the president on July 24 and just two weeks later Nixon was forced to resign the presidency.[1]

---

[1] *United States v. Nixon,* 418 U.S. 683 (1974).

The Docket

A case begins its journey through the Supreme Court decision-making process when the party wishing review files initial papers with the clerk's office to docket the action. The nature of these papers depends upon the jurisdiction that is invoked. The first distinction is whether the suit falls under the Court's original jurisdiction or is being appealed from a lower court.

ORIGINAL JURISDICTION   The original jurisdiction cases are those that have not been heard by any other court. As we noted in the previous chapter, Article III of the Constitution authorizes suits involving ambassadors and those to which a state is a party to be heard by the Supreme Court on original jurisdiction. In such suits the initial papers consist of a motion to file the action and the written pleadings in the case. The opposing party then has sixty days to respond in writing, after which the legal battle is joined.

The Court is generally hesitant to hear original jurisdiction cases for both substantive and procedural reasons. Substantively, these cases do not often present issues of significance to anyone beyond the actual parties to the suit. The Court is understandably reluctant to devote its scarce resources to these cases when more deserving ones are available on the appellate docket. For example, in May 1991 the Court handed down its decision in the original jurisdiction case of *Illinois v. Kentucky.* The dispute focused on the exact position of the boundary between the two states. Both states acknowledged that the boundary was the low water mark on the northerly side of the Ohio River. However, the river's low water mark changes from time to time. Illinois argued that the boundary should be set at the low water mark as it existed in 1792, the year of Kentucky statehood. Kentucky, on the other hand, contended that the boundary should be set at the low water mark as it exists at any given time. Speaking for a unanimous Court, Justice David Souter, in one of his first opinions, ruled in favor of the Illinois position. This suit is typical of original jurisdiction cases. They tend to be technical in nature and rarely involve any issues of general importance.

Procedurally, the Supreme Court is simply not well equipped to hear a case on original jurisdiction. The Court is designed to be an appellate tribunal and evaluate the actions of a lower court where a full record of what has transpired below is available for review. The Court must function as a trial court on original jurisdiction cases, accepting evidence and establishing a factual record. Normally, the justices cope with this task by appointing a special master (usually an established attorney or retired judge) to hold an initial hearing on the case, develop the factual record, and submit a recommendation to the Court. After the special master has completed this work the case comes to the Court in much the same form as do appeals. There is a transcript of testimony, a record of the entire hearing, and a written opinion recommending a particular decision. The justices can then review the record and treat the recommendation in the same manner as the lower court records and opinions are reviewed in a standard appeal.

APPELLATE JURISDICTION   The appellate docket contains cases in which a party dissatisfied with a lower court ruling requests a review and reversal by the Supreme Court. Following the changes approved by Congress in 1988, almost all of these appealed cases must go through the writ of certiorari procedure discussed in Chapter 3.

When a case seeking review is submitted to the clerk's office, it is given an identification number on the appellate docket. The numbering system distinguishes between paid appeals and *in forma pauperis* (proceeding as a pauper) appeals. Paid appeals are submitted by parties who have the economic resources to comply fully with Court rules on the number of documents to be filed, the format in which they must be presented, and the filing fees charged. *In forma pauperis* appeals are filed by parties who are indigent or who otherwise do not have the financial capability to meet all of the costs of printing and duplicating the required documents. Parties proceeding *in forma pauperis* are exempt from many of the procedural rules and court costs that economically advantaged litigants must satisfy. Most of the *in forma pauperis* appeals are filed by prison inmates who are challenging the legality of their incarceration. In recent years the *in forma pauperis* filings have exceeded paid appeals, but those filed by prisoners and other indigents are much less successful in part because they frequently present frivolous issues.

Beginning in 1980 and continuing to the present, the Supreme Court has faced a docket in excess of 5,000 cases. Most of these, of course, consist of new filings, but about 700 to 800 cases each year are carried over from the prior term. A summary of the Court's docket and action taken on the cases filed is found in Table 4-1. As we learned in the previous chapter, only a select few of the cases will receive a review and decision by the Court. A handful of the cases accepted by the Court are decided without a full-dress review. These cases present issues that the justices believe can be settled on the basis of the materials contained in the initial papers filed by the parties. Cases terminated at this point in the process are said to be summarily decided. Only about 150 of the cases on the Court's annual docket are finally decided with a signed opinion following a full plenary review. Although this number is small, the questions decided in these cases involve some of the most controversial and important issues confronting the American republic.

Arguments: Written and Oral

The parties to cases given full review by the Supreme Court have two methods of presenting their arguments to the justices. They first submit written arguments, called briefs, that fully document their positions. Later the attorneys for both sides appear before the justices in an open, public session to present their arguments orally and submit to questions posed by the members of the Court. The presentations in both formats are carefully governed by Court rules.

TABLE 4-1
The Supreme Court's Docket, 1985–1989 Terms

	1985	1986	1987	1988	1989
Paid appeals	2,571	2,547	2,577	2,587	2,416
Review granted	166	152	157	130	103
Summarily decided	78	71	66	75	44
Not acted upon	386	358	353	316	320
In forma pauperis appeals	2,577	2,564	2,675	3,056	3,316
Review granted	20	15	23	17	19
Summarily decided	24	38	21	32	35
Not acted upon	388	314	412	418	425
Orginal jurisdiction cases	10	12	16	14	14
Decided	2	1	5	2	2
Cases scheduled for argument	276	270	280	254	204
Cases argued	171	175	167	170	146
Cases dismissed	4	4	8	3	1
Cases remaining	101	91	105	81	57
Cases decided by signed opinion	161	164	151	156	143
Cases decided per curiam	10	10	9	12	3
Number of signed opinions	146	145	139	133	129
Total cases on docket	5,158	5,123	5,268	5,657	5,746

Source: Harold W. Stanley and Richard G. Niemi, *Vital Statistics on American Politics* (Washington, D.C.: CQ Press, 1992), 299–300.

THE BRIEFS   Once the Court issues an order granting certiorari or noting probable jurisdiction in the case, the appealing party (known as the *appellant* or *petitioner*) has forty-five days to submit a written brief on the merits making the case for reversal or modification of the lower court ruling. The appellant's brief is filed with the clerk's office and a copy is also presented to the opposing party. From this point, the opposing party (known as the *appellee* or *respondent*) has thirty days to file a brief presenting arguments urging the affirmance of the lower court ruling.

The Court has specific and demanding rules covering the presentation and format of the briefs. For example, the briefs of both appellant and appellee must be submitted in forty copies and not exceed fifty pages in length. There are detailed instructions covering the size of the paper, size of print, and binding. In addition, there are even rules regarding the color-coding of the cover page based on the type of brief and the nature of the party submitting it. These requirements ease the handling of the case by the justices and supporting staff, but add significantly to the costs of bringing an appeal to the Court. Those parties proceeding *in forma pauperis* are exempt from such regulations. They are only required to submit one typewritten copy of the brief to the clerk's office and one copy to each of the opposing parties. In addition, the Court normally appoints an attorney to handle indigent appeals.

The rules of the Court explain in careful detail what is to be included in the briefs on the merits. This required material covers such matters as the questions presented, the facts in the dispute, the legal authorities governing the questions, the argument of the party, and the relief the party believes he or she is entitled to. This indeed is a great deal to cover adequately in the fifty pages allotted, and the Court admonishes the authors to be as clear and concise as possible.

The briefs provide the most effective opportunity for the parties to convince the justices of the merits of their cases. In drafting these written arguments the attorneys have control over what is said and how it is presented. This is frequently not the case at the oral argument stage where the give-and-take of questioning can lead the session in unpredictable directions. Consequently, the briefs represent the clearest and most complete statement of the parties' arguments. They are submitted to the justices, who normally study them prior to oral argument, frequently helping structure the issues that the justices pursue during the oral argu-

Box 4-2

A SUPREME COURT BRIEF

When the justices of the Supreme Court accept a case for review, the appellant and appellee are required to submit legal briefs presenting their arguments on the merits of the case. Rule 34 of the Supreme Court outlines the necessary material that must be included in such briefs. The appellant's brief must include the following:

1. A description of the questions presented for appellate review.
2. A list of all the parties to the proceeding in the court whose judgment is being reviewed.
3. A table of contents and list of legal authorities.
4. Citations to the opinions and judgments issued by the courts below.
5. A statement describing the Supreme Court's jurisdiction over the case.
6. A description of all the constitutional provisions, treaties, statutes, ordinances, and administrative regulations relevant to the case.
7. A concise statement of the case, including the relevant facts and other matters material to the appeal.
8. A summary of the appellant's argument.
9. The detailed argument of the appellant, including the points of fact and law presented.
10. A conclusion stating the relief the appellant is seeking.

The brief of the appellee is required to cover the same points. However, the appellee need not restate any material presented by the appellant with which the appellee agrees or has no objection.

ment phase. Additionally, the briefs, as a permanent record of the arguments of the parties, are available for the justices to consult during the decision-making conference and opinion-writing stages. A well-constructed brief can place into the hands of the justices arguments, legal references, and suggested remedies that later may be incorporated into the opinion deciding the case.

In addition to briefs submitted by the parties to the appeal, Court rules allow interested persons, organizations, and governmental units to participate. These parties may submit briefs as "friends of the Court" (amici curiae) upon receiving the written permission of the parties to the appeal or, alternatively, of the Court itself. The federal government and the state governments, however, are not required to obtain such permission before filing amicus briefs. Occasionally the justices may even ask an outside party (usually the federal government) to submit an amicus brief. The briefs filed by the interested parties are normally limited to thirty pages.

ORAL ARGUMENT   When a case is accepted for full review, the clerk of the court places it on the calendar for oral argument. Unless there are reasons to expedite a particular case, the scheduling of oral argument dates generally follows the chronological order in which the appeals are accepted for review. A wait of about four months between case acceptance and oral argument is not unusual. While there are differences of opinion as to the effectiveness of oral argument and its role in actual decision making, the very fact that it is the only stage of the process that occurs in public makes it important.

In the early years, oral arguments in significant cases were considered important public events. The most prominent lawyers of the times participated in these cases and sometimes the presentations continued for several days. In the famous commerce case of *Gibbons v. Ogden* (1824), for example, Daniel Webster and other prominent attorneys argued for the better part of five days; and in *McCulloch v. Maryland* (1819), a case challenging the constitutionality of the national bank, oral argument extended over nine days. Over the years, however, the amount of time devoted to oral argument has been reduced in order for the Court to keep up with its workload. The most recent reduction occurred in 1970 when the amount of time given to each side was halved from one hour to thirty minutes, although extensions can be granted when necessary.

The Court is normally quite strict about lawyers staying within their allotted time. Some chief justices have been ruthless in their enforcement. Charles Evans Hughes is said to have cut off one attorney in the middle of the word *if.* Others have been more lenient. Warren Burger's policy was to allow the attorney to finish any sentence in progress when time expired. Once when Chief Justice William Rehnquist allowed an attorney to extend her remarks fifteen minutes into the justices' lunch hour, two members of the Court walked out when the normal time limit expired.[2]

---

[2] David M. O'Brien, *Storm Center,* 2nd ed. (New York: W. W. Norton, 1990), 272.

In years past, several lawyers might appear on behalf of one side or the other. With the new time limits imposed in 1970, however, it became impractical for multiple lawyers to represent one side, and by current Court regulations this is not permitted except in extraordinary circumstances. Similarly, while in the past oral argument by attorneys representing amicus curiae parties was permitted, this rarely takes place today. On those occasions when the Court does allow the presentation of an amicus argument it is usually to hear the views of attorneys for the federal government.

On those weeks in which oral argument occurs, the Court reserves three days for these presentations. Arguments are heard from 10:00 A.M. to 12:00 P.M. and again from 1:00 P.M. to 3:00 P.M. This allows the Court to consider presentations on four cases a day, or twelve in a typical oral argument week. The schedule obviously requires the justices to move quickly from case to case. Throughout this public session the chief justice presides in the center chair, flanked on each side by the eight associate justices, whose seats are determined by their seniority on the Court.

The rules of the Court instruct lawyers appearing before it to prepare their oral arguments on the assumption that the justices have read and are conversant with the material provided in the submitted briefs. The degree of the justices' preparation, of course, will vary from justice to justice and even from case to case. The rules, however, reflect the fact that the justices clearly want the presentations to provide amplification and clarification rather than a simple duplication of material already available in the written arguments. Attorneys are expected to be well prepared and able to discuss the case skillfully without excessive reliance on written materials. In fact, the rules explicitly state that attorneys should not read their remarks from a prepared text.

Presenting oral argument before the Supreme Court is a task best left to experienced appellate court advocates. Although lawyers must be prepared to discuss their positions for the full time allotted, it is rarely the case that they will be able to use the entire time as their own. The justices on the Court are allowed to interrupt the lawyers' remarks at any time with comments and questions. In many cases the justices pepper the attorney throughout the presentation, allowing almost no time for the lawyer to make prepared points. Justice Felix Frankfurter was fond of reminding attorneys that the Supreme Court "was not designed as a dozing audience for the reading of soliloquies." Responding to this questioning can be extremely demanding, requiring the lawyer to react knowledgeably and nimbly. Justices generally unsupportive of the lawyer's position may grill the attorney with difficult and critical questions, but it also often happens that justices with supportive views will ask friendly questions or suggest lines of response that might prove effective. It is difficult to predict a final vote based on the justices' comments, but the subjects pressed by the members of the Court are usually good indicators of what the justices believe are the central issues in the case.

Although the oral argument stage, with an advocate for each side standing before the bench of nine justices, is most impressive, there remains controversy over its importance. The justices have given us conflicting views. Some, such as William O. Douglas and William Brennan, have argued that it is extremely important. Others, including Earl Warren, have held that it makes little difference in the final outcome. Having already read the briefs and studied related cases, most justices undoubtedly have relatively firm predispositions on how the case should be decided. Probably few minds are significantly changed. However, a commonly held theory is that an attorney is much more likely to lose votes by giving a bad presentation than to convert votes by a good one.

The Conference

The decision-making activities of the Court take place during its regularly scheduled conferences. In the early years these conferences often took place on nights or weekends. This was especially the case in the early nineteenth century, when the justices met during only a small portion of the year and lived in the same boarding houses while in Washington. At the present time the justices have conferences on Wednesday afternoon and all day Friday during the weeks that oral arguments are held (see Box 4-1). Cases argued the previous Monday are decided at the Wednesday afternoon conference, and those argued on Tuesdays and Wednesdays are decided at the Friday conference. There is also frequently a conference on the Friday immediately before the beginning of each two-week oral argument session, during which certiorari petitions and other matters are handled.

In these days of "government in the sunshine," the judiciary stands alone in its insistence that decisions take place in private. Congress has agreed to this position by exempting the federal courts from open government and freedom of information legislation. There are two basic reasons for this secrecy. First, the Supreme Court was not structured as a democratic decision-making body. The justices are supposed to make their decisions based upon legal scholarship, wisdom, and adherence to the Constitution. The justices are not representatives in the same manner as members of Congress. Given the decisions it makes, the Court's deliberations can best take place outside the public spotlight. Public opinion and press scrutiny are not supposed to have a direct impact on the judges' deliberations. Second, although in conference the Court will reach tentative decisions on cases, the opinions explaining the decisions still remain to be written. This process often takes a good number of weeks or even months, and it is not until the opinions have been written, circulated, and approved that the decision is final. Since the decisions of the justices can have a major impact on politics and the economy, any party having advance knowledge of likely case outcomes could use that information for unfair business and political advantage. Unlike other agencies of government, the Supreme Court's rules of secrecy are uniformly obeyed. With few exceptions the justices have not had to deal with the problem of information leaks that have plagued Congress.

At the appointed hour the justices assemble for their conference. Tradition started by Chief Justice Fuller in 1888 dictates that each justice shake hands with every other justice upon entering the conference room. The justices then take their seats around a large conference table. Aides to the justices have already placed inside the room a number of carts loaded down with records, documentation, and law books relevant to the cases about to be discussed. When the door closes, no other person is in the room but the nine justices. Earlier in the Court's history two pages were allowed to be present to run errands for the justices during the conferences, but to reduce the possibility of leaks, this practice was stopped. No official record of the deliberations is kept. The justice with the least seniority is the Court's link to the outside, acting as the doorkeeper for the other eight.

Any official action taken by the Court is handled during these conferences. In a typical Friday session the justices may discuss administrative and scheduling matters, dispose of hundreds of writ of certiorari actions, and respond to various motions presented by counsel. But the central event in each session is the discussion of and preliminary vote on cases that have been argued.

The procedures used by the Court during conference are generally known, but we certainly do not know exactly what occurred in the deliberation of any particular case. The chief justice presides over the deliberations and is responsible for maintaining order and keeping the process moving with sufficient speed to ensure the completion of the Court's business. Clearly, some of the issues left at the Court's doorstep are so controversial and are of such complexity that they could be debated for weeks, but the justices certainly do not have this luxury. The chief justice calls up a case for discussion and then presents his views on the issues and how the case should be decided. The remaining justices then articulate their views and tentative votes in order of seniority. There is an expectation that the justices will not be interrupted when presenting their individual positions. On most cases the discussion needs to go no farther. The views expressed generally indicate not only how the justices tentatively line up on the disposition of the case, but also reveal the majority's rationale for that decision. On some cases extended discussion and deliberation are necessary, but this does not happen routinely.

While we often think of the Court's conference as a session at which the justices actually debate cases at length, attempting to convince one another of the proper way a case should be decided, there is surprisingly little of this today. All of the justices have read the briefs in the case and have been present during oral arguments. They have also discussed the case with their law clerks and have sorted out the main issues in their minds. Few cases present issue areas that are completely novel. Instead, most are related to general legal controversies with which the justices have had considerable experience. Consequently, the members of the Court already have a basic jurisprudential position on the general principles at issue. All of this means that it would be somewhat unusual for a justice to enter the conference room without having reached at least a tentative position on the cases to be discussed. It is more likely the case that fairly firm predispositions are already in place. This is not to say that the justices cannot be swayed or have their opinions modified by what is said in conference, but wholesale conversions are extremely rare. This also means that the Court is much less of a deliberative body than we would normally expect. Conference sessions are better described as statements of individual opinions rather than give-and-take discussion. If for no other reason, the crush of the Court's caseload means that the full debate of issues is not possible; and in any event, given the justices' strongly held positions, it is unlikely that devoting more time to the exchange of views would result in different case outcomes.

The Opinions and Final Decision

The conference session only determines a tentative outcome and vote. There is still much work to be done as the justices enter the final phase of disposing of a case—opinion writing. Each case given full treatment is finally announced by a written opinion drafted and signed by one of the justices who joined the majority. The written opinion of the Court is a significant document, not only for announcing and explaining the case outcome, but for articulating an authoritative statement of the law. The Court's opinion, if subscribed to by a majority of its members, becomes precedent, binding all lower court judges to apply its principles in future cases presenting similar issues.

OPINION ASSIGNMENT   A significant stage in the decision-making process is the assignment of a justice to take on the task of writing the opinion of the Court. The procedure used to determine the assignment is well established. When voting with the majority, the chief justice assigns the responsibility of writing the opinion. The chief justice may keep the opinion for himself or assign it to one of the other justices who voted with the majority. If the chief justice has voted with the minority, then the assignment task falls to the most senior member of the Court who voted with the majority. Some accounts have described Chief Justice Burger as attempting to alter this tradition by trying to assign the opinion when he voted in the minority or when he "passed" when the initial vote was taken.[3] This strategy, if successful, would have allowed him to select the opinion writer for the opposing side in the Court's vote. The rest of the Court firmly objected to these attempts and the traditional assignment procedures were maintained. In actual practice, the chief justice assigns slightly more than four-fifths of all majority opinions.

In assigning the opinion-writing task, the chief justice (or other justice if the

---

[3] Bob Woodward and Scott Armstrong, *The Brethren* (New York: Simon and Schuster, 1979).

chief dissents) may take several factors into account.[4] These factors involve institutional concerns as well as the advancement of the chief's own policy preferences.

First, in the course of an annual term the chief justice must make sure that the overall workload of the Court is not disproportionately distributed among the justices. The work of a Supreme Court justice today is extremely burdensome, and there is a great need to make sure that the work gets done as efficiently as possible. This cannot occur if some justices are given much greater opinion-writing responsibilities than others. This is, of course, a far cry from what occurred during the early days of the Court. For example, in John Marshall's thirty-five years on the bench he wrote almost half of the majority opinions. While a relatively even distribution of the workload may on its face appear easy to accomplish, this is not always the case. If the Court is badly divided, with a subgroup of justices regularly voting in the minority, the members of that group are not available to be assigned opinions in a great number of cases. In addition, newly appointed justices may need a decreased opinion-writing load until they become fully acclimated to life on the Court.

Second, some cases present important, challenging issues and others more technical routine matters. All justices desire their share of significant cases. A failure to make an effort to distribute the premier opinion-writing opportunities with some equity can cause ill will. No member of the Court wishes to be assigned opinions only in the more mundane cases, and some assignments are considered just plain drudgery. Some justices, for example, have confessed that they would rather wash windows than be assigned opinions in tax cases. With a group of nine individuals who must work so closely together on such intense issues, chief justices realize how important it is to avoid actions that cause strained relations among the justices.

Third, the assigning justice must remember that whoever writes the opinion must be able to keep the majority intact. The selection of an opinion writer with extreme views on the case may be the first step in the unraveling of the majority. If the opinion writer drafts a statement of the case with which other members of the majority are uncomfortable, some may refuse to join it, leaving the opinion with only plurality support and little precedential value. In extreme cases, a draft of a majority opinion may actually drive some justices to join the other side and can even alter the outcome of the case. A good example is provided by the case of *Bowers v. Hardwick* (1986), a decision that upheld the constitutionality of the Georgia state sodomy act. In the conference voting Justice Lewis Powell indicated that he would vote with the majority to strike down the law, but later when the drafted opinions were circulated he changed his mind. In doing so a 5–4

---

[4] See S. Sidney Ulmer, "The Use of Power in the Supreme Court: The Opinion Assignments of Earl Warren, 1953–1960," *Journal of Public Law* 19 (1970): 49–67; Elliot E. Slotnick, "The Chief Justices and Self-Assignment of Majority Opinions: A Research Note," *Western Political Quarterly* 31 (1978): 219–225.

vote to strike down the law became a 5–4 vote to uphold it. Interestingly, after leaving the Court in 1986, Powell expressed the view that he was probably right the first time.

Fourth, in some areas of the law, certain members of the Court, by interest or past experience, have special expertise.[5] Justice Harry Blackmun, for example, spent years as general counsel for the Mayo Clinic, frequently dealing with questions of medical law. It is not surprising, then, that Justice Blackmun was assigned the task of writing many of the initial abortion decisions, including *Roe v. Wade* (1973), which initially extended constitutional protection to a woman's decision to terminate a pregnancy. Justice William Brennan, an accomplished student of the First Amendment, was responsible for writing the Warren Court's most significant decisions on obscenity law. The chief justice where appropriate may take into account the various talents and backgrounds of the justices in deciding who should write the opinion.

Fifth, consideration may also need to be given to the question of compliance. Unpopular rulings may be better received by the public if presented by some justices rather than others. A classic example is provided by the case of *Smith v. Allwright* (1944), in which the Court struck down a practice in the state of Texas that kept blacks from voting in the Democratic party's primary elections. Chief Justice Harlan Fiske Stone initially assigned the task of writing that opinion to Justice Felix Frankfurter. Justice Robert Jackson responded by writing the chief justice a memorandum asking him to reconsider the assignment. Frankfurter was a northeastern Jew who was officially a political independent. Jackson argued that in a matter so delicate and arousing such opposition in the South the Court would be better served by having a different justice announce the decision. Stone agreed and reassigned the opinion to Justice Stanley Reed, a Protestant and Democrat from Kentucky.

Sixth, there is no doubt that in allocating the opinion-writing task, the policy preferences of the opinion assigner can be advanced. This can be accomplished by the selection of a justice whose views most closely approximate those of the assigner. Or, if the case involves issues of special personal salience, the assigning justice may keep the opinion rather than entrust it to another member of the Court. Assignments may also be used as a reward for justices who unexpectedly vote with the chief justice on an issue, thereby encouraging future defections from the other wing of the Court.

THE DRAFTING AND CIRCULATION OF OPINIONS   Once the opinion is assigned, the justice given the task will work on a draft over the next weeks or even months. Opinion writing is the most difficult, important, and enduring part of a justice's work. The opinion must summarize the relevant facts, present the is-

---

[5] Saul Brenner, "Issue Specialization as a Variable in Opinion Assignment on the U.S. Supreme Court," *Journal of Politics* 46 (November 1984): 1217–1225.

sues, review the applicable constitutional provisions, statutes, and precedents, and, most importantly, interpret and apply the law to settle the dispute. The statement must be written in such a fashion that it can be understood and used by lawyers and judges. It must also be true to the views expressed in conference by the other members of the majority in order to ensure that five or more justices will finally agree to support it. The draft of the opinion is usually written with the help of the justice's law clerks. The clerks contribute research to the drafting stage and critique the initial version of opinions. In many offices the clerks are given some opportunities to help write sections of opinions in accord with the supervising justice's instructions. The clerks and the justice may spend considerable time discussing how certain passages should be structured and presented.

When the justice has completed a satisfactory draft of the opinion, it is circulated to the members of the Court for their reactions and suggestions. Other justices who voted with the majority may offer suggestions ranging from matters of style to threats to vote with the minority if certain changes are not made. Each justice has his or her own style in responding to circulated drafts. Some curry favor with great praise. For example, Justice Douglas wrote on the back of Harlan Fiske Stone's draft of *United States v. Darby Lumber* (1941), "I heartily agree. This has the master's real touch!" To that same draft Justice Frankfurter added, "This is a grand plum pudding. There are so many luscious plums in it that it's invidious to select."[6] Other justices may take a different approach. The cantankerous James McReynolds penned on one circulated draft, "This statement makes me sick."[7] Once the draft makes it back to the author, work on necessary revisions begins. The revised draft is also circulated for comments. Just how many such drafts will be necessary varies from case to case. Justice Brennan indicated that in one case his opinion went through ten different versions that were circulated among his colleagues.[8]

At the same time that the draft of the majority opinion is being circulated, other opinions in the case are also making the rounds. Those justices who voted in the minority in the case are free to write and distribute dissenting opinions expressing their views. Additionally, justices who agreed with the final outcome of the case, but disagreed as to the proper reasoning for reaching that decision, may author concurring opinions explaining their alternative approach. Consequently, many different opinions on the same case, at various stages of development, may be circulating over the course of several months. This same process is replicated for each case the Court decides with a formal written opinion. At any

---

6 Reported by Walter F. Murphy in *Elements of Judicial Strategy* (Chicago: University of Chicago Press, 1964), 51.

7 Quoted in Merlo Pusey, *Charles Evans Hughes* (New York: Macmillan, 1951), vol. II, 671.

8 William J. Brennan, Jr., "State Court Decisions and the Supreme Court," *Pennsylvania Bar Association Quarterly* 31 (1960): 405.

one point in time scores of different opinions may be working their way from office to office.

A justice who agrees with a colleague's drafted opinion will signify that approval by signing on to the opinion. In every case each justice will ultimately express a position by authoring an opinion or signing on to an opinion written by another justice. This is how the final vote is taken. When all of the justices have declared themselves in this fashion, the opinions are sent via the Court's computer system to the Supreme Court printing department. In addition to the opinions of the justices, the reporter of decisions will write a summary of the decision and the positions taken by the justices. These summaries will be issued with the opinion at the time of formal announcement.

The opinion-writing system that the Court now uses was first initiated shortly after John Marshall was appointed chief justice in 1801. Prior to that time the Supreme Court followed the English practice of issuing seriatim opinions. That is, each justice wrote an opinion in each case, expressing individual views. Marshall did not think the Court could grow in stature and influence by using this procedure and adopted the new practice of having a single opinion expressing the collective position of the Court. This practice placed a great value on unanimous decisions and opinions. Dissent was only tolerated in the nineteenth century, and kept at low levels. Concurring opinions were viewed as unnecessarily detracting from the majority's position and as a rule were disfavored by the justices throughout most of the Court's history.

During the last half century, however, the norms of the Court have significantly changed. Decisions now are commonly filled with dissenting and concurring opinions. These occur at a rate that would have been unacceptable to the justices of an earlier time. Many causes of this change have been suggested, including the growing number of controversial and difficult cases, the Court's exploding caseload, and the justices' discretion over their own docket that allows them to discard easy cases. In addition to these possible factors, studies have demonstrated the importance of leadership in changing the Court's norm of unanimity. Especially contributing to this change was Harlan Fiske Stone, under whose tenure as chief justice (1941–1946) the number of dissenting and concurring opinions exploded (see Figure 4-1). With the chief justice not attempting to enforce the norms of unanimity that began with John Marshall, the justices felt free to express their views when not in accord with the majority of the Court. While Stone's immediate successor, Fred Vinson, made an attempt to reimpose the norm of consensus, he was not successful. Those following Vinson (Chief Justices Warren, Burger, and Rehnquist) took no significant actions to restrain the justices from writing separate dissenting or concurring opinions when they differed from the majority. It is unlikely that the Court will reimpose the consensus expectation any time in the foreseeable future.[9]

---

[9] Thomas G. Walker, Lee Epstein, and William J. Dixon, "On the Mysterious Demise of Consensual Norms in the United States Supreme Court," *Journal of Politics* 50 (May 1988): 361–389.

FIGURE 4-1

The Increase in Dissenting and Concurring Opinions on the Supreme Court

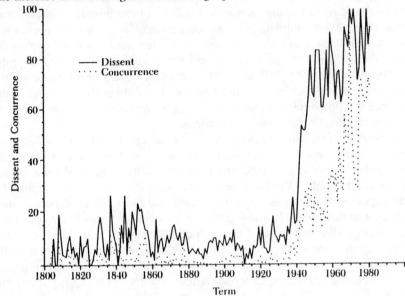

Dissent and concurrence are measured as the number of dissenting and concurring opinions per 100 opinions of the Court.

Source: Thomas G. Walker, Lee Epstein, and William J. Dixon, "On the Mysterious Demise of Consensual Norms in the United States Supreme Court," *Journal of Politics* 50 (May 1988): 363.

OPINION ANNOUNCEMENT   When the opinion-writing and approval stages are completed, the only remaining step is the announcement of the decision. During its formative years, the Court made public its decisions as the justices finished work on each case. Then in the 1850s the Court initiated the practice of reserving Monday as the day on which final decisions would be announced. The "Decision Monday" tradition continued until 1965 when the Court returned to the practice of announcing decisions as they became ready.

The Court pulled back from the "Decision Monday" system in order to improve public awareness of its decisions. When a significant number of decisions were announced on a single day, the press would tend to pick out one or two of the most important for significant coverage. The others were relegated to a mere journalistic mention. Often some of the decisions that did not receive full treatment in the press involved very significant issues. By spreading the public announcement of final decisions throughout the week, there is a much better chance that all significant decisions will receive proper press coverage and consequently there will be more public awareness of the Court's actions.

In earlier periods of history, the justices would hold a public session to announce their decisions, with the author of the Court's opinion frequently reading the entire text of the statement. The justices who wrote concurring or dissenting opinions were also free to read from their works. Today, however, the practice of reading full opinions does not occur. In most instances the author of the majority opinion simply delivers a short summary of the way the appeal was resolved, with those dissenting or concurring often adding a word or two describing their separate views. Such announcements usually take only a few minutes. When making public particularly important or controversial decisions, the justices may partially revert to earlier practices and read portions of their opinions. Once the decisions are announced by the Court they are final and become precedent binding on all lower court judges.

To assist the press in covering the Court's rulings the reporter of decisions prepares a summary of each decision and these are distributed to the media immediately following the announcement. In addition, the full texts of the opinions are available. Later the opinions will appear in three publications. The official reporter of Supreme Court decisions is the *United States Reports,* which is printed and distributed by the federal government. In addition, two commercial operations distribute bound volumes of all Supreme Court decisions, *The Supreme Court Reporter* published by West Publishing Company, and the *United States Supreme Court Reports, Lawyers' Edition,* published by the Lawyers' Cooperative Publishing Company. These reports can be found in any law library.

CONCLUSION

A common characteristic of legal institutions is a devotion to procedural regularity and tradition. The processes by which decisions are made adhere to custom and are not readily changed in response to political expediency. The U.S. Supreme Court, as a legal institution, conducts its business within such a tradition-rich environment. Although some concessions are made to the needs of efficiency, the justices today decide cases following procedures that largely have been in effect for the Court's entire history.

Beginning in October of each year the Court begins a new annual term, during which it will sift through almost 5,000 petitions for review and will ultimately resolve about 150 cases with full opinions. These cases are settled after the parties involved have submitted written briefs and have orally argued their cases before the justices. The members of the Court meet in closed sessions to decide the cases. One of the justices who voted in the majority is assigned the task of writing the opinion of the Court explaining the outcome. Justices not in agreement are free to write separate concurring or dissenting opinions. After the opinion-writing stage has been completed a public announcement is made as to the resolution of the case. This same procedure is repeated each time justices grant full review to a petitioner's appeal.

ADDITIONAL READINGS

Barth, Alan. *Prophets with Honor: Great Dissents and Great Dissenters in the Supreme Court* (New York: Random House, 1974).

Louthan, William C. *The United States Supreme Court: Lawmaking in the Third Branch of Government* (Englewood Cliffs, N.J.: Prentice-Hall, 1991).

Murphy, Walter F. *Elements of Judicial Strategy* (Chicago: University of Chicago Press, 1964).

O'Brien, David M. *Storm Center,* 2nd ed. (New York: W. W. Norton, 1990).

Woodward, Bob, and Scott Armstrong. *The Brethren: Inside the Supreme Court* (New York: Simon and Schuster, 1979).

Five ✑

DECISION-MAKING FACTORS

I n the previous chapter we examined the formal processes the justices follow in order to reach decisions on the disputes brought before them. That material answered basic questions about the institutional procedures that the Court uses to carry out its responsibilities. It addressed the Court as a legal institution. What that material did not answer were questions such as: Why do the justices reach the decisions they do? What forces play a role in determining the alternatives the justices choose in settling disputes and interpreting the law? How can we account for the presence of individual justices taking opposite positions when deciding the same case? These questions force us to confront the interaction between the legal and political aspects of the Supreme Court.

In each case we start with a set of facts that gave birth to the dispute and a relevant statute or constitutional provision. The parties to the dispute may present conflicting interpretations of the facts, disagree over what particular legal provisions should govern, or argue what the relevant law means as applied to the facts. It is the duty of the justices to sort out these conflicts and answer the questions presented. Of course, the cases that survive the obstacles of the American judicial system to be placed on the Supreme Court's docket present only the most important and difficult legal issues.

Students of the Court have done a great deal of research in attempting to unravel the mysteries of judicial decision making and to identify those factors that determine case outcomes. This research task is a difficult one because the justices make their decisions in private and they do not answer questions about what prompted them to decide a dispute as they did. The only evidence the justices leave is one or more written opinions describing the resolution of the case and their recorded votes. The rest of the puzzle we must piece together.

In general, we can categorize the research on judicial decision making into two groups: studies that emphasize the importance of legally relevant factors and those that focus on extralegal factors. Scholars who have explored these influences on court decisions have developed rich literatures, but in spite of the substantial research completed there is not unanimous agreement or even a consensus as to what actually causes judges to behave as they do.

LEGALLY RELEVANT FACTORS

The first group of decision-making factors we examine are those considered to be legally relevant. They are derived from certain normative expectations of how our society expects judges to behave, what elements should be part of judicial decision making, and how the judicial process should operate. Because the legally relevant factors are considered acceptable and appropriate criteria for use in judicial decision making, judges often use them to describe their approaches to resolving legal disputes. In fact, entire jurisprudential schools have been built around them. We will discuss four of the most prominent legally relevant factors and describe the judicial philosophies that support their use in legal decision making. Each, of course, emphasizes the legal nature of the Court.

Original Intent

The doctrine of original intent suggests that in interpreting the law, judges ought to take into account the intentions of those who drafted it. Each provision of the law was adopted in order to accomplish a particular purpose. The purposes of those who wrote the language should be determined and the words ought to be judged with those intentions in mind. We often hear that the Supreme Court should be true to the "intention of the Framers," which is a plea for the justices to take into account what the Philadelphia Convention was trying to do when it scrapped the Articles of Confederation and drafted an entirely new document. A related term, *legislative intent,* refers to the aims of a legislative body when proposing a constitutional amendment or drafting a statute.

Using original intent in judicial decision making can lead to much different results than relying on a literal interpretation of the words. For example, an "originalist" might conclude from the historical record that the Framers had no intention of providing constitutional protection for obscenity, libel, or seditious speech when they drafted the First Amendment. Consequently, such a person would undoubtedly argue that the absolute language of the amendment should not be literally applied in such cases. Similarly, a literalist would permit the Fourteenth Amendment's Equal Protection Clause to apply to all classes of people because it is generally worded to include protections for all "persons." An originalist, however, would likely reason that because this clause was proposed as a way to assist the former slaves, it offers protections only for blacks.

Two of the more contemporary advocates of an original intent approach to constitutional interpretation are Reagan administration attorney general Edwin Meese[1] and former Supreme Court nominee Robert Bork.[2] The Framers, they argue, considered each provision at length and in great depth. They knew ex-

---

[1] Edwin Meese III, Address before the American Bar Association, Washington, D. C., July 9, 1985.

[2] Robert Bork, "Neutral Principles and Some First Amendment Problems," *Indiana Law Journal* 47 (1971): 1–35; see also Raoul Berger, *Government by Judiciary* (Cambridge: Harvard University Press, 1977).

actly what they were proposing when they drafted the Constitution and it is incumbent on future generations to interpret their words as they meant them to be interpreted. In addition, the originalist approach is promoted as a way to decrease the influence of the judge's personal attitudes in interpreting the Constitution. If the purposes and philosophies of the Framers are given center stage in the decision-making calculus, the biases of the judge do not determine the outcome of the case. The end result, it is argued, is to eliminate value-laden interpretations. Adherence to the intent of the Framers also keeps the law more stable than in allowing the changing philosophies of the day to enter the process.

A judge's duty, according to the originalists, is to search the historical record to determine what the drafters of the law intended by acting as they did. For interpreting the Constitution, a judge would likely consult the notes of James Madison, or those of some of the lesser-known members of the Convention. Also regularly consulted are the *Federalist Papers,* a series of articles written under the pen name of Publius by James Madison, Alexander Hamilton, and John Jay, explaining the proposed document and urging its ratification by the states. For the amendments to the Constitution, the records of congressional actions and debates at the proposal stage are the best guide. Similarly, for statutes the records of the legislature, including committee reports, debates, and votes on various amendments, often reveal some indication of the reasons why the law was passed and what it was intended to accomplish.

Few would argue that the purposes of the people who wrote the law should be ignored. Court decisions often make specific references to the intentions of the Framers. Many, however, are critical of excessive reliance on original intent. A number of weaknesses in this approach are cited as reasons to avoid full reliance on it. First, it is difficult, and some would say impossible, to determine with any precision just what the intentions of the Framers were. The records of the Constitutional Convention, after all, are not complete, nor do we know how validly they reflect what actually occurred. The *Federalist Papers,* while helpful, were political arguments written after the Convention by three politically active persons who were not always on the winning side of the various votes in Philadelphia. Similarly, the congressional records for constitutional amendments and federal statutes are neither comprehensive nor of proven reliability. We might be able to discern what was said by some members of Congress on the floor of the House or Senate, but we have no way to determine the real motives that might have been expressed in closed sessions or in private legislative negotiations.

Second, some hold that even if the records were complete, it is impossible for us to put ourselves in the minds of the Framers. We come from a different time and have systematically different experiences. Justice William Brennan, an opponent of original intent, argued that "we current justices read the Constitution in the only way that we can: as Twentieth Century Americans."[3] Similarly,

---

[3] William J. Brennan, Jr., Address to the Text and Teaching Symposium, Georgetown University, Washington, D.C., October 12, 1985.

some contend that it would be wrong to impose an eighteenth-century perspective on a Constitution governing twentieth-century America. The perspective of the leaders of a foundling nation of small farmers geographically isolated from the world's center of commerce, culture, and politics may have no relevance to a large, diverse, industrial nation of the current century.

Third, some question the validity of the "value free" nature of original intent decision making. The advocates of original intent, it is argued, support that doctrine only because it is consistent with their own political views. In the case of people such as Bork and Meese, those political views are distinctly conservative. The Framers of the Constitution, after all, had a restricted view of civil liberties, did not think the government should impose restraints on contracts and other economic activity, firmly supported limited government power, and placed a great emphasis on private property. These values might well be consistent with the policy agendas of Meese and Bork, but they are out of line with the positions of most Americans.

Literalism

In most Supreme Court cases there is little disagreement over the facts in the case. This is not to say that there are no disagreements over the meaning of the facts or the relative importance of certain facts, but the lower courts normally produce a reasonably reliable factual record for the justices' use. It is customarily the case that the primary task of the justices is to interpret the law and apply it to those facts. In the United States we have a written Constitution and codified statutes. This means that justices must interpret legal prescriptions that have been reduced to writing. What does the Eighth Amendment's prohibition against *cruel and unusual punishments* mean as applied to the death penalty? What is an *unreasonable search and seizure* under the Fourth Amendment? When the First Amendment prohibits Congress from *abridging the freedom of speech* does that mean that burning an American flag in political protest is protected against government sanctions? Is a state affirmative action program giving hiring preferences to certain minority applicants in violation of the Fourteenth Amendment's command that all persons receive the *equal protection of the law*?

Many judges and lawyers have viewed judicial decision making as essentially a process of applying the words of the relevant law to the factual case presented. Perhaps the most explicit statement of this approach was offered by Justice Owen Roberts in his majority opinion in *United States v. Butler*.[4] This 1936 case presented a challenge to the constitutionality of the Agricultural Adjustment Act, one of Franklin Roosevelt's most important New Deal programs. In writing for the majority striking down the law, Justice Roberts described the duty of the Court in responding to constitutional challenges:

---

[4] 297 U.S. 1 (1936).

There should be no misunderstanding as to the function of this court in such a case.... When an act of Congress is appropriately challenged in the courts as not conforming to the constitutional mandate the judicial branch of the Government has only one duty,—to lay the article of the Constitution which is invoked beside the statute which is challenged and to decide whether the latter squares with the former.

Roberts's position is easily understood. He asserted the view that decisions can be reached by a relatively simple application of the plain meaning of the words of the Constitution and statutes.

Justice Hugo Black, who served on the Supreme Court from 1937 to 1971, is often identified as the most significant advocate of a literal approach to constitutional interpretation. His position was based on a commonsense application of the words. He believed that the Framers were intelligent men who understood the English language and used plain words in their drafting of the Constitution. To Black it was essential to apply the Constitution as written. This keeps the interpretation as close as possible to the text of the Constitution and minimizes the role of the justices' personal views.

Black's loyalty to the literal interpretation of the Constitution is exemplified best in cases calling for an interpretation of the First Amendment, an article that commands Congress to pass "no law" abridging freedom of religion, speech, press, peaceful assembly, and petition. Most justices and constitutional scholars believe that this absolute ban should not be interpreted literally, that there are certain forms of expression and religious practice (obscenity, libel, the handling of poisonous snakes in religious worship services, etc.) that can be prohibited by the government. To Black, any such watering down of the words of the First Amendment was unacceptable. His own words describe his position best:

My view is, without deviation, without exception, without any ifs, buts, or whereases, that freedom of speech means that government shall not do anything to people ... either for the views they have or the views they express or the words they speak or write. Some people would have you believe that this is a very radical position, and maybe it is. But all I am doing is following what to me is the clear wording of the First Amendment.... As I have said innumerable times before I simply believe that "Congress shall make no law" means Congress shall make no law.... Thus we have the absolute command of the First Amendment that no law shall be passed by Congress abridging freedom of speech or the press.[5]

Adherence to a literal approach to constitutional interpretation can, of course, lead to some seemingly inconsistent outcomes. Justice Black, for instance, would defend to the end those publishing obscene materials, arguing

---

[5] Hugo L. Black, *A Constitutional Faith* (New York: Knopf, 1968), 45–46.

that the First Amendment allows no exception in its prohibition against abridging freedom of the press.[6] On the other hand, he might well vote to uphold restrictions on political demonstrations that use means of expression other than words on the grounds that the First Amendment protects *speech,* not *action.*[7] A good example of Black's speech/action distinction is provided by the case of *Tinker v. Des Moines Independent Community School District* (1969). It that case three children were suspended from their public schools for wearing black arm bands in protest against the war in Southeast Asia in violation of school regulations. A seven-justice majority held that the school district violated the student's constitutional rights to freedom of expression. But Black dissented. For him, wearing black protest arm bands to school was not *speech.*

Black's literalism was not confined to First Amendment interpretations. In 1965 Black was one of only two members of the Court who refused to recognize a right to privacy.[8] His reason: the right to privacy did not appear in the words of the Constitution and therefore should not be interpreted as part of that document. In his dissent he wrote:

> The Court talks about a constitutional "right of privacy" as though there is some constitutional provision or provisions forbidding any law ever to be passed which might abridge the "privacy" of individuals. But there is not. . . .
> I like my privacy as well as the next one, but I am nevertheless compelled to admit that government has a right to invade it unless prohibited by some specific constitutional provision.

Justices, Black believed, must stay true to the text of the Constitution. By doing so, the personal views of the justice were minimized in the decision-making process. If the Court reached decisions unacceptable to the people, the remedy was clear—amend the words of the Constitution.

While no serious jurist or scholar would argue that the words should be ignored, many reject the literal interpretation mode of analysis. Objections to it focus on the fact that the English language is filled with imprecision and ambiguity. Words have multiple meanings. The drafters of statutes and constitutional articles may have made errors in the way provisions have been written. The record may show that certain important legal terms have been used in different ways during different historical periods. All of this leads many to conclude that interpreting the law requires more than a literal application of the words.

The Meaning of the Words

The meaning of the words approach to legal decision making, like literalism, places a high priority on the text of the Constitution, but it rejects the notion that

---

[6] See, for example, his dissent in *Ginzburg v. United States,* 383 U.S. 463 (1966).

[7] See, for example, his opinion for the Court in *Adderley v. Florida,* 385 U.S. 39 (1966).

[8] *Griswold v. Connecticut,* 381 U.S. 479 (1965).

the words can be applied directly without additional interpretation. Proponents of this view believe that the language of the law can be understood only by examining the historical context in which it was written.[9] Some words have rich traditions in legal history. They have evolved over time through legislative and judicial usage to acquire special meanings that might not perfectly correspond to a "plain meaning of the words" approach characteristic of literalism. Examples might include such terms as *a jury of peers, privileges and immunities,* and *due process of law.* The meaning of the words approach "attempts to define the words of the Constitution according to what they meant at the time the document or its amendment was written."[10] This school of interpretation recognizes that certain words may have meant something different at the time the Constitution or statute was drafted than they mean today. Consequently, it is argued that historical development and context must be taken into account in any application of constitutional or statutory words.

Chief Justice William Howard Taft provided one of the better descriptions of this approach to interpreting the Constitution. He did so in his opinion for the Court in *Ex parte Grossman* (1925), a dispute over the scope of the president's power to issue pardons:

> The language of the Constitution cannot be interpreted safely except by reference to the common law and to British institutions as they were when the instrument was framed and adopted. The statesmen and lawyers of the Convention who submitted it to the ratification of the Conventions of the thirteen States, were born and brought up in the atmosphere of the common law, and thought and spoke in its vocabulary. They were familiar with other forms of government, recent and ancient, and indicated in their discussions earnest study and consideration of many of them, but when they came to put their conclusions into the form of fundamental law in a compact draft, they expressed them in terms of the common law, confident that they could be shortly and easily understood.

The meaning of the words approach, then, is closely related to both literalism and original intent. Its emphasis on the text of the Constitution adopts the same values as the advocates of literalism, but its focus on the meaning of the words to those who drafted the law accepts some of the reasoning of the originalists.

Precedent

Read any Supreme Court opinion and you will find it richly laced with citations to the Court's previous decisions. The reason for all of these references

---

[9] See W. W. Crosskey, *Politics and the Constitution in the History of the United States* (Chicago: University of Chicago Press, 1953).

[10] David W. Rohde and Harold J. Spaeth, *Supreme Court Decision Making* (San Francisco: W. H. Freeman, 1976), 41.

to the past is that we expect our judges to adhere to the doctrine of *stare decisis,* or precedent.

Stare decisis ("let the decision stand") is a principle that holds that once a court has interpreted the law a particular way, that same interpretation should be applied to similar cases in the future. For example, in 1954 the Supreme Court held that public schools officially segregated on the basis of race were in violation of the Equal Protection Clause of the Fourteenth Amendment. Having made that decision, we would expect the Court to issue the same ruling in subsequent school desegregation cases. Following the doctrine of *stare decisis* provides stability and consistency to the law. The justices look to past rulings for guidance. What the Court decides the Constitution means today, we can reasonably expect the Court to adhere to tomorrow. Consequently, the law will not radically and unpredictably change and we can plan our lives with some reasonable expectation of what the law is.

Following precedent, while a general guide, is not an absolute rule of judicial decision making. The justices have always been mindful that as humans they make mistakes, occasionally setting unwise policies. Sometimes the decisions of the past no longer meet contemporary situations. In these instances, the justices will alter or overrule precedent. The 1954 school desegregation case of *Brown v. Board of Education,* for example, overruled the separate but equal precedent handed down by the Court in 1896 in *Plessy v. Ferguson.* Perhaps the most controversial constitutional battle fought in the courts in the 1980s and 1990s focused on the question of whether the Court would overrule its 1973 decision of *Roe v. Wade,* which legalized elective abortions. Formally altering precedents, however, is the exception rather than the rule; and justices go to great lengths in writing their opinions to document how each part of the ruling is supported by the Court's previous interpretations.

In presenting arguments to the Court, both written and oral, attorneys also comply with the expectations of *stare decisis.* Their briefs and presentations in open court largely center on how previous Supreme Court rulings should determine the outcome of the case at bar. As advocates, however, the attorneys select for emphasis those precedents that if followed will most likely result in a victory for their clients. The doctrine of *stare decisis* leaves to the justices the final task of deciding which of perhaps many prior decisions most appropriately controls the dispute needing resolution.

Not all students of the Court, however, place much stock in the rule of precedent. The criticism does not so much center on what the doctrine advises as it does on the doctrine's inability to describe or explain adequately the way judges make decisions. The controversy boils down to a question of the role of precedent in the processes by which justices arrive at their conclusions. There are two possibilities. In the first, the justices, confronted with a legal question, search the Court's past rulings for guidance in arriving at a decision. In the second, the justices have a predetermined notion of how they want the case to be decided and search for those precedents that support their position, in effect acting in much the same advocacy mode as does an attorney. In either case, the final court opinions are filled with case citations that either explain or justify the Court's decision.

Almost all justices publicly adhere to the position that they use precedent to arrive at decisions rather than to justify their preexisting preferences.[11] This position, of course, is in line with societal expectations of how the justices should carry out their responsibilities. The critics, however, are not convinced. Certainly, after two hundred years of handing down rulings, the Court has left an abundance of precedents covering almost every conceivable subject. Regardless of their ideological preferences, the justices have little difficulty finding ample precedent to justify their positions.

EXTRALEGAL FACTORS

Many contemporary scholars assert that legally relevant factors are not the dominant influences on judicial decision making. They argue instead that although the justices work in the context of constitutional provisions, the intentions of the Framers, and the application of precedent, the forces that really drive their decisions are behavioral and political in nature, not legal.

The application of judicial behavior theories to Supreme Court decision making began in the 1940s, largely initiated by the work of C. Herman Pritchett.[12] Pritchett and those who followed him were dissatisfied with the traditional legal explanations of how the justices decide cases. Their dissatisfaction was driven by the frequency of dissenting votes on the Court in the 1940s. If the nine learned justices were applying the same constitutional provisions, with the same records of the Framers' intent, and having the same precedents with which to work, why did they reach different conclusions on the same cases? Furthermore, why was there such consistency in voting, with liberal and conservative blocs forming on important issues of civil liberties and economic regulation? Clearly there was more to the decision-making process than we had previously believed. This initial research gave birth to a field of scholarship that remains active today. It focuses on the search for nonlegal factors that explain why judges vote the way they do.

The behavior of present-day justices presents the same puzzle that Pritchett faced in the 1940s, but perhaps even more so. Consider that between 1986 and 1988 William Rehnquist and Thurgood Marshall sat together on the Supreme Court hearing the same cases and having access to the same materials. In the eighty-two nonunanimous criminal rights cases decided during that time,

---

[11] An exception was Justice William O. Douglas, who frequently indicated that he would much rather create a precedent than follow one.

[12] See, for example, C. Herman Pritchett, *The Roosevelt Court* (New York: Macmillan, 1948), and *Civil Liberties and the Vinson Court* (Chicago: University of Chicago Press, 1954).

Rehnquist voted in favor of the criminal defendant 10 percent of the time. Marshall, in those very same cases, decided in favor of the criminal defendant 93 percent of the time. Such startling differences make us search for explanations beyond what the legal factors can provide. Research on these issues can be categorized into studies that examine behavioral and political factors affecting the decisions of the justices. Both emphasize the political nature of the Court.

Behavioral Factors

Scholars who think behavioral factors motivate judicial decision making look to influences found within the individual justice or in the decision-making environment. Such factors are background experiences, attitudes, role orientations, and small group influences. We discuss each of them briefly in this section.

BACKGROUND CHARACTERISTICS   Among the first studies attempting to find explanations for why justices decide cases in systematically different ways were those that examined the impact of social background differences. Researchers who take this approach posit that justices, like the rest of us, are the product of their past experiences. The justices do not join the Court bringing only their legal educations. Instead, they bring with them their childhood experiences, the training provided by their parents, their religious values, their educational accomplishments, the experiences of their legal and political careers, and their political party loyalties. All of these relationships and events have contributed to the judges' value systems, perceptual processes, and ways of reasoning. The social background approach appeals to our commonsense ideas of how people behave. We know that our background attributes affect how we think and act. Studies of electoral behavior have long demonstrated that common citizens respond to candidates and political issues according to party, religion, economic status, region, education, and other characteristics. Why should members of the Supreme Court be any different? The notion that a justice who grew up in a well-to-do Republican family in urban New York might decide cases differently than a black Democrat who grew up in the rural South should not be surprising. They may work with the same body of law and precedent but they evaluate case facts and the law in a systematically different fashion.

Paging through the reports of Supreme Court decisions gives us ample incidents of judicial behavior that seem to indicate that background experiences make a difference. For example, in *Buck v. Bell* (1927) the Court upheld a Virginia statute that imposed compulsory sterilization on certain mental patients. The vote was 8 to 1. The only dissenter was Pierce Butler. Justice Butler did not write an opinion expressing why he thought the sterilization statute was unconstitutional, but knowing that Butler was the Court's only Roman Catholic gives us a clue. It is reasonable to hypothesize that his membership in a church that condemns such procedures might have affected his vote. Potter Stewart's record provides another example. Justice Stewart was generally a moderate on most civil liberties issues, but on one, freedom of the press, he took more liberal positions. Why? Perhaps it was because one of Stewart's first jobs as a young man was as a newspaper reporter. Sometimes the justices even admit to the impact backgrounds have on their decisions. In *Edwards v. South Carolina* (1963) the Court reversed the breach of peace convictions of civil rights demonstrators who protested outside the South Carolina capitol building. Justice Tom Clark, a Southerner, cast the only vote in favor of the city authorities putting a stop to the demonstration. His dissenting opinion clearly refers to his own experiences in the South when he admonishes that "anyone conversant with the almost spontaneous combustion in some Southern communities in such a situation will agree that the City Manager's action may well have averted a major catastrophe."

The examples we have cited, of course, are anecdotal. Social background researchers have gone beyond this type of evidence in an attempt to discern if there are systematic decision-making propensities that are associated with certain background experiences. The results have been mixed, but there does seem to be an association between a handful of factors and the way judges vote. For example, in civil liberties disputes, justices who are Democrats, who are from non-Southern states, and who have had extensive judicial experience tend to have liberal voting records; whereas Republicans, Southerners, and those with extensive prosecutorial experience generally have more conservative decision-making patterns. In economic cases, those justices who have records sympathetic to government control of the economy are Democrats, former elected officials, and those who had prestigious college educations. Those who take the more conservative position on economic issues are Republicans, those who have had a background in prosecutorial work or have held nonelected offices, and those who received their educations from schools of average prestige.[13]

Of all the background factors, political party affiliation has received the most attention. This certainly makes intuitive sense. A person who is attracted to the Democratic party probably begins with interests and values associated with the goals and priorities of that party. Spending decades in service to that party only serves to reinforce those values. The same process works with the Republican party. Since these political organizations take positions on the types of issues that the Supreme Court decides, it is not unreasonable to expect that Democratic and Republican justices would have different voting records, with the Republicans being the more conservative. In general, this tendency holds true, but there are enough exceptions to cause us to treat political party affiliation with some caution. For example, Earl Warren, who led the civil liberties revolution of the 1953–1969 period, was a Republican. And two of the most conservative oppo-

---

[13] See, for example, C. Neal Tate, "Personal Attribute Models of the Voting Behavior of U.S. Supreme Court Justices: Liberalism in Civil Liberties and Economics Decisions, 1946–1978," *American Political Science Review* 75 (June 1981): 355–367; S. Sidney Ulmer, "Social Background as an Indicator to the Votes of Supreme Court Justices in Criminal Cases, 1947–1956 Terms," *American Journal of Political Science* 17 (August 1973): 622–630.

nents of Franklin Roosevelt's New Deal economic policies were Democrats James McReynolds and Pierce Butler.

ATTITUDES   Attitude theorists find the social background approach unsatisfying. They argue that even if personal attributes are somewhat predictive of judicial decisions, the background experiences themselves are not the cause of the behavior. Instead, they assert, the judges' attitudes or ideologies are what really determine how cases are decided. Background factors correlate with certain decisional patterns only because personal experiences are part of a socialization process that contributes to the development of attitudes. But it is those attitudes that control the judge's decisions, and attitude differences among the justices account for the voting divisions on the Court.

Attitude theorists explain judicial decision making in a very simple way. Justices come to the Court with a set of political attitudes about a number of issues. These attitudes combine to form a general political ideology with corresponding policy preferences. When a case comes before the Court each justice evaluates the facts of the dispute and arrives at a solution to the case consistent with his or her personal ideology. In other words, their attitudes on the issue of criminal rights explain why Chief Justice Rehnquist supported criminal defendants only 10 percent of the time and Justice Marshall did so in 93 percent of the cases. Rehnquist's value system places a high priority on "law and order"; whereas Marshall's ideology emphasizes "due process of law." These personal attitudes shape the way they evaluate the facts in a case, the credence they give to various kinds of evidence and argument, and the final policy outcomes they envision. To a believer in judicial attitude theory, little else in the decision-making process is important except judicial ideology. The legal factors, they claim, are just a myth.

Scholars involved in this line of research have employed various psychological theories and have developed relatively sophisticated statistical techniques to improve our understanding of the way judicial ideologies shape decision making. In general they have been quite successful at mathematically explaining and predicting how Supreme Court justices decide cases.[14] Nonetheless, attitude approaches have had their critics. Some claim that attitude research is inherently circular; that is, attitude proponents essentially argue that "a justice is a liberal because he's a liberal." Other critics claim that the research on judicial attitudes errs in overemphasizing the importance of ideology and refusing to accept the other factors that have a bearing on the judicial decision.

Regardless of the value of these criticisms, it is clear that the attitude approach to judicial decision making has been accepted in the political world. In the last several Senate hearings on the nominations of Supreme Court justices,

---

[14] See Glendon Schubert, *The Judicial Mind* (Evanston, Ill.: Northwestern University Press, 1965); David W. Rohde and Harold J. Spaeth, *Supreme Court Decision Making* (San Francisco: W. H. Freeman, 1976).

discussions of the nominee's ideology and values took center stage. The senators constantly attempted to get the nominees to discuss their attitudes on subjects that might come before the Court. Interest groups of all stripes delved into the nominees' past to discover ideological values. And, of course, the president selected the nominees with the same close attention to attitudes and ideologies. All of these participants in the selection process are obviously acting on the assumption that a justice's attitudes largely control how he or she will decide cases coming before the Court.

ROLE ORIENTATIONS   Each Supreme Court justice has a view of his or her role. This view is based upon fundamental beliefs of what a good justice should do, or what the proper role of the Court should be. These orientations, some Court observers argue, have an influence on how the justices carry out their duties and decide cases. A member of the Court, for example, who believes that precedent should guide the Court's decision making may be much less likely to reverse previously established Court policy than will a justice who does not place such a high value on *stare decisis*.

There have been studies of a number of different role orientations, but the differences between activist justices and restraintist justices have received the most attention. An activist justice is one who believes that the proper role of the Court is to assert its own independent positions in deciding cases, to review the actions of the other branches vigorously, to strike down unconstitutional acts willingly, and to impose far-reaching remedies for legal wrongs whenever necessary. Restraint-oriented justices take the opposite position. Courts should not become involved in the operations of the other branches unless absolutely necessary. The benefit of the doubt should be given to actions taken by elected officials. Courts should impose only remedies that are narrowly tailored to correct a specific legal wrong. As a consequence of these beliefs an activist judge will be one who votes to exercise judicial review at a much higher rate than will a restraint-oriented jurist.

In the past we have normally associated activism with liberal decisions. After all, when the Supreme Court took actions to desegregate schools, impose reapportionment, ban school prayer, modify police investigation procedures, and strike down abortion restrictions, the justices were negating actions taken by the legislative and executive branches of the national and state governments to accomplish liberal policy outcomes. The dissenters in those cases were urging restraint, but also voting to impose a conservative policy outcome. It is important to keep in mind, as we shall see in the next chapter, that conservatives can be activists too, and liberals can take restraintist positions.

An interesting example of this is provided by the life of Thurgood Marshall. As a crusading civil rights attorney of enormous accomplishment, Marshall built his career on urging judicial activism in order to produce liberal civil rights policy. He repeatedly asked the Supreme Court to exercise the power of judicial review to strike down laws passed and enforced by the political branches of government that discriminated against racial minorities. His support for this approach continued during most of his years on the Supreme Court. He and the other members of the Warren Court were quite successful at establishing liberal policies and encouraging federal and state governments to establish liberal civil rights programs. In his final years on the Court, however, he was forced to take a different posture. Marshall now found himself outnumbered by conservative justices who actively began to hand down decisions modifying precedents and striking down government programs Marshall favored. Ironically, Marshall ended his tenure on the Court urging judicial restraint and calling for the justices to have more respect for *stare decisis*.

SMALL GROUP INFLUENCES   Some researchers believe that the group context in which the Court reaches its decisions has an impact on how the justices behave. This line of thought is based on the recognition that the Court is a collegial body. A justice can do nothing acting alone. It takes a majority vote to decide a case and a majority agreeing on a single opinion to set a firm precedent. Under such conditions, human interaction is important and case outcomes can be influenced by the nature of the relations among the members of the group.[15]

The Supreme Court meets on a regular basis for nine months a year. The justices must deal with controversial and difficult questions. They must resolve disputes working together as a group. Justices who develop good relationships with their colleagues, are effective in oral and written communications skills, and are adept at bargaining and compromise will undoubtedly have more influence within the Court than those justices who fail at these measures. Of course, these influences are very difficult to research, since scholars are unable to directly observe the internal workings of the Court. Instead, scholars must attempt to reconstruct what occurs on the Court from the private papers of the justices and from what can be learned from occasional interviews with the justices or their law clerks.

Perhaps the most important group factor in the Court's performance is its leadership. Studies have demonstrated that the Court requires effective "task leadership" to keep up with the workload demands, and effective "social leadership" to maintain harmony among the justices.[16] The chief justice, of course, is in the best position to exercise such leadership. Known as "first among equals," the chief justice has certain built-in advantages in influencing how the Court operates. The chief presides at oral argument, chairs the conference, initiates the "discuss list," and assigns the opinion of the Court when voting in the majority. In addition, he has certain ceremonial duties that add to his prestige and administrative responsibilities that affect the justices' resources. The leadership styles that

---

[15] See Walter F. Murphy, *Elements of Judicial Strategy* (Chicago: University of Chicago Press, 1964).

[16] David J. Danelski, "The Influence of the Chief Justice in the Decisional Process of the Supreme Court," in Thomas P. Jahnige and Sheldon Goldman, eds., *The Federal Judicial System* (New York: Holt, Rinehart and Winston, 1968).

chief justices impose and the intragroup norms they enforce largely structure the internal operations of the institution and can have enormous consequences.[17] A chief justice who is able to provide effective intellectual and social leadership can not only keep the Court operating effectively but can also use this influence to lead the Court in the chief's preferred policy direction.

This is not to say that only the chief justice can exercise influence within the group context. Research conducted by Walter Murphy, David Danelski, J. Woodford Howard, and others into the private papers of former justices has consistently shown that through intellectual persuasion, effective bargaining over opinion writing, informal lobbying, and other interpersonal techniques all justices have the capability of increasing their influence on the Court.[18] Willis Van Devanter's intellectual leadership on the Taft Court in the 1920s is a good example. At the other extreme, justices who are incapable of operating effectively within the group context may have a minimal impact on the law beyond casting their own votes. A case in point is James McReynolds, who served from 1914 to 1941. He was nearly devoid of interpersonal skills and consumed with various prejudices. As might be predicted, McReynolds exerted almost no independent influence over Court decisions.

Political Factors

One of the major differences between the Supreme Court and the more political branches is that there is no direct electoral connection between the justices and the public. Once appointed, justices may serve for life. They are not accountable to the public and are not required to undergo any periodic reevaluation of their decisions. Divorcing the Court from direct political pressures was, of course, intended by the Framers. Interpreting the law, they thought, should not be subject to the vagaries of public opinion. Yet the Court remains a political institution and is certainly not immune to political pressures.

Unlike the behavioral factors that have their origins within the justices themselves or their group context, political pressures originate outside the Court. We will take a brief look at three sources of such influence: public opinion, the other branches, and interest groups.

PUBLIC OPINION   The president and members of Congress are always trying to keep in touch with what the people are thinking. Public opinion poll watching is a never-ending task. There is good reason for this. The political branches are supposed to represent the people and the incumbents' reelection

---

[17] See Thomas G. Walker, Lee Epstein, and William J. Dixon, "On the Mysterious Demise of Consensual Norms in the United States Supreme Court," *Journal of Politics* 50 (May 1988): 361–389.

[18] Murphy, *Elements of Judicial Strategy;* Danelski, "The Influence of the Chief Justice"; J. Woodford Howard, Jr., "On the Fluidity of Judicial Choice," *American Political Science Review* 62 (March 1968): 43–56.

prospects can be jeopardized by straying too far from what the public wants. Federal judges, however, are not dependent upon pleasing the public in order to stay in office. A Supreme Court justice does not serve in the same kind of representative capacity that the legislators do. We do not expect the justices to use the latest poll results as an aid in determining what the law means.

Are the justices affected by public opinion? Certainly we can think of times when the Court has handed down rulings that fly in the face of what the public wants. The most obvious example of such behavior occurred immediately after the onset of the Great Depression and the election of Franklin Roosevelt. In spite of the fact that the American people had elected Roosevelt by a wide margin and had sent to Washington large numbers of Democratic legislators, the Court remained unmoved by the public's endorsement of the New Deal. Time after time, until 1937, the justices struck down legislation and administrative programs designed to get the nation moving again economically.

On the other hand, there have been times when the Court seems to have embraced public opinion—especially under conditions of extreme national stress. One example is the Court's 1944 endorsement of the government's program to move all Japanese-Americans from the Pacific Coast states to inland relocation centers during World War II.[19] The justices were obviously swept away in the same wartime mind-set as was the rest of the nation. Another example is the Court's generally supportive position toward the government's anticommunist programs of the 1940s and 1950s. Justice Black even called attention to this in 1951 when he dissented from a decision in which the Court upheld the conviction of individuals charged with advocating the violent overthrow of the government. Black wrote:

> Public opinion being what it now is, few will protest the conviction of these Communist petitioners. There is hope, however, that in calmer times, when present pressures, passions and fears subside, this or some later Court will restore the First Amendment liberties to the high preferred place where they belong in a free society.[20]

Several studies have systematically examined the extent to which the decisions of the Court have been in agreement with public opinion.[21] In general, the results have shown that the Court's rulings do not deviate excessively from the views of the citizenry. On major issues (e.g., school segregation, abortion) there

---

[19] *Korematsu v. United States,* 323 U.S. 214 (1944).

[20] *Dennis v. United States,* 341 U.S. 494 (1951).

[21] See, for example, David G. Barum, "The Supreme Court and Public Opinion: Judicial Decision Making in the Post–New Deal Period," *Journal of Politics* 47 (May 1985): 652–666; Thomas Marshall, *Public Opinion and the Supreme Court* (New York: Unwin Hyman, 1989); Benjamin I. Page and Robert Y. Shapiro, "Effects of Public Opinion on Policy," *American Political Science Review* 77 (1983): 175–190.

is evidence that the Court has acted consistent with public opinion majorities or in line with rising opinion trends.

There are a number of reasons why the Court's decisions may stay relatively close to public opinion preferences. First, the justices are part of the public. They are affected by the same forces as are others in society. There is no reason to believe that they are (or even should be) insensitive to the events and conditions that surround us. Second, the justices obtain their positions through a process that has an electoral connection. They are nominated by an elected president and confirmed by an elected Senate. There is every reason to expect presidents and senators to place individuals on the Court who have views consistent with the voters who elected them. Third, the justices must be aware of popular reaction to their decisions. Many Court rulings require public acceptance and compliance to be effective. A Court that continually hands down decisions that the public resists will inevitably lose legitimacy. Fourth, the Court's own jurisprudence in some areas of the law requires adherence to public views. In the obscenity cases, for example, the justices have underscored the importance of community values and opinions. When deciding which rights in the Bill of Rights should be accorded fundamental status, the justices have often turned to the views of the public for assistance. In the death penalty cases, the justices have also consulted the public's opinion as to contemporary standards of cruel and unusual punishment.

THE POLITICAL BRANCHES OF GOVERNMENT   The Supreme Court operates fully within the checks and balances system imposed by the Framers. This, of course, means that the legislative and executive branches possess certain weapons that can be used against the judiciary. The executive branch, for example, holds the key to the enforcement of Court decisions. The legislative branch can pass laws or propose constitutional amendments reversing Court rulings, alter the Court's appellate jurisdiction, and restrict the Court's budgetary allotments. Congress can even alter the size of the Court or remove justices through the impeachment power. All of these potential threats could be used if the Court's decisions consistently ran contrary to the will of the president and Congress. While most are used only on rare occasion, their presence makes it important for the justices to keep a watchful eye on the other branches. Roosevelt's 1937 Court-packing plan provides the most notable example.

On a day-to-day basis, however, the executive branch is the primary source of political influence on the justices. The bearer of this influence is the solicitor general. As we explained in Chapter 3, the solicitor general is the legal representative of the federal government before the Supreme Court. Members of the solicitor general's office argue all cases in which the federal government is a party. And frequently the solicitor general appears as amicus curiae urging the justices to decide a case consistent with the views of the executive branch. As a political appointee of the president and the number-three-ranking member of the Justice Department, the solicitor general speaks with considerable authority and normally does so consistent with the views of the administration.[22]

Numerous studies have demonstrated that the solicitor general enjoys considerable success in arguing the government's case.[23] Research by Jeffrey Segal revealed the extent of the solicitor general's effectiveness.[24] The results of his study are summarized in Table 5-1. During the Eisenhower, Kennedy, and Johnson administrations the solicitor general was victorious more than 80 percent of the time. The success rate was into the 70 percent range when the White House was occupied by Nixon, Ford, and Reagan. Only during the Carter years did it drop below 70 percent.

In addition, there is some evidence that the materials included in the briefs submitted by the solicitor general have been influential when the justices drafted their opinions in key cases.[25] Occasionally, the Court even acknowledges reliance on the solicitor general's submissions. For example, after discussing various alternatives to settling the dispute over control of Richard Nixon's private papers in the case of *Nixon v. Administrator of General Services* (1977), Justice Brennan for the Court said: "We think that the Solicitor General states the sounder view, and we adopt it."

The reasons for the tremendous success of the solicitor general in influencing the Court's decisions on the merits are the same factors noted in Chapter 3 as contributing to the federal government's success in the case selection phase. First, as a representative of the federal government, the solicitor general speaks on behalf of very substantial interests that are respected by the justices. Second, the solicitor general's office has a long tradition of treating the Court with respect and integrity, thus developing a sound and trusted relationship with the justices. And finally, the solicitor general's office specializes in appearing before the Supreme Court and as a consequence has developed a great deal of expertise in Supreme Court advocacy.

INTEREST GROUPS   In the previous chapter we saw that interest groups had an impressive effect on the Court's docket, both by generating cases and by successfully urging the justices to accept certain appeals for review. Not surprisingly, many organizations also participate as the Court considers cases on their merits. In general, group participation takes one of two forms, with the filing of amicus curiae (friend of the court) briefs the more common. Groups also spon-

---

[22] For the political nature of the solicitor general's office, see Lincoln Caplan, *The Tenth Justice* (New York: Knopf, 1987).

[23] See, for example, Steven Puro, "The United States as Amicus Curiae," in S. Sidney Ulmer, ed., *Courts, Law, and Judicial Processes* (New York: Free Press, 1981).

[24] Jeffrey A. Segal, "Amicus Curiae Briefs by the Solicitor General during the Warren and Burger Courts," *Western Political Quarterly* 41 (1988): 135–144.

[25] See Jeffrey A. Segal, "Courts, Executives, and Legislatures," in John B. Gates and Charles A. Johnson, eds., *The American Courts* (Washington, D.C.: CQ Press, 1991).

TABLE 5-1
Solicitor General Record by President, 1952–1982 Terms

Administration	Percentage Lost	Percentage Won	#
Eisenhower	16.7	83.3	42
Kennedy	12.5	87.5	48
Johnson	17.1	82.9	41
Nixon	29.1	70.9	79
Ford	28.9	71.1	38
Carter	34.9	65.1	86
Reagan	22.0	78.0	59

Source: Jeffrey A. Segal, "Amicus Curiae Briefs by the Solicitor General during the Warren and Burger Courts," *Western Political Quarterly* 41 (1988): 135–144.

sor cases, that is, they provide litigants with attorneys and the money necessary to pursue their cases.

Throughout the Court's history, we can point to many examples of interest group participation as amicus curiae and as sponsors. Indeed, an unusually large number of landmark cases handed down by the Court have been managed and successfully argued by the legal staffs of interest groups. Among those are two cases brought by the NAACP Legal Defense Fund—the 1948 case in which the Court struck down racially based restrictive covenants[26] and the 1954 school desegregation cases,[27] and the Jehovah's Witnesses' challenge to the compulsory flag salute in public schools.[28]

Even so, prior to the 1960s, interest group participation in court litigation was probably the exception rather than the rule; for example, between 1928 and 1968, amici were present in only about 18 percent of all cases.[29] But, as we illustrate in Table 5-2, this has changed markedly. Today organized interests participate in the vast majority of cases that come before the Court in a wide range of issue areas. In the 1987 Term of the Court, as the table shows, almost 80 percent of the cases decided had amicus curiae briefs filed by one or more interest groups; 65 percent were sponsored by groups. To put it another way, over the course of the 1987 Term, the justices heard from nearly 1,600 groups and governmental interests![30]

The explosion of pressure group participation in Supreme Court litigation raises at least two questions. The first is this: Why do groups, in ever-increasing

---

[26] Clement E. Vose, *Caucasians Only* (Berkeley: University of California Press, 1959).

[27] Richard Kluger, *Simple Justice* (New York: Knopf, 1976).

[28] David Manwaring, *Render to Caesar: The Flag Salute Controversy* (Chicago: University of Chicago Press, 1962).

[29] Nathan Hakman, "The Supreme Court's Political Environment: The Processing of Non-Commercial Litigation," in Joel B. Grossman and Joseph Tanenhaus, eds., *Frontiers of Judicial Research* (New York: John Wiley, 1969).

[30] Lee Epstein, "Courts and Interest Groups," in John B. Gates and Charles A. Johnson, eds., *The American Courts* (Washington, D.C.: CQ Press, 1991).

TABLE 5-2

Participation of Organized Interests as Sponsors and as Amici Curiae during the 1987 Term of the Supreme Court by Issue Area

Issue	Cases Sponsored by Groups[a]		Cases with Amicus Briefs		Total No. Cases[b]
	%	N	%	N	
Religion	100.0	(4)	100.0	(4)	4
Environment	100.0	(8)	87.5	(7)	8
Procedure	100.0	(8)	75.0	(6)	8
Labor relations	91.7	(11)	100.0	(12)	12
Finances	85.0	(17)	65.0	(13)	20
Freedom of expression	76.9	(10)	100.0	(13)	13
Benefits	71.4	(5)	85.7	(6)	7
Discrimination	69.2	(9)	92.3	(12)	13
Property/Boundaries	66.7	(2)	100.0	(3)	3
Torts	60.0	(3)	60.0	(3)	5
Immigration/Deportation	25.0	(1)	50.0	(2)	4
Federalism/Institutionalism	25.0	(1)	100.0	(4)	4
Criminal law	22.6	(7)	64.5	(20)	31
Total	65.1	(86)	79.5	(105)	132

Source: Lee Epstein, "Courts and Interest Groups," in John B. Gates and Charles A. Johnson, eds., *The American Courts* (Washington, D.C.: CQ Press, 1991), 358.
[a]Excludes litigation sponsored by state, local, and federal governments.
[b]Four cases did not fit compatibly into any of the above categories. Three of the four were sponsored by organized interests. All four contained at least one amicus curiae brief, raising the total percentage to 80.1.

numbers, go to Court? On some level, the answer to this seems obvious. They want to influence the outcome of the Court's decisions. And, to be sure, the primary concern of most groups is "winning" their cases, but they also go to the Supreme Court to achieve other, more subtle ends. One of these is something we described in Chapter 3: setting institutional agendas. That is, by filing amicus curiae briefs at the case selection stage, groups seek to influence the Court's agenda-setting process.

Another end groups seek to achieve is to provide a counterbalance to other interests that may have competing goals. Table 5-3 provides an excellent example of this. Here we display those interests filing amicus curiae briefs in support of the pro-life and pro-choice positions in the 1989 abortion case, *Webster v. Reproductive Health Services* (1989). Of course, it is interesting that amici as diverse in goals and constituencies as the environmentally concerned Sierra Club and the religious-oriented American Jewish Congress participated in *Webster.* But what may be even more intriguing, and certainly indicative of the "balancing" goal, is that the pro-choice and pro-life sides matched constituency for constituency; as noted, both had civil liberties groups, governments, legal organizations, and so forth filing briefs on their behalf.

So, too, groups go to the Court to publicize their causes and, of course, their organizations. The NAACP Legal Defense Fund's legendary litigation campaigns

TABLE 5-3
Types of Interests Filing Amicus Curiae Briefs in *Webster*

Group Type	Pro-Choice Amicus	Pro-Life Amicus
Religious	American Jewish Congress, et al. Americans United for Separation of Church and State Catholics for a Free Choice, et al.	Agudath Israel of America Catholics United for Life, et al. Catholic Health Association Christian Advocates Serving Evangelism Covenant House, et al. Holy Orthodox Church Lutheran Church-Missouri Synod, et al. Missouri Catholic Conference New England Christian Action Council Rutherford Institute, et al. U.S. Catholic Conference New England Christian Action Council Knights of Columbus
Civil liberties/ First Amendment	ACLU, et al. American Library Association, et al.	Free Speech Advocates
Academics/Research	281 American Historians Group of American Law Professors Bioethicists for Privacy	
Science/Medical/ Hospital	American Medical Association, et al. American Public Health Association, et al. American Psychological Association 167 Scientists and Physicians National Association of Public Hospitals American Nurses Association	American Academy of Medical Ethics American Association of Pro-Life Ob-Gyns, et al. Doctors for Life, et al. National Association of Pro-Life Nurses
Population/Family/ Family planning	International Women's Health Organizations National Coalition Against Domestic Violence National Family Planning and Reproductive Health Association Population-Environmental Balance, et al. Association of Reproductive Health Professionals Center for Population Options, et al.	American Family Association Focus on Family, et al.
Labor	Americans for Democratic Action, et al.	

TABLE 5-3
Continued

Group Type	Pro-Choice Amicus	Pro-Life Amicus
Women	California NOW Canadian Women's Organizations National Association of Women Lawyers, et al. NOW 77 Organizations Committed to Equality	Feminists for Life of America, et al.
Government	Attorneys General of California, Colorado, Massachusetts, New York, Vermont, Texas 140 Members of Congress 608 Legislators from 32 States	Attorneys General of Louisiana, Arizona, Idaho, Pennsylvania, Wisconsin Center for Judicial Studies (for 56 Members of Congress) 250 State Legislators 69 Members of the Pennsylvania State Legislature 127 Members of the Missouri General Assembly United States
Lawyers/Other	Committees of the Association of the Bar of the City of New York	National Legal Foundation Alabama Lawyers for Life
Legal/Civil rights	Council of Negro Women, et al.	Southern Center for Law and Ethics
Abortion	2887 Women Who Had Abortions and 627 Friends	American Collegians for Life, et al. American Life League Association for Public Justice, et al. Birthright, Inc. Human Life International International Right to Life Federation National Right to Life Right to Life Advocates Right to Life League of Southern California Southwest Life and Law Center Crusade for Life

Source: Lee Epstein and Joseph F. Kobylka, *The Supreme Court and Legal Change* (Chapel Hill: University of North Carolina Press, 1992).

in the housing access and school desegregation cases again provide excellent examples: they not only resulted in favorable policy decisions and moved civil rights issues to the forefront of the policy agenda, but they also established the NAACP Legal Defense Fund as the foremost organizational litigator of these issues. The litigation itself brought favorable publicity to the organization and to its cause.

These are some of the reasons why groups go to Court. In general, by communicating the political and social concerns of their members, they seek to attain a wide range of goals. This, then, brings us to a second question: Are they successful? Put another way, can groups influence the outcome of Supreme Court rulings? The answer to this question is difficult to determine. On the one hand, there is some evidence that cases sponsored by interest groups have a greater chance of success than those brought by private parties. This seems to be the lesson, for example, of the litigation campaigns of the NAACP Legal Defense Fund. More recently, scholars have identified the Women's Rights Project of the American Civil Liberties Union, which brings cases of sex discrimination into Court, as unusually adept at Court litigation.[31] By the same token, some research suggests that arguments raised in amicus curiae briefs often find their way into the final opinions of the justices.

On the other hand, there is equally compelling evidence suggesting that groups are no more successful than other interests. One study paired similar cases decided by the same district court judge, the same year, with the only major difference being that one was sponsored by a group, the other by a nongroup. It found no major differences between the success of the two.[32] Research by Donald Songer and Reginald Sheehan reaches virtually the same conclusion about the effectiveness of amicus curiae briefs in Supreme Court litigation.[33]

In sum, the evidence is quite mixed. Given the other factors we have reviewed in this chapter (e.g., the justices' political views), it does seem doubtful that Supreme Court justices will often change their views on important legal questions because of a brief submitted by an interest group. Still, it is clear that these briefs do supply important legal arguments, evidence, and suggested remedies that the justices may consider when fashioning an opinion deciding a case.

CONCLUSION

There is a considerable amount of disagreement in the scholarly community over the reasons why the justices decide cases the way they do. Some support the traditional legal approach that says that justices examine such factors as the literal wording of the legal provision, the intent of the Framers, and the governing legal precedents. Other scholars hold that the justices evaluate legal claims on the basis of certain behavioral factors, including their background experiences, attitudes and ideologies, role orientations, and interactions with their colleagues. Still other researchers have examined the impact of political influences, as represented by public opinion, the other branches of government, and

---

[31] For a list of the success rates of various organizations, see Susan E. Lawrence, *The Poor in Court* (Princeton: Princeton University Press, 1990).

[32] Lee Epstein and C. K. Rowland, "Debunking the Myth of Interest Group Invincibility in the Courts," *American Political Science Review* 85 (1991): 205–217.

[33] Donald R. Songer and Reginald Sheehan, "The Impact of Amicus Briefs on Decisions on the Merits," paper presented at the 1990 Annual Meeting of the American Political Science Association.

interest group activity. In the next chapter we will examine how many of these same factors affect the policy output of the Court.

ADDITIONAL READINGS

Berg, Raoul. *Government by Judiciary* (Cambridge: Harvard University Press, 1977).

Caplan, Lincoln. *The Tenth Justice* (New York: Knopf, 1987).

Murphy, Walter F. *Elements of Judicial Strategy* (Chicago: University of Chicago Press, 1964).

Rohde, David W., and Harold J. Spaeth. *Supreme Court Decision Making* (San Francisco: W. H. Freeman and Company, 1976).

Schubert, Glendon. *The Judicial Mind* (Evanston, Ill.: Northwestern University Press, 1965).

Steamer, Robert J. *Chief Justice: Leadership and the Supreme Court* (Columbia: University of South Carolina Press, 1986).

Six ✑

THE COURT'S POLICIES: INTERPRETATION, IMPLEMENTATION, AND IMPACT

I n the previous chapter, we explored those factors affecting the decision-making process of the Supreme Court and its members. In our discussion we were less concerned with what the Court said than with why it reached the conclusions it did. In this chapter we place emphasis on the policies resulting from Court decisions, the "what the Court said" part. In particular, we consider three questions surrounding Supreme Court policies: What sorts of policies does the Supreme Court make, what kinds of trends or patterns can we discern in its policy-making process, and to what extent do Court policies affect our lives? As we shall see, the answers to the first two questions speak to the political nature of the Court: put quite simply, justices of recent eras have set policy in a wide range of issues of public concern and have often done so in ways that are related to their particular ideological and partisan tendencies and, on occasion, to their vision of what role the Court should play in American society.

In answering the final question—to what extent do Court decisions affect our lives—we once again confront the fact that the Court is, indeed, a legal institution. It cannot implement its own decisions nor can it force others to comply with them. As a result, the reach of any given ruling is largely left up to various political and legal actors to determine. In the second part of this chapter, then, we explore how others go about interpreting and implementing Supreme Court policies, with an eye toward addressing the larger question of their impact on the lives of Americans.

THE COURT AS A POLICY MAKER

Scholars disagree over the role that the Supreme Court can play in the governmental process. Some argue that it is an important policy maker; others suggest that because it lacks the ability to implement its decisions, it cannot possibly be an effective one. What is virtually incontestable—at least since the 1950s—is that the U.S. Supreme Court has spoken authoritatively on an increasing number of significant issues of public policy and, in the opinion of many, has decisively entered the political fray once largely reserved for the elected branches of government. At the very least its decisions on many social and political issues have generated a great deal of substantive debate and set political agendas for years to come. A short list of such Supreme Court decisions would include:

Brown v. Board of Education (1954) in which the Court eradicated "separate but equal" schools.

Baker v. Carr (1962) in which the Court set the stage for demanding that states must reapportion their legislative districts in a way that guarantees "one person, one vote."

Gideon v. Wainwright (1963) in which the Court gave indigents accused of committing certain crimes the right to counsel at government expense.

Engel v. Vitale (1962) and *Abington School District v. Schempp* (1963) in which the Court proclaimed that prayer in public schools violated the First Amendment.

Miranda v. Arizona (1966) in which it mandated that before questioning a suspect, police must read a set of rights.

Roe v. Wade (1973) in which the Court legalized abortions performed during the first six months of pregnancy.

Texas v. Johnson (1989) in which the Court held that flag burning was a constitutionally protected form of expression.

To be sure, these represent extreme examples—those cases that have attracted a huge amount of scholarly, journalistic, political, and public attention. Nonetheless, it is probably true that the average Supreme Court term in the 1990s results in at least a half dozen important rulings. During the 1990 Term, for instance, the Court held that:

▶ the government could take away federal dollars from family clinics in which workers and doctors discussed abortion with their clients.

▶ companies could not maintain fetal protection policies—those that prohibited fertile women from being employed in positions that might expose them to substances dangerous to a fetus.

▶ prisoners could be limited in the number of appeals they initiated in the federal court system.

▶ states could detain criminal suspects—without officially accusing them of a crime—for up to forty-eight hours.

The list could go on, but the point is a simple one. Today, the Supreme Court generates important public policy or, at minimum, is a significant participant in the policy process; its decision in the fetal protection case, for example, could prevent the loss of thousands of jobs for American women.

This, interestingly, was not always the case. The earliest Supreme Courts primarily concerned themselves with resolving issues of private law, issues of little concern to anyone but the particular parties involved. Between 1793 and 1800, almost 50 percent of the Court's cases involved maritime/admiralty disputes and the other half involved common law issues of contracts, debts, and property.[1] And, as we depict in Figure 6-1, this trend continued into the mid-1930s. Economic disputes (and pretty ordinary ones at that) continued to occupy a large space on the Court's agenda (around 50 percent) through the early 1930s; by the 1980s, though, the Court was resolving very few such cases. At that same time, its civil liberties agenda (which includes cases of rights, liberties, and justice) witnessed a steady increase. In short, it has only been over the past half century or so that the Court has moved from a resolver of private law disputes to a policy maker on important social and political questions.

Given this rather extraordinary transformation of the Court's agenda and, concomitantly, of the policy role it now plays in American society, it should come as no surprise that many Court observers have tried to explain it. They have sought to determine why the Court's agenda moved from one primarily centered on private, economic issues to one chock-full of important matters of rights and liberties.[2] They have identified several possible answers, many of which are quite similar to those factors (reviewed in Chapter 3) that contributed to the Court's caseload growth. Three have been major contributors to the agenda shift: the Court itself, the federal government, and interest groups.

The Court

Because the Court has so much discretion over its own docket, it is not surprising that it helped usher in the transformation observed in Figure 6-1, and did so in a number of ways. First, and perhaps most important, was the Court's nationalization of the Bill of Rights. Prior to the 1930s the Supreme Court held, with only a few exceptions, that the states did not have to guarantee to their citizens those rights contained in the federal Bill of Rights. So, for example, while federal agents had to conduct searches and seizures in line with the precepts of the Fourth Amendment, state police had no such constraints. One of the effects of this duality was that it generally kept state criminal cases, in this example, off the Supreme Court's docket. Because states did not have to abide by federal constitutional guarantees, there was little room for U.S. Supreme Court involve-

---

[1] Sheldon Goldman, *Constitutional Law and Supreme Court Decision-Making* (New York: Harper and Row 1982), 167.

[2] Among the best studies is Richard L. Pacelle, Jr., *The Transformation of the Supreme Court's Agenda* (Boulder, Colo.: Westview Press, 1991).

FIGURE 6-1
Supreme Court's Civil Liberties and Economic Agendas, 1930s–1980s

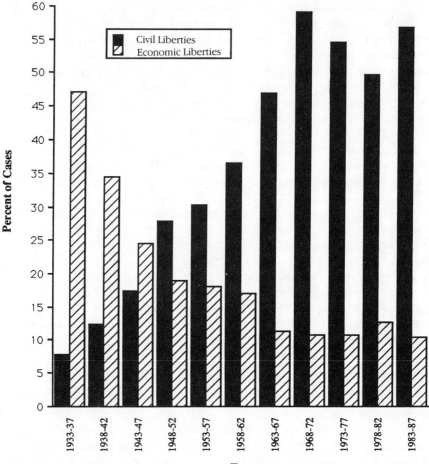

Terms

Data Source: Richard L. Pacelle, Jr., *The Transformation of the Supreme Court's Agenda* (Boulder, Colorado: Westview, 1991), 56–57.

ment. Since most crimes involve violations of state law, rather than federal, the Court's docket contained very few criminal disputes. The same was true for most other sorts of civil liberties issues.

This changed rather dramatically in the decades of the 1930s through the 1960s. As we illustrate in Table 6-1, the Court began to apply (or "incorporate") the federal Bill of Rights to the states, thereby forcing them to follow its provisions. Individuals convicted of state offenses were now guaranteed that the procedures surrounding the criminal justice process conformed to federal con-

TABLE 6-1
Incorporation of the Bill of Rights

Constitutional Provision	Case	Year
First Amendment		
Religious freedom (generally)	*Hamilton v. Regents of California*	1934
Religious establishment	*Everson v. Board of Education*	1947
Free exercise	*Cantwell v. Connecticut*	1940
Freedom of speech	*Gilbert v. Minnesota*	1920
	Gitlow v. New York	1925
	Fiske v. Kansas	1927
Freedom of the press	*Near v. Minnesota*	1931
Assembly	*DeJonge v. Oregon*	1937
Petition	*Hague v. CIO*	1939
Fourth Amendment		
Search and seizure	*Wolf v. Colorado*	1949
Fifth Amendment		
Double jeopardy	*Benton v. Maryland*	1969
Self-incrimination	*Malloy v. Hogan*	1964
Just compensation	*Missouri Pacific Railway v. Nebraska*	1896
	Chicago, Burlington & Quincy v. Chicago	1897
Sixth Amendment		
Speedy trial	*Klopfer v. North Carolina*	1967
Public trial	*In re Oliver*	1948
Impartial jury	*Parker v. Gladden*	1966
Jury trial in serious crimes	*Duncan v. Louisiana*	1968
Notice	*Cole v. Arkansas*	1948
Confrontation	*Pointer v. Texas*	1965
Compulsory process	*Washington v. Texas*	1967
Counsel in capital cases	*Powell v. Alabama*	1932
Counsel in felony cases	*Gideon v. Wainwright*	1963
Eighth Amendment		
Cruel and unusual punishment	*Robinson v. California*	1962
Ninth Amendment		
Privacy	*Griswold v. Connecticut*	1965

stitutional standards. If, for example, an officer arrested individuals on the basis of evidence gathered illegally, the defendants could mount a challenge based on their Fourth Amendment rights and have their cases reviewed in the federal courts. That would have been almost impossible prior to incorporation. Not surprisingly, this had the effect of increasing the number of rights and liberties cases that the Court could decide, especially in the area of criminal rights.

The Court's incorporation of the Bill of Rights was not the only way it helped to transform its own agenda. In recent decades, it has demonstrated a willingness to "open the windows" on salient policy issues, windows that it had previously nailed shut.[3] Reapportionment—the manner in which states draw legislative districts and allot representatives within them—provides an excellent example. Prior to the 1960s, the Court rejected the claim that the failure of legislators to apportion representation on the basis of population violated the constitutional rights of any voter. In the eyes of the Court such disputes were nonjusticiable because they involved political questions, constituting a "political thicket" into which "courts ought not enter."[4] However, in *Baker v. Carr* (1962), the Court did enter this thicket, holding that legislative redistricting was a justiciable issue. In so doing, the Court "opened the window" to reapportionment, ensuring that such cases would become a regular part of its plenary docket.

Reapportionment is a prominent, but certainly not the only, example of how the Court has transformed its agenda by taking on new issues. Indeed, in each decade since the 1950s, the Court has entered new territory. A few examples include:

▶ In the 1950s, the Court overturned the "separate but equal doctrine" of *Plessy v. Ferguson* (1896), and thus opened itself up to numerous cases challenging state practices as racially discriminatory.

▶ In the 1960s, the Court applied the judge-made exclusionary rule—which prohibits the introduction of illegally seized evidence into trial—to the states. This had the effect of dramatically increasing the number of Fourth Amendment cases making their way onto the plenary docket.

▶ In the 1970s, the Court legalized abortion during the first two trimesters of pregnancy. In so doing, it created a new legal area, the effects of which it continues to feel into the 1990s.

▶ In the 1980s, the Court continued where it had left off in *Regents of the University of California v. Bakke* (1978). By striking down quota systems as unconstitutional, but permitting entities to consider race and sex as factors in their decision-making processes, the Court carved out for itself another new area requiring adjudication—affirmative action.

What the remainder of the 1990s will bring remains a subject on which we can only speculate. Suffice it to say that the Rehnquist Court is seeking to shut the window on some of the issues noted above. Its ruling in *Webster v. Reproductive Health Services* (1989), for example, may indicate that it will no longer be as willing to consider cases challenging certain state regulations on abortion services. But, if it shuts the window on abortion, the Rehnquist Court will—like its predecessors—inevitably open one for some other policy issue.

---

[3] Ibid.

[4] *Colegrove v. Green*, 328 U.S. 459 (1946).

The Federal Government

The more political branches of government also have contributed to the transformation of the Court's agenda. First, let's think about Congress. On the one hand, the national legislature has provided fodder for the Court's increasing policy role by passing legislation requiring judicial interpretation. A most poignant example of this is the Civil Rights Act of 1964. In some ways, this act is quite clear. It prohibits discrimination on the basis of race, color, religion, national origin, and sex in many spheres of American life. On its face, then, it provided a vehicle for numerous challenges to discriminatory practices, many of which reached the Supreme Court's doorstep. But those cases asking the Court to reach some conclusions on things the act does not specify also take up a good deal of the Court's time. For example, while the act explicitly prohibits discrimination in employment, it did not describe how people can go about proving that they were the victims of discrimination. As a result, the Supreme Court has had to issue policy on the kinds of standards plaintiffs must meet to prove violations of the law.

On the other hand, Congress has transformed the Court's agenda by *not* acting in certain policy areas. Once again, abortion provides an excellent example. Because Congress took no action—either for or against legalized abortion—litigants desiring social change took to the courts. To be sure, the Court did not have to take up the subject. But in the absence of legislative action, there was a great deal of pressure for the judiciary to resolve the issue. At the time the Court decided *Roe v. Wade* (1973), a dozen or so abortion cases were pending before it, not to mention the many that were working their way up the state and federal judicial ladders.

Now let us consider Congress in tandem with the president. Over the past few decades, the federal government has not been uniformly of the Republican or Democratic party. Rather, what we have seen are divided governments, with presidents coming from the ranks of the Republican party and Congresses full of Democrats. How has this contributed to the Court's shift from a private law to a constitutional law Court? Largely because of these partisan differences, we have seen an increasing number of interinstitutional disputes. Some examples include:

> *Buckley v. Valeo* (1976). Did 1974 Federal Election Campaign Act Amendments infringe on executive power because Congress provided that it would appoint four of the five members of the Federal Election Commission? The Court ruled that it did.
>
> *Immigration and Naturalization Service v. Chadha* (1983). May one house of Congress veto the rulings of executive branch agencies? The Court held that such one-house vetoes violate the separation of powers doctrine.
>
> *Bowsher v. Synar* (1986). Did Congress infringe on presidential power when it gave the comptroller general (an office over which Congress has removal

power) the ability to inform the president where to cut the federal budget? The Court ruled that it did.

Morrison v. Olson (1988). Did the Ethics in Government Act, which authorizes a panel of judges to appoint special prosecutors to investigate allegations of wrongdoing by public officials, violate the doctrine of separation of powers? According to the Court, it did not.

Mistretta v. United States (1989). By authorizing the creation of a commission to set sentencing guidelines for the federal judiciary, did the Sentencing Act of 1984 violate the separation of powers doctrine? The Court ruled that it did not.

By resolving these and other cases, the Supreme Court has emerged as something of an umpire between the two feuding branches; and, in playing that role, it has established significant constitutional policy.

Interest Groups

Interest groups also have played a role in the transformation of the Court. Although organizations turned to the Supreme Court as early as the 1800s, it has only been in recent decades that they have done so in great numbers. In fact, today most cases ultimately resolved by the Court are brought or supported by organized interests. This, in itself, reveals a good deal about the change in the Court's agenda. By their very nature, interest groups seek to represent something more than mere private interests. They want to see certain policies etched into law. When they litigate, they are asking the Court to make policy, and not necessarily to resolve disputes that have little or no interest to anyone outside of the immediate parties. Hence, the more litigation sponsored by interest groups and the more such cases the Court accepts for review, the greater opportunity for the Court to set policy.

To be even more concrete, over the last several years interest groups have brought to the Court the majority of those cases used by the justices to enunciate their most significant (and controversial) policy decisions. Virtually all major abortion cases, including *Webster v. Reproductive Health Services,* were sponsored by one or more pro-choice organizations, including the American Civil Liberties Union, Planned Parenthood, or the Center for Constitutional Rights. By the same token, the NAACP Legal Defense Fund and the Women's Rights Project play an important role in bringing race and sex discrimination cases, respectively, to the Court's attention. And there is hardly a religious liberty case decided by the Court that is not supported by the American Jewish Congress, the American Jewish Committee, Americans United, or the ACLU. Undoubtedly, then, by viewing the Court as an important policy-making body and, in turn, bringing cases to its attention, groups have contributed to the agenda transformation observed in Figure 6-1.

TRENDS IN SUPREME COURT POLICY MAKING

Now that we know something about why the Court has emerged as an important policy maker, let us consider whether it exhibits trends in the way it resolves such issues. Scholars have generally explored policy-making trends along three distinct dimensions: partisanship, ideology, and judicial role.

Partisanship

In the previous chapter, we saw that the party identification of the justices provides a reasonably good predictor of the way they will vote in cases. Put simply, justices affiliating with the Republican party tend to be more conservative than their Democratic counterparts. The question we consider here is a bit different: does partisanship affect the policies emerging from the Court? The answer, nonetheless, is quite similar. The political party of the majority of the Court does seem to have an impact on the kinds of policies it will enunciate.

Indeed, the relationship between partisanship and policy making has been manifest since the earliest days of the republic when, in the dying days of his administration, President John Adams installed his secretary of state, John Marshall, as chief justice of the United States. Through the Court, Marshall kept the Federalist agenda alive for over thirty years. In case after case, he was more than willing to elevate the powers of the federal government above the states; his most significant statement on national supremacy came in *McCulloch v. Maryland* (1819).[5] In *McCulloch* the Court addressed the question of whether Congress could create a Bank of the United States (even though the Constitution did not explicitly grant it that power) and, then, whether states could tax federal banks that were located within their borders. By holding, first, that Congress possessed powers beyond those enumerated, that it has implied powers (and, thus, could create a bank), Marshall set into law a largely Federalist version of congressional authority. And, because of *McCulloch,* Congress now exercises a whole series of powers not enumerated within the Constitution but "implied" from it. For example, Article I, section 8 provides Congress with the power to raise and support armies, to provide and maintain a navy, and to declare war. From these, we can infer a power to conduct a draft, even though that power is not explicitly included within Article I.

McCulloch also served as Marshall's vehicle for expounding national supremacy over the states. That occurred because of Marshall's treatment of the two relevant constitutional provisions:

---

[5] We derive this from Lee Epstein and Thomas G. Walker, *Constitutional Law for a Changing America: Institutional Powers and Constraints* (Washington, D.C.: CQ Press, 1992).

▶ The Tenth Amendment, which says that powers not granted to the federal government are reserved for the states, stands as no significant bar to congressional exercise of its power.

▶ The Supremacy Clause places the national government as supreme within its sphere of operation, a sphere—again given his interpretation of the Necessary and Proper Clause—that is quite broad. No state may "retard, impede, burden, or, in any manner, control the operations of the constitutional laws enacted by Congress."

McCulloch's holdings—supporting congressional creation of the bank and negating state taxation of it—were not particulary surprising. They reflected the tenets of Marshall's party—the Federalists—even though it had long since disappeared as a force in American politics. And while Marshall was chief justice of the United States, it was his view of nation-state relations that found its way into law. By the last days of the Marshall Court in the 1830s, however, the political environment in the United States had turned. It was Jacksonian Democracy—which stressed the rights of states—that now reflected the views of the populace. So it was to no one's real surprise that President Andrew Jackson chose his loyal supporter, Roger Taney, to succeed Marshall.

Taney and Marshall held distinctly different perspectives, particularly on issues of federalism. Whereas Marshall viewed the federal government as supreme, Taney (and Jackson) thought states' rights were not incompatible with those possessed by the national government. The two chief justices' views on the Bank of the United States provide a wonderful juxtaposition. In *McCulloch,* Marshall lent his full support to it; in 1832, Taney "coauthor[ed]" President Jackson's veto message in which he "condemned the Second Bank of the United States," and refused to recharter it.[6]

Had Taney been President Jackson's only appointment to the Court, he might not have been able to change the course of the federalism doctrine. But that was hardly the case. By 1841 Joseph Story was the only justice remaining from the Marshall Court that decided *McCulloch;* the balance were, like Taney, schooled in Jacksonian Democracy. And, not surprisingly, the Court shifted its interpretative direction away from Marshall's determined nationalism. The policy changes ushered in by the Taney Court, especially on federal-state relations, were quite substantial. Although there is no true Taney corollary to Marshall's *McCulloch,* examples of his views abound. In many opinions, he explicated the doctrine of dual federalism, that national and state governments are equivalent sovereigns within their own spheres of operation. Unlike Marshall, he read the Tenth Amendment in a broad sense, that it reserved to the states certain powers and limited the power of the federal government over them.

Undoubtedly, then, the policy positions of the earliest Courts tended to

---

[6] R. Kent Newmyer, *The Supreme Court under Marshall and Taney* (New York: Crowell, 1968), 93.

reflect their partisan composition, especially when it came to nation-state relations. This general trend continued into the 1930s, when the Court's policies
reflected its dominant party affiliation. But the issues changed. With the advent of
the Industrial Revolution and the emergence of big business, the Court was
placed in the position of determining the extent to which governments—both
federal and state—could regulate corporate interests. Though it could have
adopted the position that Congress and state legislatures possess certain policy
powers enabling them to place restrictions on what employers could and could
not do, the Court chose not to take this route. Rather, it generally struck down as
violative of the Constitution state and federal regulatory efforts to do so, such as
maximum hour and minimum wage laws.

Why it chose this policy posture is not all that difficult to discern. With only a
few exceptions, between the late 1800s and the 1920s this was the view held by
the dominant political party, the Republican party. And many of the justices
(twenty-two out of the thirty-five appointed between 1874 and 1932 were Republicans) certainly reflected the "business of America is business" philosophy in
their opinions. Some examples include:

▶ *Lochner v. New York* (1905) in which the Court struck down a state
  maximum hour work law as a violation of the liberty of contract that the
  justices proclaimed as embedded in the Fourteenth Amendment.

▶ *Pollock v. Farmers' Loan and Trust Co.* (1895) in which the Court struck
  down the federal income tax as violative of the Constitution.

▶ *Hammer v. Dagenhart* (1918) in which the Court struck down a congressional attempt to limit child labor.

▶ *Adkins v. Children's Hospital* (1923) in which the Court struck down
  minimum wage laws as violative of the Constitution.

In short, the Court, composed largely of Republicans, generally etched that
party's positions into law.

With the Depression of 1929 and the emergence of President Franklin Roosevelt's popular New Deal philosophy, the Court too changed. Its initial move from
a probusiness to a proregulation stance came in 1937 with the famous "switch in
time that saved nine." That trend continued largely because the president had an
opportunity to appoint virtually an entire Court (eight justices, plus the elevation
of Harlan Fiske Stone to the chief justiceship) over the course of his twelve years
in office. Not surprisingly, the Court that Roosevelt built reflected his policies, at
least on economic issues. As Sheldon Goldman wrote, "All nine were known
New Deal supporters and only one, Harlan Fiske Stone, was a Republican. With
the exception of Stone and Rutledge, the appointees were personal friends of
Roosevelt and politically close to him."[7]

---

[7] Goldman, *Constitutional Law and Supreme Court Decision-Making,* 330.

Hence, once again the Roosevelt Court demonstrates the importance of partisanship as a determinant of the Court's policy-making trends. Interestingly, though, we cannot say that political party is all that helpful in understanding the policies emanating from the most modern Court eras, the Warren, Burger, and Rehnquist Courts. Just consider the fact that Earl Warren, who presided over a Court generating arguably the most liberal policies in American history, was a Republican, appointed by a Republican president, Dwight Eisenhower. So too, while Republican president Nixon appointed party member Warren Burger to replace Warren, the Court over which Burger presided—as we describe below—did not necessarily follow the party line. The Rehnquist Court may be the closest to past eras in that its decisions tend to reflect the partisan affiliation of most of its members, again Republicanism. But it is probably safe to say that partisanship does not provide the best explanation of Supreme Court policies. Rather, ideology seems to be more powerful.

Ideology and Policy Making

As we noted above, it would be a relatively difficult task to try to explain the Warren Court's (and, to a lesser extent, the Burger Court's) policies through a partisanship lens. About a third of the justices who sat with Warren were Republicans or appointed by Republican presidents; indeed, President Eisenhower—who appointed Warren and another of the Court's most liberal members, William Brennan—once responded to the question of whether he had made any mistakes in office: "Yes, two and they are both on the Supreme Court." Clearly, the Republican president was not all that happy with the Republican chief justice he had appointed.

What we see during the Warren Court era is the beginning of a modern-day trend that continues today in which ideology, and not necessarily partisanship, is an important indicator of Court policy positions. As Table 6-2 illustrates, during the 1950s and 1960s the Court's majority was composed of some of the most liberal justices in its history. Chief Justice Warren and associates Black, Douglas, Brennan, Fortas, and Marshall forged the way, supporting the interests of the disadvantaged in an unusually large percentage of the cases. Although the Warren Court was not monolithically left of center, Table 6-2 shows that it contained a core of six liberals who energized it.

Though the Court's liberalism left virtually no policy area untouched, among its more noticeable manifestations were within the area of criminal law and procedure. Not only did it support the incorporation of the guarantees contained in the Fourth, Fifth, Sixth, and Eighth Amendments (which contain rights afforded to the criminally accused), but it read them in a very expansive fashion. Among those policies generated by the Warren Court in this area were:

▶ the state must provide indigents with counsel
▶ police must read warnings to those they wish to question in conjunction with a crime

TABLE 6-2
From the Warren to Burger to Rehnquist Courts

	Percent Support for Liberal Positions[a] in Non-Unanimous Cases				
	Civil Liberties		Economics		Baum Ranking[b]
	%	#	%	#	
Justices of the Warren Court[c]					
Warren (1953–1969)	77.6	576	79.2	457	8/26
Black (1937–1971)	74.7	582	83.6	450	9/26
Douglas (1939–1975)	96.1	583	86.4	455	1/26
Harlan (1955–1971)	22.1	551	20.9	402	15/26
Brennan (1956–1990)	76.0	509	71.5	382	5/26
Stewart (1958–1981)	39.6	424	33.8	299	11/26
White (1962–	44.2	278	62.9	175	14/26
Fortas (1965–1969)	81.1	159	51.1	90	7/26
Marshall (1967–1991)	83.5	79	56.0	25	3/26
Justices of the Burger Court[d]					
Burger (1969–1986)	17.6	1,099	25.0	328	21/26
Rehnquist (1971–	5.6	959	22.8	285	25/26
Stevens (1975–	61.4	676	52.6	211	10/26
Powell (1971–1987)	31.2	940	29.7	256	16/26
Brennan (1956–1990)	85.5	1,086	74.2	329	5/26
Stewart (1958–1981)	43.6	782	32.1	234	11/26
White (1962–	33.7	1,103	50.6	328	14/26
Blackmun (1970–	39.5	1,056	46.5	310	13/26
Marshall (1967–1991)	88.5	1,078	68.2	321	3/26

Justices of the Rehnquist Court[e]

	Criminal Rights		Civil Rights		
	%	#	%	#	
Rehnquist (1971–	9.8	(82)	29.6	(27)	25/26
Stevens (1975–	65.9	(82)	72.4	(28)	10/26
White (1962–	16.0	(81)	40.7	(27)	14/26
Blackmun (1970–	62.2	(82)	89.7	(29)	13/26
Marshall (1967–1991)	92.7	(82)	93.1	(29)	3/26
O'Connor (1981–	19.5	(82)	35.7	(28)	20/26
Scalia (1986–	19.5	(82)	25.0	(28)	Not Ranked
Kennedy (1988–	14.7	(34)	21.4	(14)	Not Ranked
Souter (1990–					Not Ranked
Thomas (1991–					Not Ranked

[a] Source for Warren and Burger Court data: Jeffrey A. Segal and Harold J. Spaeth, "Decisional Trends on the Warren and Burger Courts: Results from the Supreme Court Data Base Project," *Judicature* 73 (1989): 103–107. Source for Rehnquist Court data: Lee Epstein and Joseph F. Kobylka, *The Supreme Court and Legal Change* (Chapel Hill: University of North Carolina Press, 1992).

[b] Source: Lawrence Baum, "Comparing the Policy Positions of Supreme Court Justices from Different Periods," *Western Political Quarterly* 42 (1989): 509–521. Baum devised a technique for comparing the ideological behavior of justices across courts. These rankings represent the "adjusted scores" of 26 justices' pro–civil liberties voting in cases decided between the 1946 and 1985 Terms. So, for example, Douglas's ranking of 1/26 asserts that he was the most liberal member of the Court during the period under analysis.

[c] Data are for nonunanimous cases decided between 1953 and 1969.

[d] Data are for nonunanimous cases decided between 1969 and 1986.

[e] Data are for nonunanimous cases decided between 1986 and 1988.

▶ judges must not allow the admission of illegally obtained evidence or of coerced confessions into a proceeding

We can also see this at a more aggregated level. In Figure 6-2 we display the overall percentage of cases in which the Warren Court, its predecessors, and its successors ruled in favor of the criminally accused. As noted, it was far more liberal than Courts before or since.

Many applauded these and other Warren Court policies, particularly those eradicating discrimination against minorities. Others, though, were far less enchanted. As we noted in Chapter 1, Richard Nixon—as a candidate for the presidency in 1968—vowed to appoint justices who would restore law and order, and who would change Warren Court policies governing the rights of the criminally accused. Nixon had the chance to make good on his promise as he appointed four justices, three of whom were Republicans, to the Court.

With those members in place, coupled with President Ford's appointment of Republican John Paul Stevens, a partisan model of policy making would surely predict the adoption of the Republican party's positions. Some of this did occur. For example, the Court generated more conservative policies in criminal law and procedure. Moreover, it significantly changed the liberal standard the Warren Court had developed to define obscenity. Still, it did not overrule important Warren Court decisions. Perhaps even more interestingly, the Court continued to generate liberal policy in a variety of issue areas: it legalized abortion, upheld the underpinnings of affirmative action, liberalized standards to evaluate claims of sex discrimination, and validated busing plans to achieve racial balance in public schools.

Why the relatively Republican Burger Court did not become uniformly conservative, thus, has less to do with partisanship and more with ideology. As we can see in Table 6-2, some of the Burger Court justices were quite moderate (for example, Republicans Potter Stewart, John Paul Stevens, and Harry Blackmun). And when they joined with the more liberal Warren Court holdovers, policies often tended toward that end of the spectrum.

This has changed rather dramatically since 1981. Presidents Reagan and Bush effectively transformed the Court, appointing collectively six of the Court's nine members. In doing so they replaced such strong liberals as William Brennan and Thurgood Marshall, as well as moderates Lewis Powell and Potter Stewart. As of the beginning of the 1991 Term, Byron White was the only member of the Court who had served under Earl Warren, and he represents little of what that Court has come to symbolize.

Whether the Rehnquist Court's policies reflect the ideology of its members or their partisanship is difficult to determine. Party and ideology usually overlap. Unlike some of the Warren Court justices, who were Republicans and liberals, thereby making rather easy the task of determining whether ideology or partisanship was more significant, the Rehnquist Court justices are, as Table 6-2 indicates, Republican and conservative. What we can say is that they are blazing a far more

FIGURE 6-2

Support for the Rights of the Criminally Accused, 1945–1985

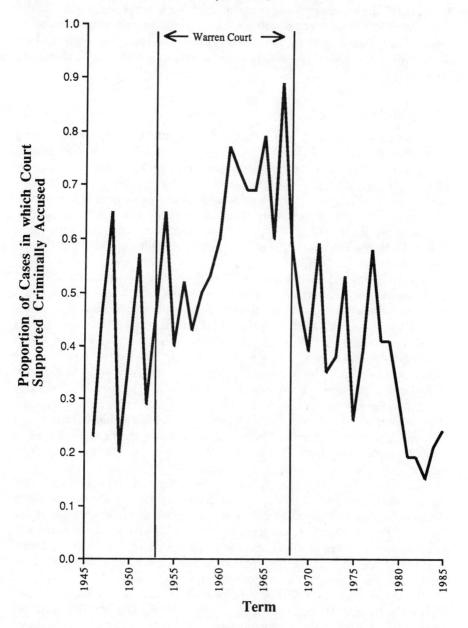

Source: Lee Epstein, Thomas G. Walker, and William J. Dixon, "The Criminal Justice Disputes: A Neo-International Perspective," *American Journal of Political Science* 33 (1989): 834.

conservative policy trail than that of their predecessors. Just as there were few policy areas untouched by the Warren Court's liberalism, there are few that the Rehnquist Court's conservatism has not affected. Some are predicting that, by the end of the 1990s, the justices will have overturned or substantially modified many of the Warren (and Burger) Court's important precedents—particularly those involving criminal law and procedure, religious liberty, federalism, and abortion.

The Judicial Role

While those examining policy making from an ideological perspective tend to ask "are the Court's policies liberal or conservative?" those contemplating policy making through a judicial role approach question whether the Court is behaving in an *activist* or *restraintist* manner. A problem with asking this question, as you may imagine, is that some disagreement exists over how to define activism and restraintism. Let us first consider the predominant definitions: activist courts are those willing to strike down policies or laws enacted by majoritarian institutions; restraintist courts would generally defer to the popularly elected branches.

Legal analysts and observers have long debated whether courts *should* act in an activist or restraintist manner. This is something we discussed in Chapter 1 and we shall take it up again at the end of this volume. For now, though, the more relevant question is whether certain Courts have evinced extreme levels of activism or restraintism. Using the definition outlined above, we can see in Figure 6-3 that the answer is somewhat mixed. On the one hand, prior to the 1920s the Court rarely struck down federal laws and only occasionally overturned state legislation or local ordinances. This changed for a while in the 1920s and 1930s, largely because holdover justices from past Republican administrations struck down much of Roosevelt's New Deal legislation, most of which was economic in nature. After the "switch in time," however, the Court began to uphold congressional laws. That is why we see a decrease in the use of judicial review in the 1940s and 1950s.

Courts of the 1960s, 1970s, and 1980s—albeit of different ideological stripes—were far more active than their predecessors. The absolute numbers displayed in Figure 6-3 speak to this, as do the percentages of federal laws struck down. While it is difficult to compare the ratio of laws passed to laws struck in any given period (this is so because the Court can strike down legislation anytime after it was passed), it is true that Congress is passing fewer and fewer laws, while the Court is striking down more and more of them.

To be sure, then, the Court over the past few decades has been more "active" than at any other point in history. But, as we would expect, that activism has not been uniform across issues. Not unexpectedly, earlier courts were far more prone to strike down laws restricting economic liberties, and the Warren Court, civil liberties. But beginning in the 1980s, we see precisely the opposite trend.

FIGURE 6-3

Laws Overturned by the Supreme Court: Civil and Economic Liberties

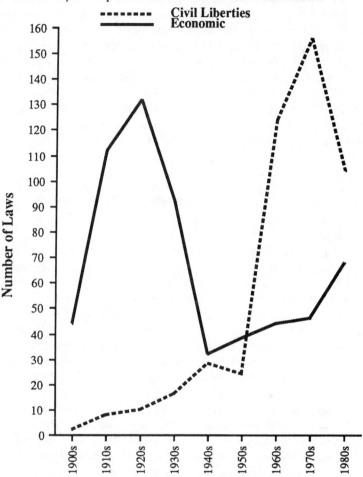

Source: Lawrence Baum, *The Supreme Court,* 4th ed. (Washington, D.C.: CQ Press, 1992), 197.

The Burger and now Rehnquist courts are increasingly less inclined to strike down restrictions on rights and liberties and more likely than their predecessors to do so in cases challenging regulations on economic liberties.

But the bottom line still remains: at least under the most conventional definitions of activism and restraint, the Warren and Rehnquist Courts are quite similar—they are both actively scrutinizing and striking down governmental policies. This may strike you as strange. After all, we tend to equate liberalism with activism and conservatism with restraint. The actions of our most recent Court belie that notion. Conservatives can be equally as activist as their liberal counterparts, at least when it comes to striking down legislation.

If this is so, then why does it always seem to be conservatives who clamor for judicial restraint? President Ronald Reagan once said that he would appoint a Court of "Felix Frankfurters" (a justice many identify as the quintessential restraintist) if he could. Part of the explanation lies in the way that Reagan and others define judicial restraint. To them, upholding legislation is not necessarily the hallmark of a restraintist Court. To the contrary, they fully approve of Court decisions that overturn legislation (or even previous Court rulings) if to do so eradicates liberal policies and doctrines. Seen in this way, classically defined "activism" may be a vehicle to return to restraintism. The Rehnquist Court's decision in *City of Richmond v. Croson* (1989), in which it struck down a city's affirmative action program designed to help minority interests, provides a good example.

SUPREME COURT POLICIES: INTERPRETATION AND IMPLEMENTATION

Thus far, we have paid a great deal of attention to the kinds of policies the Supreme Court has generated and to patterns underlying those policies. In so doing, we raised a number of specific issues and concerns with the Court's policy-making process. But one general point is this: the process is a highly political one. The particular partisan or ideological makeup of the Court, for example, has a great deal to do with the ultimate policies it adopts. Seen in this way, the court is not so different from its legislative or executive counterparts.

What is unique about the Court's policies is that the institution—as a legal body—lacks any way to enforce them. When the Court outlawed prayer in public school, for instance, it would have been out of the question for Chief Justice Earl Warren to enter every schoolroom in the United States to force teachers to comply with the ruling. The Warren Court ran headfirst into this problem when the Southern states rebelled against the desegregation decisions. Moreover, it is often true that Court policies are quite vague, requiring—just like congressional laws—interpretation. The problem, of course, is that sometimes the Court does not realize just how much room for interpretation exists in its rulings. When Chief Justice Warren wrote in *Brown v. Board of Education* (1955) that school systems should be desegregated "with all deliberate speed," he may have thought he was being reasonably precise—that this should be done with dispatch. Nonetheless, "deliberate speed" turned out to be a vague term, open to different interpretations by a diverse range of legal and political actors.

In this section, we explore the twin issues of interpretation and implementation. What our discussion indicates is this: however political the Court might be, its inability to enforce its own decisions significantly constrains the effect it might have on society. It is this issue of effect, of "impact," that we will consider in the final section of the chapter.

A Framework for Understanding Interpretation and Implementation of Court Policies

What happens when the Supreme Court hands down a decision? Different things do. In fact, we could go so far as to say that because many rulings are unique, they follow distinct paths. But examining the aftermath of *every* judicial decision not only would be beyond the scope of this book but would also not be very useful in helping us to understand what occurs in the aftermath of Supreme Court rulings. Rather, we will make some general observations.

One way we can do this is by considering a framework for the study of judicial interpretation and compliance, one that was proposed by Charles Johnson and Bradley Canon. As we illustrate in Figure 6-4, their framework focuses on how different actors ("populations") respond to Supreme Court rulings and ultimately shape judicial policy. Each of these actors has a role in the interpretation and/or implementation of Supreme Court decisions.

The first, the interpreting populations, generally consist of lower court judges who have the responsibility of applying Supreme Court decisions to disputes before them. For example, when the Supreme Court ruled in *Mapp v. Ohio* (1961) that evidence gathered illegally by law enforcement officers should not be used against the defendants, it fell to trial court judges to interpret and apply that command at the trial court level.

FIGURE 6-4
The Implementation and Interpretation of U.S. Supreme Court Decisions

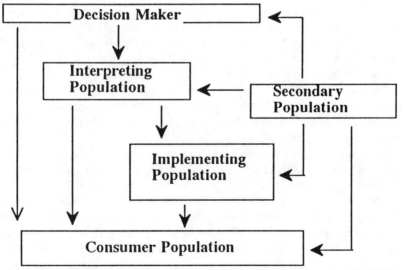

Source: Charles A. Johnson and Bradley C. Canon, *Judicial Policies* (Washington, D.C.: CQ Press, 1984), 15.

Implementing populations are something of a mixed bag. In general, as Johnson and Canon tell us, this population is "made up of authorities whose behavior may be reinforced or sanctioned by the interpreting population."[8] Under the *Mapp* example, we can say that police constituted the major implementing population. They knew they should no longer gather evidence illegally and that if they did the interpreting population (the criminal court judges) could penalize them by refusing to admit it at trial.

The consuming population is that which stands to gain or lose as a result of a Court decision. In *Mapp,* the clear winners were criminal suspects against whom the police had gathered illegal evidence.

Finally, there is a secondary population composed of everyone who is not in the interpreting, implementing, or consuming populations, but nonetheless may react to the Supreme Court's rulings. Members of this population include government officials, interest groups, the media, and the public.

Identifying the relevant actors is important, but to understand fully the interpreting/implementing process, we must consider a number of factors emanating from their specific roles and how they ultimately come together to affect the way policies are transmitted to us. In particular, how do these populations react to Supreme Court decisions and why? What explains their varying responses?

The Responses of the Populations to Supreme Court Policies

Despite the fact that the actors depicted in Figure 6-4 play distinct roles in the interpretive/implementation process, the range of responses available to them is roughly similar: all of them can reject, accept, or enthusiastically endorse Supreme Court policies. Before we take a more detailed look at how and why the specific populations make these decisions, you may be wondering why they even have these choices in the first instance. After all, as we noted in Chapter 1, the Court sits atop both federal and state judicial ladders, meaning—at least theoretically—that *all* courts and other actors are bound by its rulings. They, especially interpreting populations, are supposed to accept and apply Supreme Court decisions to cases before them. They are not supposed to reject Supreme Court precedent. Yet they sometimes do. Why?

The answer centers on something to which we alluded at the introduction to this section. Supreme Court policies are often vague, complex, or just not very applicable to situations that arise in their aftermath. Let us return to *Mapp v. Ohio* as illustrative. Once again, in that case, the Court held that evidence obtained illegally could not be admitted at trial; it must be excluded. To be sure, the policy resulting from *Mapp*—the so-called exclusionary rule—on its face was quite clear. But was it? As we show in Table 6-3, between 1961 and 1969, state supreme courts had to deal with many issues flowing from *Mapp,* but not quite clearly

---

[8] Charles A. Johnson and Bradley C. Canon, *Judicial Policies* (Washington, D.C.: CQ Press, 1984), 17.

TABLE 6-3
State Supreme Court Responses to *Mapp v. Ohio,* 1961–1969

Legal Question before the State Supreme Court	No. of States Applying Exclusionary Rule	No. of States Not Applying Exclusionary Rule
1. Does the failure of the defendant to make a timely motion for supression of illegally seized evidence waive his or her right to invoke the exclusionary rule?	2	21
2. Can one spouse waive the Fourth Amendment rights of the other and consent to a search of the home?	4	16
3. Is evidence secured during a routine noncriminal search—a building inspection, for example—admissible in criminal prosecutions?	1	4
4. Is *Mapp* retroactive? That is, does it apply to cases where the trial occurred before the Supreme Court's decision?	5	11
5. Is evidence secured from one who was stopped for "suspicious behavior" admissible under the Fourth Amendment?	3	6
6. Are searches of automobiles following a traffic arrest valid?	4	7
7. Must appellate courts overturn convictions in which illegally obtained evidence was introduced but did not constitute a vital or major proportion of the evidence upon which the verdict was based?	3	5
8. Does a defendant who does not reside on the premises from which the evidence was illegally seized have standing to object to its admission?	12	16
9. Are warrants issued or searches made on the basis of anonymous tips valid?	3	3
10. Can evidence be admitted that is secured in good faith but nonetheless illegally (that is, the warrant is later determined to be void)?	3	3
11. When a defendant is under arrest or in custody, is a waiver of Fourth Amendment rights presumed to have been coerced and thus void unless the state can rebut the presumption?	8	5
12. Is testimony about illegally seized evidence admissible?	6	1
13. Is evidence seized in the course of an invalid arrest admissible?	5	1

Source: Charles A. Johnson and Bradley C. Canon, *Judicial Policies* (Washington, D.C.: CQ Press, 1984), 53–54.

covered by it. And as we can see, they responded in varying ways—sometimes they excluded the evidence and sometimes they did not. Reactions of the other populations were equally varied. Some police officers implemented the dictates of *Mapp* and others did not. Certain legislators strongly supported *Mapp;* others were quite opposed. By the same token, many interest groups, such as the American Civil Liberties Union, hailed *Mapp* and sought immediately to invoke it on behalf of clients; others, like Americans for Effective Law Enforcement, have sought to narrow *Mapp's* scope. Does this *necessarily mean* that they were ignoring the Court? Usually not. To reiterate, it is just that the Court's decisions cannot cover all the bases, or they are complex or vague, and not amenable to easy interpretation. They also are not self-implementing. *Mapp* required endorsement by judges and the compliance of police officers and others to be effective.

The important question, then, turns on whether there is any pattern to the way the various actors respond and react. For example, why is it that some supreme courts excluded evidence and others did not (see Table 6-3)? One explanation centers on the political and environmental pressures to which many of the populations are susceptible, with the ebb and flow of ordinary politics inevitably affecting their responses. Consider interpreting populations. Though we tend to think of judges as immune from political pressures, we know that they are not. Indeed, they can be just as responsive to the political environment as Supreme Court justices, perhaps more so in the case of elected state judges. A major difference, of course, is that the decisions of lower court judges may reflect regional, state, or local trends, rather than national ones. As a result, the actual application of Supreme Court rulings can vary from state to state, or even from city to city. One study, for example, found that judges in California tended to vary in the severity of the sentences they gave for offenses involving marijuana, depending on public opinion. Judges in Los Angeles were more severe than their counterparts in San Francisco.[9] Another study, conducted by Beverly Blair Cook, indicated that the sentences meted out to draft resisters by federal court judges also reflected trends in the public's views.[10]

Implementing populations are equally sensitive to political or even judicial pressure. Suppose that a police department knew that the courts in its city were quite supportive of *Mapp v. Ohio.* The chances that the department would instruct officers to abide by the ruling would, then, be much higher. Why would officers gather evidence illegally if they suspected that a trial court would exclude it? By the same token, we know that public school administrators charged with enforcing Supreme Court decisions that struck down prayer in school faced immense local pressure, especially in the South, to resist. Finally, and most obviously, the secondary population—particularly legislatures—is by its very

---

[9] James H. Kuklinski and John E. Stanga, "Political Participation and Government Responsiveness," *American Political Science Review* 73 (1979): 1090–1099.

[10] Beverly Blair Cook, "Sentencing Behavior of Federal Judges: Draft Cases—1972," *University of Cincinnati Law Review* 42 (1973): 597–633.

nature sensitive to the political environment. Elected officials must pay some attention to the climate of the times, to the opinions of their constituents.

Another explanation takes us back to the individual attitudes held by the varying populations. We cannot ignore the fact that like Supreme Court justices, interpreters and implementors may have their own views toward specific policies and tend to act accordingly. "If the judge," for example, "is favorably disposed toward a higher court policy, then his or her interpretations may be more expansive or positive than the norm; the reverse would be true for judges unfavorably disposed toward a policy."[11] Research by Alumbaugh and Rowland provides a good example of the extent to which this may affect judicial decision making.[12] They explored how lower federal court judges resolved abortion cases. They found that Reagan appointees—presumably rather conservative jurists—were far more likely to take a pro-life stance than their presumably more liberal Carter-appointee counterparts.

A third explanation for the varying responses of the implementing and interpreting populations, though, has less to do with their particular attitudes and more with the attributes of the specific policy. For one, some Supreme Court rulings are inherently more controversial than others. When the Court issues a decision on an antitrust dispute, for example, it is far less likely to generate a significant reaction—even if it is an important decision—than, say, when it delves into affirmative action, prayer in school, and the like. Why? One answer is that the decision must be perceived to have the potential of affecting many people, or at least those beyond the parties to the litigation. Another is that when the Court significantly alters past policies—for example, a *Roe* or a *Mapp*—responses tend to be wider in range. Some will inevitably oppose them; others will support them. So, too, we cannot forget the role played by the media. Journalists are far more likely to report on certain Court decisions, those that they perceive as "salient," than they are on others. Which decisions they choose to publicize or ignore, of course, has an effect on the various populations. For example, if the public does not know about a particular ruling, then it will not be in a position to pressure any of the actors to take a specific stance.

Another policy attribute that may affect the responses of interpreters and implementors is the degree to which the Supreme Court supports its own ruling. Some analysts suggest that when the Court issues a unanimous decision, legal and political actors are more likely to comply with it. Conversely, if the decision represents the views of only a bare majority of the justices, all the various populations may be a bit more suspicious, perceiving the decision as one that may change within the near future. *Texas v. Johnson* (1989), in which the Court struck down, by a 5 to 4 vote, a state law barring flag desecration,

---

[11] Johnson and Canon, *Judicial Policies,* 66.

[12] Steve Alumbaugh and C. K. Rowland, "The Links between Platform-Based Appointment Criteria and Trial Judges' Abortion Judgments," *Judicature* 74 (1990): 153–162.

provides a good example. After that ruling was issued, Congress immediately enacted a federal flag protection statute that, in the eyes of many, was equally as repugnant to the Constitution as the Texas law. Had a unanimous Court produced the *Johnson* ruling, under this explanation, then Congress may not have taken the action it did. It would have recognized the improbability of five justices changing their minds. The one-vote margin in *Johnson* gave the legislature hope—a hollow one as it turned out—that this law would pass muster.

A final policy attributed worthy of consideration is that of clarity. How clear is the policy enunciated by the Court? It is only axiomatic that the more "ambiguous, vague, or poorly articulated" a policy, the more likely it is "to produce dissimilar" responses by the interpreting and implementing populations.[13] Once again, *Roe v. Wade* provides a good example of what can occur when a policy possesses these traits. In that decision, the majority asserted that during months four through six of pregnancy (the second trimester), the state "in promoting its interest in the health of the mother, may, if it chooses, regulate the abortion procedure in ways that are reasonably related to maternal health." While the meaning of the term "reasonably related to maternal health" may have been clear to the majority, it was not to some interpreting and implementing populations. Indeed, based on what you have just read, see if you could answer the following questions:

- ▶ Can a state outlaw certain abortion procedures on the ground that they may be dangerous to the mother's health?
- ▶ Can a state require that all abortions after the first three months of pregnancy be performed in a hospital, rather than a clinic?
- ▶ Can a state require doctors to perform medical tests to determine if a fetus is viable (capable of living on its own) on those women who are seeking second-trimester abortions?
- ▶ Can a state require doctors to inform women of the risks entailed by the abortion procedure?

These are difficult questions to answer based solely on the rather vague language used in the Court's opinion. Nonetheless, after *Roe,* lower court judges had to answer them. It should, thus, not surprise you too much that they did so in very different ways.

THE IMPACT OF U.S. SUPREME COURT POLICIES

Based on the discussion above, what can we now say about the impact of U.S. Supreme Court decisions? Quite clearly, we see that the impact of any decision

---

[13] Johnson and Canon, *Judicial Policies,* 49.

has a good deal to do with the reactions of the different populations, which in turn depend on views and preferences of the involved actors, the political environment in which they work, and the attributes of the policy itself. But are those reactions alone determinant of the impact of a specific policy? When the Supreme Court outlawed prayer in school, for example, and many public school officials chose to ignore the Court, could we not argue that the decision had no impact? That would be a reasonable conclusion for those noncomplying schools, but surely not for those that followed the Court's rulings and eliminated prayer. Moreover, it would not adequately describe the impact the decisions had on the political environment. Prayer in school suddenly became a hot topic. Congress considered a constitutional amendment to overturn the Court's decisions, pollsters surveyed Americans to gauge their opinions, public officials voiced their views, and so forth. To be sure, then, the impact of Court rulings does depend on the way actors deal with them. But at the same time it can transcend those actors as well. At least according to some, Court policies can actually alter how the public perceives particular issues, can change governmental agendas, and ultimately can have a major effect on society as a whole. Let us consider each of these claims.

Public Opinion

Can the Supreme Court change the way the public views a particular issue? To this, many say yes, that once the Court creates policy that policy has the gloss of legitimacy. After all, if the Supreme Court has lent its approval to "something," then that something must be legitimate. In the words of some, the Court, then, is "a schoolmaster," teaching the public a thing or two when it reaches a decision. On the surface, this argument has some appeal. We know that the Court is the most respected branch of government, the one in which people have expressed a high degree of confidence. So, presumably, its decisions would have some impact on the opinions the public holds about particular issues—and that impact would be to move public opinion more in line with the Court's rulings.

Some research supports this view. A study conducted by Thomas Marshall compared the results of polls taken before and after eighteen Supreme Court decisions. As we display in Figure 6-5, in some instances significant shifts—whether in the long or short term—occurred.

Despite the rigor with which Marshall and others conducted their studies, there are several problems with these kinds of analyses.[14] The first is quite visible from the data presented in Figure 6-5; the public does not always shift in favor of a Supreme Court ruling. As Marshall's study indicates, on nine occasions studied the Court's opinion was greeted by a positive or neutral response, but in nine others, the public moved in the opposite direction. This finding, of course,

---

[14] We adopt some of this discussion from Gregory A. Caldeira, "Courts and Public Opinion," in *The American Courts,* John B. Gates and Charles A. Johnson, eds. (Washington, D.C.: CQ Press, 1991).

FIGURE 6-5
Shifts in Public Opinion

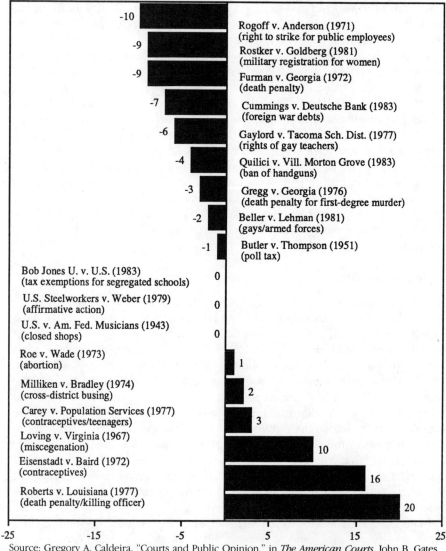

Source: Gregory A. Caldeira, "Courts and Public Opinion," in *The American Courts,* John B. Gates and Charles A. Johnson, eds. (Washington, D.C.: 1991), 308. Figure adapted from Thomas R. Marshall, "The Supreme Court as an Opinion Leader: Court Decisions and the Mass Public," *American Politics Quarterly* 15 (1987), 153.

contradicts the view of the Court as a "schoolmaster," presumably legitimating controversial policy. Rather, as Marshall argues, shifts in public opinion may be more attributable to the sort of policy generated by the Court. As he wrote, "Under limited circumstances . . . Supreme Court decisions are associated with measurable poll shifts. . . . When the Court makes liberal, activist decisions, those decisions are accompanied by significant (positive) poll shifts."[15]

Another problem with these sorts of studies has to do with the data they use. That which we present in Figure 6-5 is based on aggregated level (or macro level) public opinion polls. It considers changes in the citizenry, as a whole, not individual shifts. Such analyses are important to the extent that they can reveal something about the way the public views the Court. But, as Gregory A. Caldeira astutely notes, "stability in aggregate distributions can mask systematic and important shifts in the views of individuals in particular segments of the population. Changes at the level of individuals and in the aggregate can come about in quite different ways. The Court, like Congress and the president, has a set of constituencies, and hidden shifts in the opinions of these constituencies can have important consequences for its ability to function."[16]

Why then did scholars focus on aggregate trends, rather than individual opinions? Mostly because of the lack of available data. For many years, Gallup polls were the only polls available on particular Court opinions. And these, as you may know, are aggregated. They report what percentage of the population supports or opposes particular opinions. This situation has changed in recent years. Perhaps due to the "rise of hot issues such as abortion, affirmative action, and capital punishment,"[17] many of the surveys used by social scientists to study, among other things, why citizens vote the way they do now include questions about the Court. By the same token, scholars have devised creative schemes to try to get at individual opinion on the Court.

What have these individual level analyses revealed? In general, they do not lend much support to the "schoolmaster" perspective. In a particularly interesting study, Larry Baas and Dan Thomas asked college students about their opinions on certain controversial statements.[18] Half of the students were told nothing about the source of the statement; half were informed that a specific person or institution made the statement. For those questionnaires that attributed policy to the Supreme Court, the authors anticipated greater agreement. In their view, if the Supreme Court acted as a legitimator of policies, especially controversial ones, then it should be able to "generate consent" among those who were neutral. Their findings, however, did not support this perspective of the Court. In

---

[15] Thomas Marshall, *Public Opinion and the Supreme Court* (Boston: Unwin Hyman, 1989), 161.

[16] Caldeira, "Courts and Public Opinion," 306.

[17] Ibid., 305.

[18] Larry R. Baas and Dan Thomas, "The Supreme Court and Policy Legitimation," *American Politics Quarterly* 12 (1984): 335–360.

none of the "experiments did the Supreme Court appear to exercise even minimal abilities to legitimate controversial public policies."[19] In another study, Charles Franklin and Liane Kosaki examined whether the Court's decision in *Roe v. Wade* changed individuals' opinions on abortion.[20] In particular, they sought to discover whether Americans followed the Court and became more liberal. Franklin and Kosaki make a convincing argument that this did not occur. Rather, those who supported abortion before *Roe* became more liberal, while those opposed prior to 1973 became equally more pro-life.

Another thing that these individual-level examinations have revealed is that most people do not know about most Court decisions. Naturally, we would not expect the average American to have knowledge of rulings involving private law issues or those that have relatively little bearing on their lives. Since the media do not report on those kinds of issues, from where would they get such knowledge? More troublesome is that large percentages of individuals have not heard of salient cases, cases that received some media attention. Consider the results of a survey of St. Louis residents conducted by Franklin and Kosaki.[21]

Case Subject	Minutes on TV News	Percent Aware of Decision
Dial-a-Porn	6.3	22.1
Affirmative Action	8.8	30.4
Death Penalty	10.5	31.5
Flag Burning	74.0	71.7
Abortion	80.8	83.5

To be sure, a correlation between media time and awareness exists; but even so, we cannot ignore the fact that a large percentage of the public is not cognizant of the most salient Court decisions. If people have not heard of a ruling, then it seems only reasonable to suggest that it could not have had any impact on their opinion.

Given all of this, what can we conclude about the impact of Court decisions on the public's evaluation of particular policies? Is the Court a "schoolmaster"? The evidence, to date, is quite mixed. Perhaps the only conclusion we can reach is that the Court does seem to have an impact on public opinion. It's just that it is not always in favor of the particular policy position the justices have taken. But even that conclusion must be qualified by virtue of the fact that the public is unaware of the average Court decision, and only slightly more knowledgeable about those that receive some press.

---

[19] Caldeira, "Courts and Public Opinion," 310.

[20] Charles H. Franklin and Liane C. Kosaki, "The Republican Schoolmaster: The U.S. Supreme Court, Public Opinion, and Abortion," *American Political Science Review* 83 (1989): 751–771.

[21] Charles H. Franklin and Liane C. Kosaki, "Public Awareness of Supreme Court Decisions," paper presented at the 1991 annual meeting of the American Political Science Association, Washington, D.C., 16.

Impact of Court Policies on the Agenda of Government

To what extent do the policies enunciated by the Supreme Court help set the agendas of the federal and state governments? This is an important question, one whose answers take us back, at least in some measure, to the interpretation/ implementation process depicted in Figure 6-4. That is, the ability of the Supreme Court to shape the agenda of other institutions depends on the reactions of the secondary population, particularly of government officials and interest groups. As we described earlier, sometimes their reactions are either strongly supportive or defiant; and sometimes they do not react at all.

Presuming that a particular Court policy does elicit some response from a public official or an interest group, does that necessarily mean it has an effect on the governmental agenda? On the one hand, it is now the rare term that goes by without at least one Court ruling finding its way onto the floors of state legislatures and Congress for debate. Over the past five years, Congress alone has contemplated (and even enacted) proposals to overturn or modify Court rulings on employment discrimination, funding for family planning clinics, criminal appeals, and flag desecration. By the same token, Supreme Court rulings have become the stuff over which campaigns for public office are fought. After the Court revised *Roe* in its 1989 decision in *Webster,* groups and the populace sought to force politicians to reveal their position on abortion. And there is reason to suspect that candidates' views on that issue alone explain some election outcomes. On the other hand, we must keep in mind that cases like abortion represent the exceptions, not the rule. Of the 150 or so decisions handed down over the course of a term, there are only a few that make it to the governmental agenda. The balance may be of relevance to the legal community but are of minimal concern to the public and its representatives.

What, then, should we conclude about the Court's impact? Does it, as some suggest, act as an agenda setter for the other institutions? Again, the best response is a mixed one. Certain policies do have an enormous impact on the deliberations of the other branches, but many others fade into the legal annals.

Impact of Court Policies on Society

To what extent do Court policies change the lives of Americans? Scholars have offered three competing answers to this question. First, many believe that the Court can have a great deal of influence on American society. To support this, they point to significant policies generated by the Court in a wide range of issue areas, particularly over the past four decades. They remind us that it was the Court that legalized abortion, ordered schools desegregated, protected the rights of the criminally accused, and validated affirmative action programs. And the justices did so before any other governmental body acted. What these and other policies indicate, according to this argument, is that the Court is an important policy maker and, as such, can have a profound impact on American society. That is why, especially in recent years, we have seen such contentious fights over who gets to sit on the Court. If it were an insignificant institution, then why would the Senate, the president, and even the public care about who was appointed?

A second group is more circumspect. In its opinion, the Court's impact is mixed, varying by the particular policy it announces and by the reaction of other institutions to the policy. After examining four areas "where the judiciary is thought to make considerable policy" (freedom of expression, criminal justice, equality, and regulation of the economy), Johnson and Canon concluded that the Court's influence has not been as consistent or even as important as many assumed. They argue, for example, that when the Supreme Court enunciates policies that "have been in direct conflict with those of Congress and the president," the Court "seldom prevailed." Moreover, even when the Court announces policy of some significance with which other branches either agree or are silent, its rulings might lack force without reinforcement. Consider *Brown v. Board of Education*. To be sure, this ruling "initiated the drive for racial equality"; yet, as Johnson and Canon note, "it took the active participation of Congress and the president to sustain this effort and ensure substantial implementation of such policies." Does this mean that the Court has no impact? No. Johnson and Canon and others of this particular school would simply suggest that its influence is not as straightforward as it would appear. As Johnson and Canon conclude,

> The Courts have had and will continue to have an important impact on U.S. society. On occasion they will initiate fundamental changes in public policy. More often they will legitimize, enhance, or more fully develop policies made by other government agencies or by nongovernment institutions. . . .
> On an overall basis, the impact of Courts on U.S. society will best be understood in conjunction with an understanding of how other government agencies . . . affect society.[22]

Finally, there are some scholars who argue that the Court has had virtually no impact on American life. Representing this particular school of thought is Gerald Rosenberg, who centered his research on the question of whether the Supreme Court can be an effective policy maker.[23] He reasoned that if the answer to this question was "yes," then Supreme Court decisions should have some concrete meaning; that is, they should lead to major changes in the lives of affected populations. To determine if this was the case, Rosenberg selected legal areas on which scholars agree the Court had a major impact (e.g., civil rights, abortion), rather than those on which its effect may have been murkier. The results of Rosenberg's inquiry are somewhat shocking. He found that even in areas such as abortion, in which the Court clearly generated profound *legal* change, its ability to generate *social* change was minimal. For instance, he demonstrated that while the number of legal abortions increased after *Roe,* that

---

[22] Johnson and Canon, *Judicial Policies,* 268–269.

[23] Gerald Rosenberg, *The Hollow Hope* (Chicago: University of Chicago Press, 1991).

change was "part of a trend that started . . . three years before the Court acted."[24] This and other evidence led Rosenberg to answer his research question in the negative; that is, the Court "is far less responsible for the [social] changes . . . than most people think."[25]

CONCLUSION

In this chapter, we addressed three broad questions concerning Supreme Court policies: what sorts of policies does it generate, what kinds of trends or patterns can we discern in its policy-making process, and to what extent do court decisions affect our lives? In so doing, we covered a good deal of specific material, but can we come to any general conclusions about the Court's policies and the process by which they are translated to Americans? First, the answers to the first two questions reinforce the view of the Court as a political body: it sets policy on a wide range of issues of public concern and it often does so in ways that are related to the justices' particular ideological and partisan tendencies. In other words, conservative Courts are likely to generate conservative policies; liberal Courts, liberal policies. But that Courts—conservative or liberal—generate policy, and important policy at that, is almost beyond dispute.

A second conclusion we can reach is that in addressing the final question—to what extent do Court decisions affect our lives—we once again confront the fact that the Court is different from the other institutions of government. It is a legal body, which cannot implement its own decisions nor force others to comply with them. As a result, it is largely left to various political and legal actors to determine the force of any given policy.

But does the Court's inability to implement its own decisions necessarily mean that its impact on our lives is quite small? We have provided you with the different responses offered by scholars, yet we think it would be premature to provide any concrete answer. Rather, we leave it to you to consider. What is your view of the Court? Do you think it has had a significant effect on our governmental system, or on your life in particular?

ADDITIONAL READINGS

Becker, Theodore L., and Malcolm Feeley, eds. *The Impact of Supreme Court Decisions,* 2nd ed. (New York: Oxford University Press, 1973).

Caldeira, Gregory A. "Courts and Public Opinion," in *The American Courts,* John B. Gates and Charles A. Johnson, eds. (Washington, D.C.: CQ Press, 1991).

---

[24] Ibid., 178.

[25] Ibid., 201.

Canon, Bradley C. "Courts and Policy," in *The American Courts,* John B. Gates and Charles A. Johnson, eds. (Washington, D.C.: CQ Press, 1991).

Franklin, Charles H., and Liane C. Kosaki. "The Republican Schoolmaster: The U.S. Supreme Court, Public Opinion, and Abortion," *American Political Science Review* 83 (1989): 751–771.

Johnson, Charles A., and Bradley C. Canon. *Judicial Policies* (Washington, D.C.: CQ Press, 1984).

Marshall, Thomas. *Public Opinion and the Supreme Court* (Boston: Unwin/Hyman, 1989).

Pacelle, Richard. *The Transformation of the Supreme Court's Agenda* (Boulder, Colo.: Westview Press, 1991).

Rosenberg, Gerald. *The Hollow Hope* (Chicago: University of Chicago Press, 1991).

Wasby, Stephen L. *The Impact of the United States Supreme Court* (Homewood, Ill.: Dorsey, 1970).

Seven ✑

THE ROLE OF THE COURT IN THE GOVERNMENTAL PROCESS

T hroughout this volume we have explored many aspects of the U.S. Supreme Court, from its origins to the Rehnquist Court, from the types of cases it hears to the impact its decisions have on society. In so doing, we have stressed the dual roles the Court plays in our society—as both a legal and political institution—and how those roles affect everything from the way the Court selects its cases to how it resolves them. What we have not addressed is how those dual roles affect the Court's ultimate place in the American governmental system. While we know the Court as a political institution is similar to the other branches of government and as a legal institution is sufficiently different, we have not yet discussed how those help or hinder the Court within the broader polity.

In this chapter we address several questions relating to the role of the Supreme Court in the governmental process. First, to what extent has the Court, relative to Congress and the president, been a major policy maker? Second, what does the future hold for the Court? Will it be a restraintist body, generally acceding to the will of the elected institutions, or will it be a force that charts its own independent path?

THE COURT AND AMERICAN DEMOCRACY: TO WHAT EXTENT IS THE SUPREME COURT A MAJOR GOVERNMENT PLAYER?

The Court has several ways of checking the elected branches of government. Most important, of course, is that it can review their actions to determine their compatibility with the Constitution. Put somewhat differently, by exerting its power of judicial review the Court—at least theoretically speaking—can be a major participant in the policy-making process. Yet there exist at least two distinct schools of thought about the conditions under which the Court takes on this role. One, the "ruling regime" argument, asserts that the Court can never really be much more than a legitimator of the policies articulated by the elected branches. The other, the "independent actor" view, sees the Court as an important and influential policy maker, at times enunciating policies that undercut those desired by majority interests. These schools of thought, in turn, suggest very different responses to the question asked: To what extent has the Court been a major player? In what follows we review those schools, including the arguments they make and the evidence they bring to bear.

The Court as a Part of the Ruling Regime

As presented most eloquently by political scientist Robert A. Dahl,[1] the "ruling regime view" suggests that the Supreme Court will never be much more than a supporting actor within the governmental process. While it has the potential to play a major role by checking the other branches of government, according to Dahl, the Court will almost never take on this function. Rather, it will simply move to legitimate the actions of the other branches.

Dahl and others offer a number of explanations for this. First, presidents on average have the opportunity to nominate a new justice every two years, meaning that during the course of a term in office, the president can appoint two justices to the Court. "If this were not enough to tip the balance on a normally divided Court," as Dahl writes, "he would be almost certain to succeed in two terms."[2] Just consider the numbers of appointments made by our most recent presidents (with the notable exception of Carter):

President	Terms of Service	No. of Appointments
Hoover	March 1929–March 1933	3
Roosevelt	March 1933–April 1945	9
Truman	April 1945–January 1953	4
Eisenhower	January 1953–January 1961	5
Kennedy	January 1961–November 1963	2
Johnson	November 1963–January 1969	2
Nixon	January 1969–August 1974	4
Ford	August 1974–January 1977	1
Carter	January 1977–January 1981	0
Reagan	January 1981–January 1989	4
Bush	January 1989–	2

How does the fact that presidents usually make two appointments to the Court over a given four-year term support Dahl's view? Quite simply, as we learned in Chapter 2, "presidents are not famous for appointing Justices hostile to their own

[1] Robert A. Dahl published his views in an article ["Decision-Making in a Democracy: The Supreme Court as a National Policy-Maker," *Journal of Public Law* 6 (1957): 279–295] and in a chapter in his book [*Pluralist Democracy in the United States* (Chicago: Rand McNally, 1967)]. We rely on the latter since it updates the earlier article.

[2] Dahl, *Pluralist Democracy in the United States*, 156.

views on public policy."[3] As a result, those they put on the Court, at least theoretically speaking, will be predisposed to support the political positions of the administration. Only if the president has terribly miscalculated a nominee's ideology would we expect the justice to hand down significant rulings against the executive's policies.

A second factor to which Dahl and others point is the confirmation process, specifically the Senate's role. They argue that the president will generally nominate candidates who can win the Senate's approval. Presidents do not want to see their candidates go down in defeat and, accordingly, they will not name someone to the Court who is well out of step with the dominant majority in that body. Consequently, judicial nominees who are both ideologically compatible with the elected president and acceptable to the elected Senate will not likely assume a posture at odds with the political branches.

A final factor is one we touched on in the previous chapter: because the Court lacks any mechanism to enforce its decisions, it can never stray too far from public opinion if it hopes to retain legitimacy. Under this argument, if the Court were bent on continually resolving disputes in ways that went against the public's values and preferences, the citizenry would simply begin to ignore the justices or refuse to comply with their rulings. As a result, the Court would lose whatever legitimacy it previously enjoyed.

Taken together, these explanations suggest that the "policy views dominant on the Court will never be out of line for very long with the policy views dominant among the law-making" and public majorities of the United States.[4] Put somewhat differently, the Court can serve only as a part of the ruling regime, a legitimator of majoritarian interests, rather than as a serious check on them. As such, it can be a major policy maker only to the extent that it goes along with what others want.

Is there any evidence to support this particular perspective of the Court? Dahl relies primarily on the Court's use of judicial review (between 1789 and 1965) to strike down federal legislation, and particularly on the length of time between the enactment of laws and the Court's decisions striking them down. He stresses that many exercises of judicial review (striking down laws) have come more than four years *after* the particular law was passed. *Boos v. Barry* (1988) provides an interesting and recent example. In this case, the Court struck down a federal law of 1938 prohibiting people from displaying signs near a foreign embassy if the sign suggested negative things about the foreign government. In other words, a fifty-year gap existed between the time the law was passed and the Supreme Court's overturning of it. Cases like *Boos,* Dahl would argue, indicate that the Court is much more likely to strike down legislation passed by legislative majorities that are no longer in power than it is to void the acts of existing

---

[3] Ibid.

[4] Ibid.

Congresses. As a result, the Court—in striking down legislation at least four years after it was passed—may be reflecting the will of the *new* majority that no longer desires the legislation enacted by its earlier counterpart.

Even so, the Court has struck down a number of pieces of federal legislation almost immediately (within four years) after their passage; for example, in the 1989 case of *Sable Communications v. FCC,* the Court invalidated a 1988 congressional law prohibiting indecent (and obscene) commercial telephone recordings. And, in fact, of the laws struck down by the Court between 1789 and 1965, 44 percent had been passed by Congress within the previous four years. How do "ruling regime" theorists explain this? One argument is that the New Deal period contributes a good portion of these "exceptions." At that time the Court contained a number of holdovers from an earlier political era. Newly elected Franklin Roosevelt, the first Democrat following twelve years of Republican presidents, went an entire term without a Court vacancy to fill. At one point, these holdover justices reflected the dominant views of Congress and the president, but by the 1930s those views were outmoded. Not surprisingly, as Dahl notes, the Court eventually turned its back on its initial rulings hostile to New Deal legislation and began to uphold those laws desired by the president and Congress. Some of these reversals were quite dynamic. For example, in 1941 the Court upheld a federal minimum wage law that was more expansive in coverage than one it had struck down in the early 1920s.

Dahl also observes that those exceptions (laws struck down within four years after Congress enacted them) did not survive very long. If the Court struck down a *major* congressional law soon after its passage, then Congress often retaliated by passing legislation to overturn the Court's ruling. Hence, as we illustrate in Table 7-1, at least for the period between 1789 and 1965, Court rulings that went against the wishes of the ruling regime did not survive very long. If the justices did not reverse themselves, Congress did it for them. According to Dahl and his supporters, this indicates that the "court evidently cannot hold out indefinitely against a persistent law-making majority."[5] Rather, in all but a few instances, it will eventually accede to their wishes. If this is so, then can the Court really play a major independent role in the American governmental process?

Gerald Rosenberg's work,[6] which we described briefly at the end of Chapter 6, also lends reinforcement to the "ruling regime" view of the Court's role in American society. Rather than look at all cases in which the Court struck down acts of Congress, Rosenberg selected areas of the law in which the Supreme Court presumably acted as an innovative and influential policy maker, including abortion, the environment, racial discrimination, and criminal rights. While he acknowledged that in each of these instances, the Court struck down laws passed by elected bodies (usually state legislatures, rather than Congress), he found that

---

[5] Ibid., 163.

[6] Gerald N. Rosenberg, *The Hollow Hope* (Chicago: University of Chicago Press, 1991).

TABLE 7-1

Type of Congressional Action Following Supreme Court Decisions Holding Legislation Unconstitutional within Four Years after Enactment (Other than New Deal Legislation), 1789–1965

Congressional Action	Major Policy	Minor Policy	Total
Reverses Court's policy	10	2	12
Changes own policy	2	0	2
None	0	8	8
Unclear	3	1	4

Source: Robert A. Dahl, *Pluralist Democracy in the United States* (Chicago: Rand McNally, 1967), 161.

its rulings did not differ wildly from what existing majorities desired. Let's consider one of his examples, abortion. At first blush, it would appear that the Court, in *Roe v. Wade,* acted as a major policy maker, going against the grain of existing regime preferences. After all, its decision struck down as unconstitutional the abortion laws of all fifty states. But Rosenberg argues that first appearances can be deceiving. In his view, the Court merely jumped on a bandwagon supportive of legalized abortion. Indeed, he suggests all the elements were in place for *Roe* to happen—the number of abortions performed was on the upswing, sufficient legal precedent generated from state and federal courts existed, and "large segments of the political and professional elite" were either indifferent to or supportive of expanded abortion rights.[7]

For some of Rosenberg's other issues, the Court was more clearly at the vanguard of social reform. For example, its ruling in *Brown v. Board of Education* (1954) was revolutionary. Even so, Rosenberg argues, the opinion had little impact on American life largely because the nation was not quite ready for such drastic change. As he convincingly demonstrates, *Brown* alone did not desegregate school systems, much less integrate other aspects of American life. Significant change came only after Congress and the president entered the fray in the mid-1960s. Put succinctly, the Court alone did not generate major reform in 1954, largely because the existing regime had not yet staked out a position.

Another source of support for the "ruling regime" view comes from the work of Lee Epstein and Charles Hadley.[8] They explored the Court's decisions in litigation involving major (the Democratic and Republican) and minor (the Communist, Socialist, etc.) political parties. They hypothesized that if the Court was part of the ruling regime, it would generally support the interests of major parties and rule against those of their minority counterparts. Overall their data, which consisted of all cases involving political parties decided by the Supreme Court since 1900, partially supported this proposition. Generally speaking, the justices were no more inclined to rule in favor of minor parties than major ones.

---

[7] Ibid., 189.

[8] Lee Epstein and Charles D. Hadley, "On the Treatment of Political Parties in the U.S. Supreme Court, 1900–1986," *Journal of Politics* 52 (May 1990): 413–432.

Between 1970 and 1986, though, the Court was significantly more likely to favor claims of the Democratic or Republican party over minor party interests. Perhaps even more interesting was their finding that the Court's treatment of minor parties tended to follow the larger political environment. Typically the Court ruled in favor of minor parties about 50 percent of the time. During the Mc-Carthy era, when specific minor parties—those advocating the violent over-throw of the government—were an extremely unwelcome part of the American scene, that support score fell to 25 percent.

The Independent Actor

Although many continue to subscribe to Dahl's argument that the Court acts largely to legitimate existing majoritarian interests, others argue quite the oppo-site. In their opinion, the Court is an important political and independent actor, one that can set policy on a range of issues, protect minority interests, and generate social change. To what evidence do these analysts point in support of their views?[9]

First, some assert that Dahl's analysis, in particular, was bound to the time period he was describing and, accordingly, is not particularly helpful in explain-ing Court behavior of the last three decades. Consider, for example, the data presented in Table 7-2, which updates Dahl's study to include the last thirty or so years. Recall that Dahl's argument rested heavily on the notion that when exercis-ing judicial review, Courts—with the exception of the New Deal era—tend to target laws passed in an earlier political era. Table 7-2, of course, shows a somewhat different pattern. Through the 1970s, the Court seemed to follow the trend Dahl identified; but, since 1980, the justices have often held unconstitu-tional relatively new laws.

While these data are instructive, we should also consider rulings enunciated over the last three decades because they too seem to cast doubt on the utility of Dahl's study. As political scientist Jonathan Casper put it,

> Dahl's article was published in 1957, appearing at the end of a decade that had seen one of our periodic episodes of national political repression. . . .
> The rulings of the Supreme Court in this period did not mark it as a bastion of individual rights standing against a fearful and repressive na-tional majority. . . .
>   Since then, we have witnessed the work of the Warren Court and . . . the Burger Court. The Warren Court, by general reputation at least, was quite different from most of its predecessors. Indeed, one associates with it pre-cisely the characteristics that Dahl found lacking in the Supreme Court—

---

[9] Throughout this section, we rely on what is perhaps the most comprehensive response to Dahl's work, Jonathan D. Casper's "The Supreme Court and National Policy Making," *American Political Science Review* 70 (March 1976): 50–63.

TABLE 7-2

Cases in which Federal Legislation Was Held Unconstitutional, by Time Intervals, 1789–1990 (Excluding New Deal Cases)

	1789–1957	1958–1979	1980–1990
No. of Years			
4 or less	38%	17%	47%
5–20	51	57	30
21 or more	12	26	24
Total No. of Cases	**66**	**35**	**17**

Sources: For 1789–1974, Jonathan D. Casper, "The Supreme Court and National Policy Making," *American Political Science Review* 70 (1976): 53, with Robert A. Dahl, *Pluralist Democracy in the United States* (Chicago: Rand McNally, 1967), 158 used to select out New Deal cases; for 1958–1974, Jonathan D. Casper, "The Supreme Court and National Policy Making," *American Political Science Review* 70 (1976): 53; for 1980–1990, collected by the authors.
Note: Percentages may not total 100 due to rounding.

activism and influence in national policy making and protection of fundamental rights of minorities. . . . [10]

To be sure, the Burger and Rehnquist Courts may have been less prone to protect the rights of minority interests, but they too, contrary to Dahl's expectations, have been major policy players. Just consider that many of the examples on which we have drawn throughout this book—abortion, flag burning, school busing programs—were handed down not by the Warren Court but by those under the leadership of Burger and Rehnquist.

A second interesting piece of evidence in support of the Court as an independent policy maker is that, again contrary to Dahl's expectations, Congress has not successfully overturned many of the Court's more recent decisions. If the Court were an unimportant branch or one that simply acceded to the wishes of the majority, we should find, as Dahl did, that Congress reversed its *major* decisions or the Court itself would have "a change of heart," as it did during the New Deal. But this trend did not continue into the next three decades. As we can see in Table 7-2, the Court has grown more active over time; yet Congress has become more passive. It could have, but did not, respond concretely to any number of important Supreme Court decisions.

Congress occasionally responds to Court rulings. Consider the Supreme Court's decision in *Oregon v. Mitchell* (1970), in which it ruled that Congress can lower the voting age to eighteen for federal—but not state—elections. It retaliated against this ruling by proposing a successful constitutional amendment. Another example emanates from *Texas v. Johnson* (1989), in which the Court struck down a Texas law prohibiting flag desecration. Congress sought to overturn the *Johnson* decision by enacting federal legislation that prohibited such

---

[10] Casper, "The Supreme Court and National Policy Making," 52.

conduct. But, in an action particularly damaging to the ruling regime thesis, the Court struck that law down months after it was passed. This is not to say, of course, that the legislature will not eventually take action in *Johnson* or in many others; indeed, as of this writing, it is considering several bills aimed at altering Court opinions. This is just to indicate that the Court has emerged as the final policy maker on a wide range of important issues.

A third challenge to the view of the Court as a legitimator of majoritarian preferences is that the ruling regime studies failed to consider indicators other than the Court's use of judicial review to strike down federal laws. As Casper writes, "The Court is frequently called upon to interpret the meaning of federal statutes, and in the course of doing so, important policy choices must be made."[11] In other words, the Court does not necessarily need to strike down a law to set policy; it might do so by merely construing a statute, something that Dahl's study failed to contemplate.

By way of example, consider the Supreme Court's 1991 decision in *Rust v. Sullivan.* In that case, the justices examined a directive of Ronald Reagan's secretary of health and human services, which prohibited federally funded family planning clinics from counseling women on abortions. The administration argued that this directive was consistent with a 1970 congressional law stating that: "None of the funds appropriated under this title shall be used in programs where abortion is a method of family planning." In response, some members of Congress argued that the law was not meant to prohibit abortion *counseling,* that "if the 1970 Congress had wanted to ban abortion counseling, it would have done so explicitly."[12] The U.S. Supreme Court, however, ignored this assertion and upheld the administration's directive. It did not strike down the 1970 law; it merely "interpreted" it. But, in so doing, it set an important "policy." Indeed, Congress enacted a bill aimed at reversing the Court's ruling in *Rust,* but President Bush promptly vetoed it.

We, thus, should not ignore the important role the Court can play as an "interpreter" of law, a role that may become even more important in the coming years. We write this in light of the fact that some members of the Rehnquist Court—particularly Antonin Scalia and William Rehnquist—may be seeking to push the justices to adopt a rather different approach to statutory interpretation. Historically speaking, justices have usually examined the legislative histories of laws (committee reports, debates, etc.) they are seeking to interpret. These give the justices some idea of the intent of those who wrote the legislation, an important concern given that many laws produced by Congress are quite vague. Justice Scalia, however, believes that it is unnecessary to examine legislative histories. As he wrote recently, "we are a government of laws not of committee

---

[11] Ibid., 56.

[12] This and what follows in the next paragraph draw on Joan Biskupic, "Congress Keeps Eye on Justices as Court Watches Hill's Words," *CQ Weekly Report,* October 5, 1991, 2863–2867.

reports." Rather, he thinks that the Court should base its construction on "what [legislators] write into law," and not on "what [they] say they mean."

Such a "textual" approach to statutory construction might substantially increase the Court's policy-making power. As Joan Biskupic put it, because congressional laws are so vague, "when courts rely only on the words of a statute, judges have greater latitude to make their own interpretations or to defer to the regulatory framework . . . " And, needless to say, "conservatives, who now dominate the court, are likely to interpret the law from that ideological viewpoint."[13] *Rust* provides a good example of these points.

Fourth, we can consider a body of literature that contradicts the implications of Rosenberg's study. Recall that he suggested the Court was not capable of generating major and efficacious social or legal change without assistance from the other institutions of government. Literature exploring the use of litigation by interest groups to attain policy objectives and to influence judicial outcomes counters his thesis, as well as Dahl's view of the Court as a protector of majoritarian interests. How does it do so? For one, interest group studies indicate that it is generally *disadvantaged groups* that seek refuge in the Supreme Court. As Richard C. Cortner put it,

> [Groups that] are temporarily, or even permanently, disadvantaged in terms of their abilities to attain successfully their goals in the electoral process, within the elected political institutions or in the bureaucracy . . . are highly dependent upon the judicial process. . . . If they are to succeed at all in the pursuit of their goals they are almost compelled to resort to litigation.[14]

If this is so, then we must question the assertion that the Court acts to protect majority interests. After all, why would the NAACP Legal Defense Fund, the American Civil Liberties Union, and other organizations representing disadvantaged interests take to the courts in the first place?

For another, at least during the Warren and early Burger Court eras, the justices themselves encouraged minority interests to seek refuge in its corridors. In one case, the Court went so far as to suggest that "groups which find themselves unable to achieve their objectives through the ballot frequently turn to the courts . . . [U]nder the conditions of modern government, litigation may well be the sole practicable avenue open to a minority to petition for redress of grievances."[15]

Finally, we should acknowledge that the last several decades present some interesting practical and theoretical problems in attempting to understand the role of the Court. The period from 1968 to the present has been marked by

---

[13] Ibid., 2863.

[14] Richard C. Cortner, "Strategies and Tactics of Litigants in Constitutional Cases," *Journal of Public Law* 17 (1968): 287.

[15] *NAACP v. Button,* 371 U.S. 415 (1963), 429–431.

divided government. Almost without exception, both houses of Congress have been in the control of Democratic majorities. However, in five of the six presidential elections beginning in 1968 the voters sent a Republican to the White House. Divided government makes it difficult even to determine the prevailing political majority. Is it represented by the majority of congressional seats or the majority of votes cast in the presidential election? This condition also imposes difficult obstacles for congressional attempts to reverse Court rulings. The Republican presidents, especially Reagan and Bush, have been quite supportive of the Court's conservative decisions. They have threatened or have actually used the veto to block congressional attempts to alter the Court's decisions. The aftermath of the *Rust* abortion counseling ruling is a typical example. Having a staunch ally in the White House may even encourage the justices to enact policies more independent of the prevailing views in Congress.

THE FUTURE: WHAT LIES AHEAD FOR
THE SUPREME COURT

The debate we described above is just that, a debate. Some always will take the position that the Court is an inefficacious decision maker, a mere part of the ruling regime; others will quite strongly assert just the reverse. We leave it to you to consider the evidence and make your own determination.

But are there lessons we can extract from both sides to help us understand where it is the Court might be heading? We think so. For starters, let us think about the 1992 Court. As we have suggested throughout this volume, it is, to be sure, one of the most conservative Courts in recent memory. It is also, with but few exceptions, a relatively youthful group of justices. Consider the chart below, indicating the current age of the justices and when they might leave the Court (based on an average retirement age of eighty):[16]

Justice	Current Age (1992)	Projected Year of Retirement
Blackmun	84	–
White	75	1997
Stevens	72	2000
Rehnquist	68	2004
O'Connor	62	2010
Scalia	56	2016
Kennedy	56	2016
Souter	53	2019
Thomas	44	2028

---

[16] The assumption of retirement at age 80 is not, as it may seem at first blush, unreasonable. The four justices who retired between 1986 and 1991 (Burger, Powell, Brennan, and Marshall) averaged 81.5 years of age when they stepped down. Burger was the youngest—he was 79.

Note, of course, that the justices most likely to retire the soonest (Blackmun, White, and Stevens) are among the more liberal members. So there is little chance that the Court would become significantly more liberal when they are replaced, especially if the Republicans continue to control the White House. It would more likely move in an even more conservative direction or stay about the same. Now let us think about the public and the officials its elects. During the 1980s the citizenry also appeared to have moved toward a more conservative posture. The Republican party has picked up membership and we have not elected a Democratic president since 1976.

Putting these two things together—the Court's and the public's conservatism—would lead us to conclude that we should have relative harmony in the broader governmental process. That is, the institutions of government, including the Court, would well encompass societal preferences. Such would not be unprecedented. As we have suggested throughout this volume, a similar situation existed in the 1920s when we had a relatively conservative public, a long string of Republican presidents, and a very right-of-center Court.

The "harmony" of the 1920s, of course, ended with the depression, the election of Franklin Roosevelt, and the ensuing constitutional crisis. When holdover justices from Republican regimes kept striking down New Deal legislation, Roosevelt threatened to pack the Court. Eventually, as Dahl's study details, the Court had a change of heart and "harmony"—albeit of a far more liberal nature—once again prevailed.

It was, of course, the depression that precipitated the constitutional crisis over the New Deal. But does that necessarily mean that such a showdown could not happen in the absence of something as dramatic as a depression? We think not; indeed, it may be the case that we are heading for such a Court-public battle within the not-so-distant future. While it is perhaps true that the Court is in line with the public *now,* this may well not be the case as we reach the 2000-year mark. Various scholars are predicting, for different reasons, that the now conservative populace is drifting toward liberalism, and has been for a while. Based on analyses of many public opinion surveys, political scientist James Stimson writes,

> The data do not say that an era of liberalism is coming. They say it is here. . . .
> Public opinion to this moment is moving toward liberalism . . . we can say
> with more certainty that it has rejected Reagan-style conservatism.[17]

If such assertions are correct, what might that mean for the future of the Court? What will happen if the Court continues to move to the right, while the public drifts to the left? What would be the result of the conservative Court handing down major decisions that were opposed by the public and their representatives

---

[17] James A. Stimson, *Public Opinion in America: Moods, Cycles and Swings* (Boulder, Colo.: Westview Press, 1991), 117, 126.

in Congress? What if liberal Democrats captured control of the White House as well as the Congress? Would such conditions make it possible for the Court to issue a ruling as unpopular as *Dred Scott* or the anti–New Deal decisions of previous generations and with just the same ill-fated results? To be sure, the answer largely depends on the Court itself. If the pendulum of public opinion swings sufficiently to the left, the Court may be faced with a choice of maintaining an independent conservative posture or modifying its behavior to support the ruling political majorities.

ADDITIONAL READINGS

Adamany, David. "Legitimacy, Realigning Elections, and the Supreme Court," *Wisconsin Law Review* 1973 (1973): 790–846.

Casper, Jonathan D. "The Supreme Court and National Policy Making," *American Political Science Review* 70 (March 1976): 50–63.

Dahl, Robert A. "Decision-Making in a Democracy: The Supreme Court as a National Policy-Maker," *Journal of Public Law* 6 (1957): 279–295.

Dahl, Robert A. *Pluralist Democracy in the United States* (Chicago: Rand McNally, 1967), Chapter 6.

Funston, Richard. *A Vital National Seminar: The Supreme Court in American Political Life* (Palo Alto, Calif.: Mayfield, 1978).

Gates, John B. *The Supreme Court and Partisan Realignment* (Boulder, Colo.: Westview Press, 1990).

Rosenberg, Gerald N. *The Hollow Hope* (Chicago: University of Chicago Press, 1991).

APPENDICES

THE JUSTICES OF THE SUPREME COURT

Justice	State	Political Party	Appointing President	Political Party	Years of Service
John Jay	N.Y.	Fed.	Washington	Fed.	1789–1795
John Rutledge*	S.C.	Fed.	Washington	Fed.	1789–1791
William Cushing	Mass.	Fed.	Washington	Fed.	1789–1810
James Wilson	Pa.	Fed.	Washington	Fed.	1789–1798
John Blair	Va.	Fed.	Washington	Fed.	1789–1796
James Iredell	N.C.	Fed.	Washington	Fed.	1790–1799
Thomas Johnson	Md.	Fed.	Washington	Fed.	1791–1793
William Paterson	N.J.	Fed.	Washington	Fed.	1793–1806
John Rutledge**	S.C.	Fed.	Washington	Fed.	1795
Samuel Chase	Md.	Fed.	Washington	Fed.	1796–1811
Oliver Ellsworth	Conn.	Fed.	Washington	Fed.	1796–1800
Bushrod Washington	Va.	Fed.	J. Adams	Fed.	1798–1829
Alfred Moore	N.C.	Fed.	J. Adams	Fed.	1799–1804
John Marshall	Va.	Fed.	J. Adams	Fed.	1801–1835
William Johnson	S.C.	Dem-Rep	Jefferson	Dem-Rep	1804–1834
H. B. Livingston	N.Y.	Dem-Rep	Jefferson	Dem-Rep	1806–1823
Thomas Todd	Ky.	Dem-Rep	Jefferson	Dem-Rep	1807–1826
Joseph Story	Mass.	Dem-Rep	Madison	Dem-Rep	1811–1845
Gabriel Duvall	Md.	Dem-Rep	Madison	Dem-Rep	1811–1835
Smith Thompson	N.Y.	Dem-Rep	Monroe	Dem-Rep	1823–1843
Robert Trimble	Ky.	Dem-Rep	J. Q. Adams	Dem-Rep	1826–1828
John McLean	Ohio	Dem.	Jackson	Dem.	1829–1861
Henry Baldwin	Pa.	Dem.	Jackson	Dem.	1830–1844
James M. Wayne	Ga.	Dem.	Jackson	Dem.	1835–1867
Roger B. Taney	Md.	Dem.	Jackson	Dem.	1836–1864
Philip P. Barbour	Va.	Dem.	Jackson	Dem.	1836–1841
John Catron	Tenn.	Dem.	Jackson	Dem.	1837–1865
John McKinley	Ala.	Dem.	Van Buren	Dem.	1837–1852
Peter V. Daniel	Va.	Dem.	Van Buren	Dem.	1841–1860

Chief Justices in bold type.
* Served later as chief justice.
** Served previously as associate justice.

Samuel Nelson	N.Y.	Dem.	Tyler	Whig	1845–1872
Levi Woodbury	N.H.	Dem.	Polk	Dem.	1846–1851
Robert C. Grier	Pa.	Dem.	Polk	Dem.	1846–1870
Benjamin R. Curtis	Mass.	Whig	Fillmore	Whig	1851–1857
John A. Campbell	Ala.	Dem.	Pierce	Dem.	1853–1861
Nathan Clifford	Maine	Dem.	Buchanan	Dem.	1858–1881
Noah H. Swayne	Ohio	Rep.	Lincoln	Rep.	1862–1881
Samuel Miller	Iowa	Rep.	Lincoln	Rep.	1862–1890
David Davis	Ill.	Rep.	Lincoln	Rep.	1862–1877
Stephen J. Field	Cal.	Dem.	Lincoln	Rep.	1863–1897
Salmon P. Chase	Ohio	Rep.	Lincoln	Rep.	1864–1873
William Strong	Pa.	Rep.	Grant	Rep.	1870–1880
Joseph P. Bradley	N.J.	Rep.	Grant	Rep.	1870–1892
Ward Hunt	N.Y.	Rep.	Grant	Rep.	1872–1882
Morrison Waite	Ohio	Rep.	Grant	Rep.	1874–1888
John Marshall Harlan	Ky.	Rep.	Hayes	Rep.	1877–1911
William B. Woods	Ga.	Rep.	Hayes	Rep.	1880–1887
Stanley Matthews	Ohio	Rep.	Garfield	Rep.	1881–1889
Horace Gray	Mass.	Rep.	Arthur	Rep.	1881–1902
Samuel Blatchford	N.Y.	Rep.	Arthur	Rep.	1882–1893
Lucius Q. C. Lamar	Miss.	Dem.	Cleveland	Dem.	1888–1893
Melville W. Fuller	Ill.	Dem.	Cleveland	Dem.	1888–1910
David J. Brewer	Kan.	Rep.	Harrison	Rep.	1889–1910
Henry B. Brown	Mich.	Rep.	Harrison	Rep.	1890–1906
George Shiras, Jr.	Pa.	Rep.	Harrison	Rep.	1892–1903
Howell E. Jackson	Tenn.	Dem.	Harrison	Rep.	1893–1895
Edward D. White*	La.	Dem.	Cleveland	Dem.	1894–1910
Rufus W. Peckham	N.Y.	Dem.	Cleveland	Dem.	1895–1909
Joseph McKenna	Cal.	Rep.	McKinley	Rep.	1898–1925
Oliver W. Holmes, Jr.	Mass.	Rep.	T. Roosevelt	Rep.	1902–1932
William R. Day	Ohio	Rep.	T. Roosevelt	Rep.	1903–1922
William H. Moody	Mass.	Rep.	T. Roosevelt	Rep.	1906–1910
Horace Lurton	Tenn.	Dem.	Taft	Rep.	1909–1914
Charles E. Hughes*	N.Y.	Rep.	Taft	Rep.	1910–1916
Edward D. White**	La.	Dem.	Taft	Rep.	1910–1921
Willis Van Devanter	Wyo.	Rep.	Taft	Rep.	1910–1937
Joseph R. Lamar	Ga.	Dem.	Taft	Rep.	1910–1916
Mahlon Pitney	N.J.	Rep.	Taft	Rep.	1912–1922
James C. McReynolds	Tenn.	Dem.	Wilson	Dem.	1914–1941
Louis D. Brandeis	Mass.	Dem.	Wilson	Dem.	1916–1939
John H. Clarke	Ohio	Dem.	Wilson	Dem.	1916–1922
William H. Taft	Ohio	Rep.	Harding	Rep.	1921–1930
George Sutherland	Utah	Rep.	Harding	Rep.	1922–1938

Pierce Butler	Minn.	Dem.	Harding	Rep.	1922–1939
Edward T. Sanford	Tenn.	Rep.	Harding	Rep.	1923–1930
Harlan Fiske Stone*	N.Y.	Rep.	Coolidge	Rep.	1925–1941
Charles E. Hughes**	N.Y.	Rep.	Hoover	Rep.	1930–1941
Owen J. Roberts	Pa.	Rep.	Hoover	Rep.	1930–1945
Benjamin Cardozo	N.Y.	Dem.	Hoover	Rep.	1932–1938
Hugo L. Black	Ala.	Dem.	F. Roosevelt	Dem.	1937–1971
Stanley F. Reed	Ky.	Dem.	F. Roosevelt	Dem.	1938–1957
Felix Frankfurter	Mass.	Ind.	F. Roosevelt	Dem.	1939–1962
William O. Douglas	Conn.	Dem.	F. Roosevelt	Dem.	1939–1975
Frank Murphy	Mich.	Dem.	F. Roosevelt	Dem.	1940–1949
Harlan Fiske Stone**	N.Y.	Rep.	F. Roosevelt	Dem.	1941–1946
James F. Byrnes	S.C.	Dem.	F. Roosevelt	Dem.	1941–1942
Robert H. Jackson	N.Y.	Dem.	F. Roosevelt	Dem.	1941–1954
Wiley B. Rutledge	Iowa	Dem.	F. Roosevelt	Dem.	1943–1949
Harold H. Burton	Ohio	Rep.	Truman	Dem.	1945–1958
Fred M. Vinson	Ky.	Dem.	Truman	Dem.	1946–1953
Tom C. Clark	Tex.	Dem.	Truman	Dem.	1949–1967
Sherman Minton	Ind.	Dem.	Truman	Dem.	1949–1956
Earl Warren	Cal.	Rep.	Eisenhower	Rep.	1953–1969
John M. Harlan	N.Y.	Rep.	Eisenhower	Rep.	1955–1971
William J. Brennan, Jr.	N.J.	Dem.	Eisenhower	Rep.	1956–1990
Charles E. Whittaker	Mo.	Rep.	Eisenhower	Rep.	1957–1962
Potter Stewart	Ohio	Rep.	Eisenhower	Rep.	1958–1981
Byron R. White	Colo.	Dem.	Kennedy	Dem.	1962–
Arthur J. Goldberg	Ill.	Dem.	Kennedy	Dem.	1962–1965
Abe Fortas	Tenn.	Dem.	Johnson	Dem.	1965–1969
Thurgood Marshall	N.Y.	Dem.	Johnson	Dem.	1967–1991
Warren E. Burger	Minn.	Rep.	Nixon	Rep.	1969–1986
Harry A. Blackmun	Minn.	Rep.	Nixon	Rep.	1970–
Lewis F. Powell, Jr.	Va.	Dem.	Nixon	Rep.	1971–1987
William Rehnquist*	Ariz.	Rep.	Nixon	Rep.	1971–1986
John Paul Stevens	Ill.	Rep.	Ford	Rep.	1975–
Sandra Day O'Connor	Ariz.	Rep.	Reagan	Rep.	1981–
William Rehnquist**	Ariz.	Rep.	Reagan	Rep.	1986–
Antonin Scalia	D.C.	Rep.	Reagan	Rep.	1986–
Anthony Kennedy	Cal.	Rep.	Reagan	Rep.	1988–
David H. Souter	N.H.	Rep.	Bush	Rep.	1990–
Clarence Thomas	Ga.	Rep.	Bush	Rep.	1991–

U.S. CONSTITUTION, ARTICLE III

Section. 1. The judicial Power of the United States, shall be vested in one supreme Court, and in such inferior Courts as the Congress may from time to time ordain and establish. The Judges, both of the supreme and inferior Courts, shall hold their Offices during good Behaviour, and shall, at stated Times, receive for their Services, a Compensation, which shall not be diminished during their Continuance in Office.

Section. 2. The judicial Power shall extend to all Cases, in Law and Equity, arising under this Constitution, the Laws of the United States, and Treaties made, or which shall be made, under their Authority;—to all Cases affecting Ambassadors, other public Ministers and Consuls;—to all Cases of admiralty and maritime Jurisdiction;—to Controversies to which the United States shall be a Party;—to Controversies between two or more States; [between a State and Citizens of another State;—]* between Citizens of different States—between Citizens of the same State claiming Lands under Grants of different States, [and between a State, or the Citizens thereof, and foreign States, Citizens or Subjects.]*

In all Cases affecting Ambassadors, other public Ministers and Consuls, and those in which a State shall be Party, the supreme Court shall have original Jurisdiction. In all the other Cases before mentioned, the supreme Court shall have appellate Jurisdiction, both as to Law and Fact, with such Exceptions, and under such Regulations as the Congress shall make.

The Trial of all Crimes, except in Cases of Impeachment; shall be by Jury; and such Trial shall be held in the State where the said Crimes shall have been committed; but when not committed within any State, the Trial shall be at such Place or Places as the Congress may by Law have directed.

Section. 3. Treason against the United States, shall consist only in levying War against them, or in adhering to their Enemies, giving them Aid and Comfort. No Person shall be convicted of Treason unless on the Testimony of two Witnesses to the same overt Act, or on Confession in open Court.

The Congress shall have Power to declare the Punishment of Treason, but no Attainder of Treason shall work Corruption of Blood, or Forfeiture except during the Life of the Person attainted.

---

* Changed by the Eleventh Amendment.

GLOSSARY

Advisory opinion: An opinion issued by a court indicating how it would rule on a question of law should such a question come before it in an actual case. The United States Supreme Court, and other federal courts, do not issue such opinions. The courts of some states do.

Affirm: A decision of an appellate court upholding the decision of a lower court.

Amicus curiae: "Friend of the Court." A person, group, or institution, not a party to a case, who submits views (normally in the form of written briefs) on how a case should be decided.

Appeal: The procedure by which a case is taken to a superior court for review of a lower court's decision.

Appellant: The party dissatisfied with a lower court ruling who appeals the case to a higher court.

Appellee: The party usually satisfied with a lower court ruling against whom an appeal is taken.

Article III: The section of the United States Constitution pertaining to the federal judiciary.

Brandeis brief: A legal argument that stresses sociological and economic evidence along with traditional legal authorities. Named after Louis Brandeis, who originated its use.

Brief: A written legal argument submitted to a court.

Case: A legal dispute brought to a court for resolution.

Case law: Legal rules and principles derived from judicial decisions.

Case or controversy rule: The constitutional rule that federal courts can hear only real legal disputes brought by adverse parties.

Certification, writ of: A procedure whereby a lower court requests a superior court to answer a legal question so that the lower court may correctly apply the law.

Certiorari, writ of: An order by the Supreme Court for a lower court to send up the record of a case that the justices have decided to review. This is the primary way by which the Court exercises its discretionary jurisdiction to accept an appeal for a full hearing.

Civil law: Law that deals with the private rights of individuals, as opposed to criminal law.

Class action: A lawsuit filed by a person or persons on behalf of themselves and other individuals similarly situated.

Common law: A body of legal rules and principles derived from custom, tradition, and judicial decisions. Usually associated with English legal development.

Concurring opinion: An opinion written by a judge on an appellate court agreeing with the decision of the majority but expressing different reasons for reaching that result.

Courts of appeals (U.S.): An intermediate appellate court in the federal judiciary located above the district court and below the Supreme Court.

Criminal law: A body of law governing the relationship between individuals and society. Deals with the enforcement of laws and the prosecution and punishment of those who violate them.

Defendant: The party at the trial court level who is being sued in a civil case or accused of a crime in a criminal case.

Dicta; obiter dicta: The portions of a court's opinion not essential to the decision in the case.

Discretionary jurisdiction: The right of a court to accept or reject cases brought to it for a decision. The Supreme Court's jurisdiction is almost totally discretionary.

Dismissal: An action by a court disposing of a case without deciding it.

Dissenting opinion: An opinion written by a judge on an appellate court disagreeing with the outcome of a case as supported by the majority.

District courts (U.S.): The trial courts of general jurisdiction in the federal judiciary.

Docket: The list or schedule of cases to be heard by a court.

Due process: Legal procedures designed to ensure essential fairness.

Ex parte: A legal action or hearing in which only one party is represented.

Exceptions Clause: The constitutional provision allowing Congress to alter the appellate jurisdiction of the Supreme Court.

Federal question: A legal issue based on the federal Constitution, laws, or treaties.

Habeas corpus: A writ issued to determine if a person held in custody is being illegally detained.

Holding: A rule of law used to decide a case.

In forma pauperis: "In the form of a pauper." A special status granted to indigents that allows them to proceed in a legal action without satisfying all procedural requirements and paying all fees.

Incorporation: A decision by the Supreme Court holding that a provision of the Bill of Rights applies to state and local governments through the Due Process Clause of the Fourteenth Amendment.

Injunction: A judicial order prohibiting a party from engaging in certain specified acts.

Judicial activism: A philosophy that courts should not be reluctant to review and if necessary strike down the acts of the legislative and executive branches.

Judicial restraint: A philosophy that courts should defer to the legislative and executive branches whenever possible.

Judicial review: The power of the judiciary to review the acts of the legislative and executive branches and to declare them void if found in conflict with the Constitution.

Judiciary Act of 1789: The initial act of Congress establishing the federal judicial system.

Jurisdiction: The authority of a court to hear and decide a case.

Justiciable: A legal question capable of judicial resolution.

Litigant: A party to a lawsuit.

Majority opinion: An opinion explaining the decision of an appellate court that is supported by a majority of members participating in the decision.

Mandamus, writ of: "We command." An order of a court commanding a public officer to carry out the official duties of that position.

Mandatory jurisdiction: Cases that a court by law must accept and decide.

Modify: The action of an appellate court making alterations in a lower court ruling.

Moot: A question presented to a court that cannot be answered either because the issue has resolved itself or conditions have so changed that the court is unable to grant the relief requested.

Original jurisdiction: The authority of a court to hear a case at trial, as opposed to appellate jurisdiction.

Per curiam: "For the court." An unsigned or collectively written opinion issued by a court.

Petitioner: A party seeking relief from a court.

Plaintiff: A party bringing suit in a civil case.

Plenary review: Granting a full hearing to a case, usually including the submission of written briefs and the presentation of oral arguments.

Plurality opinion: An opinion announcing the judgment of a court that is not endorsed by a majority of the court's members.

Precedent: A previously decided case that serves as a guide for deciding future cases.

Remand: An action of an appellate court sending a case back down to a lower court for additional action.

Respondent: The party against whom a legal action is filed.

Reverse: The action of an appellate court setting aside a decision by a lower court.

Ripeness: A condition in which a legal dispute reaches the point of development that it can be resolved by judicial decision.

Seriatim opinions: A practice originated in English appellate courts in which all of the participating judges write individual opinions explaining their views on deciding a case. The use of seriatim opinions on the Supreme Court was terminated during the tenure of Chief Justice John Marshall.

Standing; standing to sue: The right of parties to bring legal actions because they are directly affected by the legal issues raised.

Stare decisis: "Let the decision stand." The doctrine that once a legal question has been settled the decision should be followed as precedent for future cases presenting the same or similar issues.

Statutory construction: A court interpretation of a statute.

Summary decision: A decision by a court made without a full hearing or without receiving full briefs or having oral arguments.

Test: A criterion or set of criteria used by courts to determine if certain legal thresholds have been met or constitutional provisions violated.

Vacate: A decision by an appellate court to void or rescind a lower court ruling.

Writ: An order issued by a court commanding the party to whom it is directed to perform certain acts or refrain from certain acts.

TABLE OF CASES

About the Authors

Thomas G. Walker is a professor and former chair of the Department of Political Science at Emory University, where he teaches courses in constitutional law and the judicial process. He received his B.A. in government from St. Martin's College (Olympia, Washington) and his Ph.D. in political science from the University of Kentucky (Lexington). Professor Walker is the author or coauthor of several books on American politics and public law, including *American Politics and the Constitution* (1978), *Political Parties, Interest Groups and Public Policy* (1980), *Constitutional Law for a Changing America: Rights, Liberties and Justice* (1992), and *Constitutional Law for a Changing America: Institutional Powers and Constraints* (1992). His coauthored book, *A Court Divided: The Fifth Circuit Court of Appeals and the Politics of Judicial Reform* (1988) received the prestigious V. O. Key, Jr. award for the best book on Southern politics. His research has appeared in such journals as the *American Journal of Political Science, Journal of Politics,* and *Western Political Quarterly.*

Lee Epstein is associate professor of political science at Washington University in St. Louis. She received her Ph.D. from Emory University. She is author or coauthor of several books on law, courts, and judicial processes, including *Conservatives in Court* (1985), *Public Interest Law Groups* (1989), *Constitutional Law for a Changing America: Rights, Liberties, and Justice* (1992), *Constitutional Law for a Changing America: Institutional Powers and Constraints* (1992), and *The Supreme Court and Legal Change* (1992). She has published articles in, among other publications, the *American Political Science Review, American Journal of Political Science,* and *Journal of Politics.*

INDEX